G000168673

To Wanda
Hoping this brings
memories of the dea

Love

Joan
September 1991

Dog Easy

Dog Easy

JOAN de SMITH

SAWD
England

SAWD PUBLICATIONS
Placketts Hole, Bicknor,
Sittingbourne, Kent ME9 8BA.

British Library Cataloguing in Publication Data.

De Smith, Joan
Dog easy: the love and war letters of a
Cambridge professor.
I. Title
940.548173092

ISBN: 1-872489-06-0

Typeset in Great Britain by MediaType, Sittingbourne, Kent.
Printed in Great Britain by Biddles Ltd, Guildford, Surrey.

To Our Four Children:
Jane Catherine, Anna Margaret, Michael John and Nicholas Mark.

CONTENTS

Introduction and Acknowledgements

PART I – A STUDENT IN WARTIME

PART II – ARMY LIFE IN THE UK

PART III – THE WAR IN EUROPE

PART IV – POSTWAR/INTELLIGENCE CORPS

EPILOGUE

Bibliography

Abbreviations

Copyright Acknowledgements

Introduction and Acknowledgements

The title of the book, Dog Easy, was the name by which Stanley Alexander de Smith was affectionately known to his troops. It arose from the standard phonetic alphabet used in signalling during the war: Able, Baker, Charlie, *Dog, Easy*, Fox, etc. Frequently messages would be passed using only the first two initials of his rather odd surname as he remarks in his letter dated October, 6th '44: *'When there's a casualty the cry seems to be; Send for Dog Easy'.*

In the spring of 1988, when our old house in London was about to be sold, I discovered a large cardboard box crammed full of letters. They were sealed − three or four to an envelope and each envelope was dated − just as I had left them some forty-five years ago. Inside were the letters which Stanley had written to me during the war, starting when I was fourteen years old and ending six years later when he was demobilised in November 1946, a total of some half a million words.

I had long thought them lost and certainly he was unaware that I had kept them. Over the next few months, as I carefully unfolded the closely written pages and re-read the contents, the idea of this book began to take shape. It was clear they could not be handled by straightforward editing. For one thing they were too personal, full of love and affection, and for another the many references to a wide circle of friends, relations and places would be meaningless to the general reader. But as a background to a continuous story they presented a fascinating picture of the difficulties faced by a young man in war-time, and the impact of army life on him, his friends and his career.

The 'extracts' presented, which are based on only a small number of the total of four hundred letters which have survived, are not verbatim. Frequently paragraphs have been changed about, phrases altered or enhanced, the contents of two or three letters run together, or additional explanatory comment inserted. I offer no apology for including my own recollections of events or adding his later impressions but the spirit of the reconstituted letters is never false to his ideas.

The letters themselves would also be fairly meaningless to his children's and grandchildren's generation were they not set against a contemporary background. Though not an historian, I have endeavoured to provide that setting on three different levels: firstly by describing the major military, political and international events; secondly by outlining the living conditions in war-time Britain; and thirdly, by analysing the development of our own relationship.

Dog Easy is not intended as a balanced war history − there are those far better qualified who have already produced a wide selection of books on the subject. It is very subjective, dependent on events which impinged themselves on my memory either at the time or later. Many brave and heroic incidents and campaigns are not even mentioned, many horrors of life under Nazism and Fascism are understated, many achievements by our Allies are not given full due. For these omissions I apologise but as one lived day by day, trivia often assumed grand proportions and overwhelmed the greater moment.

In selecting historical events I have referred to a large number of books on the Second World War, the majority of which appear in the bibliography. But there are two on which I drew most heavily which deserve special mention: firstly, 'Second World War' by Martin Gilbert, which gives a most vivid and scholarly chronological account whilst not forgetting that history is made by people; the other invaluable source was Joan Strange's 'Despatches from the Home Front', edited by Chris McCooey. I acknowledge gratefully the works of these two authors.

Over the last two years the Imperial War Museum – to whom the letters will eventually go – and the Public Records Office have both provided valuable material. From the Department of Documents at the Imperial War Museum, I must thank Simon Robbins particularly for his unfailing helpfulness and encouragement. The Public Records Office at Kew – that superbly organised (and comfortable) fount of unpublished papers – provided the Regimental War Diaries. In the long task of researching these I gratefully acknowledge the help of D. A. Brace.

It gave me great pleasure to renew contact with some of Stanley's few surviving war-time friends and colleagues. Among them were Bill Bailey, Harry Duerr and Sergeant-Major Wilson of the 77th Medium Regiment, RA(DLOY). Other officers from D Troop – Roger Harrop and John Skinner – provided material and photographs to help me with my task. I am indebted also to Geoffrey Harris, who served with a field regiment in North Africa, for his comments on that campaign. I am particularly indebted to Hugh Carless, a close friend of Stanley's whom I have not seen since those days, who provided much of the background for the Intelligence section. My thanks are due to all of them.

To my publishers and in particular, Susannah Wainman, I owe an immense debt of gratitude. Having seen only a synopsis of DOG EASY they accepted my promise that I would finish the book in six months. They encouraged me at every stage and my experience was far removed from some of the hair-raising tales I had heard from fellow writers of author/publisher encounters. I did not have any such problems and enjoyed our many meetings to discuss the progress and format of the book.

But most of all I must thank my four 'Readers': Anna, our second daughter, who cast her eye relentlessly over the manuscript both as an English scholar and family watch-dog; Elizabeth Harris, herself an established author and keen literary critic; Chris McCooey, a free-lance journalist and editor of one of my main sources of material; and lastly my literary agent, Merric Davidson, for his unstinting help and enthusiasm.

Joan de Smith
Tunbridge Wells, 1991

First Meeting

'the company of friends, tennis, eating and, above all, sleeping'
July 23rd, 1941

In the heat of the debate I forgot my promise and jumped to my feet, saying:

"Surely it depends whether you're talking about England or France, doesn't it? La Place published his 'Right to Work' towards the end of the eighteenth century and this influenced French workers' attitudes to the Industrial Revolution."

The words tumbled out before I caught the Chairman's eye. Embarrassed, I resumed my seat and tried to hide. I could not have presented a very attractive picture: a gawky, blushing, dark-haired, bespectacled schoolgirl dressed in a navy blue skirt, white pullover and wellingtons.

The subject of the debate was 'Does Machinery Increase Unemployment?'. Looking back over fifty years it seems an abstruse topic to have chosen for discussion. A few months previously, in May 1940, Churchill had become the leader of the coalition government. One of his first tasks had been to organise the evacuation of the BEF from Dunkirk. Then, in June, Italy declared war on the Allies and soon invaded British Somaliland and Egypt. That summer the Battle of Britain had been fought in the skies above south-east England from where my family had moved to the slightly safer area around High Wycombe, Buckinghamshire.

The Youth Club was an escape for young people from the dreariness and horrors of war. Debates and dances, musicals and plays (the talented members included Denis Norden) relieved the monotony of blackouts, poor food, and clothes rationing. Nobody – particularly those who were about to be called up – wanted to talk about the war.

Across the room I noticed a timid young undergraduate eyeing me with interest. He was about 5′11″, with dark hair and untidy clothes but the most interesting thing about him was his face. He was certainly not handsome. His complexion was pale, he wore glasses, which enlarged his gentle hazel eyes, and his long arms protruded from the sleeves of his V-necked pullover. Yet there was something attractive about his high forehead, generous mouth and reticent smile.

"Are you a h..h..history s..s..s student?" he called as he pushed his way through the crowd of teenagers milling round the door.

In his shyness he stammered badly, a defect which was to remain with him throughout his life, making his job as a University lecturer peculiarly trying. Stanley Alexander de Smith was eighteen, in his second year at Cambridge, a brilliant but socially awkward man, who was destined to become one of the great English law writers of his time.

I was busy wrapping myself up against the autumn chill and answered cautiously,

"Well, sort of. I'm very interested in the subject."

I could hardly tell him that I was only fourteen, still at school and writing an essay on La Place for homework. That I had wormed my way into this Youth Club debate, which was for seventeen to twenty year olds. That I had bribed the Chairman, my cousin, who had admitted me on the strict understanding that I kept my mouth shut and revealed my age to no-one.

This, then, was the setting for the first meeting of two young people who, though they rarely met, were to correspond regularly and frequently for six years, and whose letters touched on matters which ranged from music and art, through bullets and bloodshed, to love and marriage.

Unfortunately my letters did not survive. Frequently, particularly in the early days, they were returned to me corrected for grammar, spelling and appropriate word usage and, after noting my errors, I threw them away. Nevertheless much of their content can be gleaned from the four hundred replies. Most of Stanley's letters I sealed in dated envelopes after reading and then hid them away, though some were carried around in my pocket to be read and re-read until they fell to pieces. One such early letter described his feelings about our relationship. I had asked why sometimes he signed himself 'yours affectionately' whilst others ended 'with love from'. The gist of his reply was as follows:

> *'You must remember that I am only nineteen and not very experienced in these matters. I am not sure what love is and even if it can be defined it may*

STANLEY DE SMITH, WESTCLIFF, 1927.

not pertain to two people so far apart in years. However given that premiss and bearing in mind that what I am about to say must be taken cautiously and without any commitment on my part, to the best of my inadequate knowledge I believe that I am in love with you.'

Stanley was born in 1922, the first child of a comfortably off, middle class couple of no great intellectual pretensions. He grew up a solitary child, marked out early by a brilliant mind. At the age of two he was reading fluently. At three he knew the names and scoring history of every team in the English Football League. His favourite game was inventing teams and playing theoretical matches between them which resulted in them moving up and down the league table. And later he would amuse himself by finding the cube roots of eight figure numbers in his head.

Adored and protected by his parents and their maid, Mabel, he made few friends at the Junior school he attended in Westcliff and had little contemporary company apart from his young sister, Sylvia. Had he been born in the post-war era he would have been classified 'exceptionally gifted'. As it was he went on to the local Grammar school, matriculated at fourteen, won two State scholarships at sixteen, and went up to Cambridge at seventeen, just after war had broken out. Fortunately he had not suffered from the lack of special provision for his talents because he was not only bright but also very self-motivated.

His family had to abandon their Westcliff home the following year when all south-east coastal areas were evacuated. Access to the beaches was to be restricted to the forces and essential workers. Westcliff was more fortunate than Bungalow Town, at Shoreham, which was completely destroyed by the Army as the buildings there obstructed the view of gunners who had to fire into the sea from the nearby Downs.

Joe and Jenny de Smith moved with Mabel and their daughter into a large old house near High Wycombe station where they shared a stirrup pump with Gillie Potter who lived in their gate-house. Though he lightened Britain's war-time gloom with his comic radio shows Gillie Potter proved a morose neighbour with suspected Mosley sympathies. And of course it was to that rented house in High Wycombe that Stanley went to spend his summer vacation in 1940 and so to the youth club where we met. His cousins, Marjorie and Sybil, were members.

Thus fate and families brought us both that October evening to a room above the bar of the Red Lion. Our first three dates were all near disasters. A week or so after the Youth Club debate, we went out for a drink together accompanied by two friends of Stanley's from University, James and Molly, who are mentioned several times in the letters. I had never drunk alcohol let alone entered a pub and replied "The same as James" to the inevitable question. The green liquid arrived – it was Benedictine – and I swallowed it straight down. The horror of that first drink never wore off and I have rarely touched alcohol since.

Our next meeting was on the tennis courts. Stanley arrived with a college sweater slung over his shoulders, carrying three rackets. I wore black school gym shoes, blouse and shorts and carried only my glasses, without which I couldn't see the ball. After playing a few strokes Stanley came round my side of the net and showed me how to hold the racket he'd lent me. I had started playing tennis the previous term at school. He was Junior County Tennis Champion. The horror of that first game stayed with me, too, and I have rarely touched a racquet since.

Our third meeting took place the following spring. We went for a walk in the country side. Unsuitably clad in borrowed high-heeled sandals, a tight skirt and wearing my mother's lipstick I struggled bravely across the ploughed fields. Stanley asked what my views were on homosexuality, an illegal activity and taboo subject in those days, of which I was totally ignorant. Although shocked at his explanation I tried to sound blasé and informed but the effect was somewhat spoilt when one of the sandal heels snapped off.

Unable to keep up the pretence any longer I collapsed on the grassy path and in a mixture of laughter and tears told him the truth about my age. But he already knew – his mother had been at school with my Aunt Gertrude and they were still in touch.

In spite of our parents' obvious disapproval at the disparity in our ages, we decided to meet as often as we could. But we never managed to be alone together for more than a few hours at a time and over the next five years we were to meet alone less than a dozen times. Letters were the lifeline that kept us together.

Those which have survived begin in July '41 a few months after that country walk, though there had been several earlier ones. The excerpts which follow in this chapter cover three months of our correspondence in the summer of 1941.

Since our first meeting Germany had occupied Rumania, Yugoslavia, Bulgaria and Greece. Coventry had been blitzed and in May '41 Rudolph Hess made his ill-conceived flight to Scotland in an effort to persuade Britain to make peace with Germany so they could attack Russia together. The same month a German submarine sank the pride of the British fleet, HMS Hood.

Cambridge   *July 23rd 1941*

J. dear
You bet I'll be in town on Saturday. I think the Regent Palace is probably the best rendezvous. Please write as soon as you can spare time from rehearsing 'George and Margaret'. (The current Youth Club production in which I was playing the lead.)
I cannot deny that I have every inducement to work hard – for example we have to keep pace with the lectures and I've bought some massive text books – but factors like the company of friends, tennis, eating and, above all, sleeping, seem to consume the greater part of my time......

You may be able to get one of those Pelican books I mentioned at Smith's or Boots. I believe I pointed out that 'The Socialist Sixth of the World' does not embody a serious exposition of socialist theory. It is concerned primarily with the ethical aspects of everyday life under a socialist system. By the way, I should advise you not to read that sort of thing too conspicuously, at any rate at home. The status of a ''respectable young man'' is liable to be forfeited in consequence of observation of the influence exercised by the said young man over a respectable young woman.

Affectionately, Stanley

But the war news was not all gloomy. Britain had obtained fifty destroyers from America in September '40 although the US Lease-Lend Act did not become law until March '41. The Italian fleet had been severely damaged by a British air attack at Taranto and in December '40 Field Marshall Wavell, then Commander-in-Chief, British Forces in the Middle East, had launched his victorious offensive against the Italians in North Africa. And Britain retaliated three days after the Hood tragedy, by sinking the Bismarck.

The author of 'The Socialist Sixth of the World' was Hewlett Johnson, then Dean of Canterbury, generally referred to as the Red Dean. The book was originally published in 1939 by Gollancz whose imprints included The Left Book Club.

It was not uncommon for politically-minded students to be extremely left-wing before the war – Cambridge in particular was the cradle of future spies like Burgess and Maclean – though party members were dismayed at Russia's alliance with Hitler. However, many still clung to a communist viewpoint, justifying this by decrying Stalin's communism as pseudo-socialism. Others, like Stanley, thought that Russia was biding her time whilst re-arming herself and would eventually turn against Germany. When Germany invaded Russia a few weeks before Stanley wrote this letter, it seemed he had been right.

Though intensely interested in politics and at first idealistically inclined towards socialism Stanley never, at any time, allied himself to or joined any political party. He found all extreme political or religious views distasteful.

Cambridge   **July 28th, 1941**

I am writing this at my earliest opportunity in case you are wondering whether I was in London during last night's raid. Well, I wasn't but neither was I in Cambridge.

I had a snack in Oxford Street and then got a lift to a roundabout on the London – Cambridge road. If you've thought that door-to-door canvassers are pathetic, compare them with people trying without success to get a lift on a main road. It took me nearly an hour to find another motorist going in the right direction. He took me about 15 miles to Ware? — yes W A R E; and it isn't funny......

Someone advised me to enquire of one Mrs Partridge. By this time I should have been grateful to anyone who could have produced a nest. The lady in question was in Salvation Army uniform. In a spirit of Christian charity she agreed to put me up, and her paying guest vacated his bed accordingly. When I thanked him with profound gratitude, he said: "Don't thank me: we are not doing this for your sake: All things are God's and they are only lent to us. Our duty is to share them with out brothers in need" (I don't mean we shared the bed).

Mrs. Partridge gave me a cup of tea and a piece of bread and butter in the morning. When I was preparing to leave, she asked me whether I would put something in the Salvation Army box. I had 11d (about 5p) on me and gave her sixpence...... "Thank you," she said, with a frozen smile, "we charge 7/6, by the way." She will receive a postal order in the morning.

All my love.

He would probably have done better to offer her some of the plums he had picked in the Wycombe garden and was taking to Cambridge. Or possibly she might have accepted his sweet coupons in lieu of money. The old-fashioned system of bartering was back in full swing with six oranges equal to three eggs, and five tomatoes worth a tennis ball.

In spite of all the raids I remember London looking surprisingly tidy in parts. Demolition of bombed buildings and rebuilding was going on spasmodically. On one occasion we visited the undamaged part of Westminster Abbey though the eastern end was all shrouded in scaffolding. But as the war proceeded it soon became clear that whole areas of the city would have to be re-planned and most of the piecemeal construction, other than essential repairs, stopped. Materials and labour, too, were both in short supply. Wild flowers quickly took over the neglected bomb sites.

August '41 was a notable month. The first act of British/USSR co-operation led to the joint occupation of Iran, forcing the abdication of the Shah, Reza. The subsequent history of Iran may have been very different if Germany had not chosen to attack Russia that summer.

Cambridge   **August 2nd, 1941**

Need I say how glad I was to receive two letters from you in such quick succession.

I've seen one outstandingly good film since we last met: 'Primrose Path'. If you haven't seen it do so at the earliest opportunity. It is a film about the lives real people live — sordid lives, frustrated lives, even wasted lives —

*each trying to shake off the trammels imposed on them by our environment
and to live more fully. The characterisation was brilliant.*

*I hope to see a photograph of you in your next letter. The best photograph
I have of myself was taken with James – and that's not a very good one.*

'Primrose Path' was an American film made just before the war. It
describes the life of a girl from a seedy shanty town whose husband leaves
her when he discovers she has lied about her origins. Forced by her family
to live with an unsavoury old man to earn money she is eventually rescued
and forgiven by her husband. The unlikely co-stars of this film which so
impressed Stanley were Ginger Rogers and Joel McCrae.

The setting could hardly have been further from the comfortable life
Stanley was living at University where in spite of the war academic life
drifted on much as before. His time was divided between lectures, sports
(such as tennis), student gatherings and friends.

Cambridge   **August 7th, 1941**

*On Saturday I shall be playing tennis for the college against the
University Air Squadron. I expect to go to a political meeting on Friday. So I
am still having a fairly busy time up here, even though about half my
friends in college have gone now. One of them has been ignominiously
thrown out: he was trying to climb into college in the early hours while in a
most unsteady condition, and managed to fetch down the black-out
arrangements and also the Chaplain who was sleeping up above.*

*I shall have to do some work away from home for two or three weeks of the
coming vacation. It would be preferable to arrange for part of the time to
coincide with the week you are away on holiday.*

Till then, all my love.

*P.S. Here is the photograph you asked for. James looks supercilious and I am
smiling at someone rather feebly. I suppose it's better than nothing.*

Cambridge   **Aug 13th, 1941**

This is the last letter you will have from me before we meet again.

*On Saturday last we played our tennis match against the Air Squadron.
Although the team just lost, my partner and I did quite well.*

*I have been offered a job in London for part of the coming vacation. It's
with the National Council for Civil Liberties who were very willing to have
my assistance although they can't promise any remuneration in excess of
travelling expenses. It should give me some invaluable experience and the
work is really important for the whole community.*

Au revoir till Monday.

JAMES CLARKE AND STANLEY, CAMBRIDGE, 1941.

Although nowadays it is common for university students to work during the vacations, either to support themselves or to earn enough for an overseas holiday, it was virtually unknown in pre-war England. Being at University in wartime granted you a short reprieve from being called up for military service. But Stanley knew that resentment was rife amongst less fortunate youngsters and felt unpaid work was the least he could do to justify his privileged position.

High Wycombe   August 26th, 1941

You know of course about my grandfather. Thank you for your sympathy. He died, rather suddenly at about 9.45 on Friday — only about three hours after you left — and the funeral took place on Monday afternoon. We shall miss his presence in the house.

For the past hour or so I have been amusing myself making notes. Apart from working there isn't much for me to do just now. I shall probably begin this job with the Civil Liberties people later this week.

The weather is not quite so bad as it was. I hope it is better in Bournemouth. I appear to have been almost devoured by midges just above the tops of my socks. I'm still wondering how that happened.

I'm looking forward to having you back with me again, but in the meantime. I'm glad you are in a comfortable hotel. My thoughts will be with you in the dark walnut room.

First Quarrel

'as you may have guessed your letter came as a hard blow'
undated (1941)

By the beginning of September the Germans had reached Leningrad and two weeks later they captured Kiev. Most of Stanley's time was taken up with his Civil Liberties job though we did manage to meet on one occasion after I returned from Bournemouth. The possibility of his being called up for the Armed Services was an ever present threat but he resolved to continue studying, hoping that his youth – he was still only nineteen – would enable him to finish his degree in the summer of 1942.

Many of his friends, however, had been called up without completing their degrees and he returned to Cambridge expecting to find the college a dull place without them. Fortunately this did not prove to be the case.

Cambridge   **October 8th, 1941**

I find that we have four lectures in the morning. Which is just too bad, for I want to hear Mr Attlee speak in the Guildhall tonight and there are many other things to do besides. For instance I have to make enquiries about the OTC. You may be sure that when I begin my training I shall give you a full account of how I get on.

I miss you very much and would give anything to have you here with me. Anyway, I'm hoping to get a letter from you before Sunday and that you will have something more interesting than this to write about – for example, the result of our history essay.

For now, my fondest love

The above reference to (our) history essay is an example of the many ways in which Stanley helped me. He usually outlined a suitable structure with section headings, listed essential points I ought to make, and provided me with a list of reference books. Given the lack of proper education that I was receiving, his assistance was quite invaluable and without it I would never have achieved any academic success.

Cambridge   **October 12th, 1941**

First, I am glad you are doing a reasonable amount of work. Keep it up! The marking of your (our) history essay interested me; but I felt slightly aggrieved at the B+. Modesty is not my greatest virtue......

The pressure on my time will further increase shortly, for I am now not only a member of the OTC but I am also a Home Guard − though my duties are confined to Cambridge. Unfortunately it will only be infantry training; not until a later stage are we allowed to take a specialised OTC course in artillery. Anyway I have my uniform, which includes greatcoat, battledress, forage cap, boots, anklets, and the necessary badges. You seem to be anxious to have a photo of me in this rig-out, but I don't think I look ridiculous enough in it to be really funny.

But don't run away with the idea that the major portion of my time is occupied by such trivialities. I am generally talking, eating or drinking or combining these functions, with my friends. We don't always discuss serious topics: often we ''reminisce'' or exchange experiences or just play the fool − a very popular way of passing the time up here. It explains how I and probably most other people manage to waste such an incredible amount of time in Cambridge − if, that is, it is really wasted.

Yesterday afternoon I played my first game of football, captaining one side in the College trials. It was quite a good game and I was still on my feet at the end. Just after I had come back from football, I had an unexpected visitor, Percy. He is at present stationed about 15 miles from Cambridge. I introduced him to some of my pals and he got on very well with them. I took him into Hall to have dinner as my guest − unfortunately they gave us what seemed to be inferior horseflesh, but the Army's used to that......

If you don't feel like working and haven't the opportunity to amuse yourself, remember that it is very important to increase one's knowledge of politics and allied topics.

Finally, my fondest love. How I miss you!

PS Your portrait is greatly admired among the gentlemen, ma'am.

Most students were obliged to eat their main meals in college unless they could afford to eat frequently in the cafés and restaurants that abounded in Cambridge. Ration cards and points coupons had to be handed in to the Junior Common Room at the beginning of term but in any case student accommodation rarely had facilities for self-catering.

Cambridge   **October 16th, 1941**

Before your letter arrived I was feeling really anxious about its non-appearance. But, as things turned out, I had placed too much confidence in the post for actually this was one of those letters which takes a day and a half to get from you to Cambridge. Now, could such things happen, could such mental cruelty be inflicted in a Socialist state?

Any intelligent person who has access to knowledge can make life at least interesting. The sort of work you do is a good deal more varied and interesting than mine, and there are so many important things in science, in history, in politics, which are quite new to you. Of course, I am in a much more congenial atmosphere – though certain aspects of life up here irritate me intensely. Well, I'm not quite sure where all these arguments are supposed to lead. If I keep on in this strain I shall soon come to the Lord's Prayer.

One thing emerges from all this incoherent waffling; and that is that I think we should definitely see each other if we get the slightest chance to do so before December even if only for a few hours. Anyway, I feel pretty strongly about it. It's for you to make the best arrangement you can, if you do want to meet me.

And so until I see you, my fondest love, dear.

PS Give my love to my cousins and tell them I'll drop them a line soon.

Cambridge   *October 21st, 1941*

I take it that your half-term runs from October 31st to November 3rd. Now, unless Mr Bradshaw isn't telling the truth – which is almost impossible – it seems that it will be quite an easy matter for Miss Natley to pay Mr de Smith a visit during those few days.

There follows two pages of timetables and travel instructions

If you agree with me, and if you are willing to come all this way just to see me, then write and tell me so. But that is really up to you, darling. I can't tell you how I shall long to get a reply from you, saying you will come up here. If you do come it will be an absolutely delightful situation, and one which is not likely to occur again.

To deal with your letter: I'm very glad you continue to develop politically and I excuse your scribble and hope you will reciprocate with mine. I go in for a certain amount of political activity – which is of unprecedented importance just now. I have played in a couple of football matches so far. And finally – today I had my first parade. It wasn't very exciting: we were instructed in the mechanism & aiming of a rifle, we were given elementary military drill, the sergeant used a lot of funny words, and so on.

Cambridge   *Date torn off 1941*

I had hoped and expected to write this letter in a happy frame of mind. But, as you may have guessed, your letter came as a hard blow. Is this going to be our first quarrel? You have made it clear that you won't travel to Cambridge by yourself. You explain that you can't possibly face such a long journey by train. Very probably, also, you have other reasons, and even better ones, for not travelling all this way in one day.

But don't draw the conclusion from what I have said that I am biting my pen in a state of pent-up fury. Before I pass on there's one remark that I certainly don't understand. You say ''the difference in our positions is greater than we at first thought − or at least, so it appears to me''. Admittedly there are difficulties in our relationship; but they are insignificant in comparison with those of many other people. Three weeks without you is bad enough but the prospect of another five more of desolation would make a stronger man than I quail.

If you still require convincing that I love you, then the uniformity of the theme which has run through my recent letters should be enough to convince you. I love you, and I love you passionately. Just like that, darling. I want nothing in the whole world so much as to be with you. You have become the centre of my life and you are going to stay there.

Cambridge   **November 2nd, 1941**

Now that the effect of a blazing fire has counteracted the cold and damp which were penetrating my loving heart, I can sit down and write more or less a decent letter.

Last week I went to two political meetings (one on India, with Harry Pollitt as principal speaker and the other an all party meeting on aid to Russia), and to a very fine play at the Arts Theatre, 'The Cherry Orchard' by Chekov. If you haven't read anything by Chekov you ought to make up for lost time. He portrays the suffering, the humour and the pathos of the purposelessness in the Russian landowning classes in the latter part of the 19th century. Recently they have broadcast some of his plays.

Although I did not see 'The Cherry Orchard' I did manage to see a performance, which I enjoyed very much, of another of Chekov's plays, 'Uncle Vanya', at the Westminster Theatre, but not till two years later. Stanley's interest in the theatre and cinema meant that our meetings usually included a visit to one or other. I failed to persuade him to come either swimming or ice skating with me though occasionally I managed to get him to go to a concert or ballet.

Ironically, it was Armistice Day when news came through that the largest British aircraft carrier, HMS Ark Royal, had been sunk. It was her torpedoes that had slowed down the Bismarck six months earlier.

For me the news was particularly poignant. A year earlier I had persuaded a young cousin of mine, with whom I was supposed to be sailing to safety in Canada, to stay with me in England. The ship we should have sailed on, the 'City of Benares', was torpedoed in the mid-Atlantic with the loss of eighty-five children's lives. Only eight of the evacuees survived. But within a few months my cousin was dead, struck down by tubercular meningitis for which there was then no treatment.

Cambridge   *Tuesday, November 11th, 1941*

I have some rather important news concerning myself, though you may have heard it already. The War Office have cancelled my enlistment notice for Wednesday. When I rang up home this evening they had heard nothing from Maidstone, where I was due to report, but in view of the War Office decision the Maidstone authorities will almost certainly do likewise. So I am still in Cambridge – and with no more idea when they will call me up than I had ten days ago. Anyway, whatever happens I owe a very pleasant journey in a very pleasant carriage to the aforesaid minor crisis.

I bought a little book, published in the Thinker's Library at the station and I've found it very interesting. It is called 'Fact and Faith' by J. B. S. Haldane, and it deals with several fundamental scientific and religious problems.

When I got back to Cambridge I remembered I was down for fire-watching duty from 11.30pm to 7am. So I didn't have much sleep last night and just now I am feeling rather sleepy. Probably you are feeling a lot more sleepy as I write these words; for it is a quarter past eleven, and every respectable young woman is in bed (by herself) at this time of night.

Life becomes a very pleasant thing for several days before I am due to see you again, and happy memories linger for a long time after we have parted.

Until about December 9th – if not before – my very fondest love, darling. Write to me, won't you?

Yours indefinitely

Cambridge   *November 16th, 1941*

I am college representative for the undergraduate Council – the student's representative body – which is organising a canvass of all Colleges to induce them to work in rest centres, give blood transfusions, cultivate allotments – in fact, to do almost anything which nobody has any time for at all. It's rather discouraging work but it's necessary in order to show that the Universities are not completely divorced from the War.

It seems that my call-up has been definitely cancelled, so that it's quite possible that I may be able to carry on up here till next June. That means I have to work for another First. The prospect doesn't exactly exhilarate me. When I get back home in about three weeks time I don't want to see you around – except when I can't do without you. If I loved you a little less than I do, I might mean something by that. But, things being what they are, it just doesn't mean a thing.

Now, remember, you've got a job to do as well. You have to get through your examinations and also to learn more about society and politics. You can't justify your existence by thinking beautiful thoughts all the time in virgin solitude. So keep at it. By writing more letters like your last you can make our period of separation seem much happier – to me at least.

PS I hope it really was me who recommended you to buy the 'Physiology of Sex'.

Writing letters was no problem because I could slouch about in school things, my straight hair dangling in my eyes. Getting ready for our rare dates, however, required some ingenuity. Finding 'glamorous' clothes to wear on outings was almost impossible. I had no sisters and my mother's clothes were several sizes too large, though I could and did borrow shoes, lipsticks and jewellery. But as for my hair, little could be done. It was extremely difficult to get hair clips, shampoo, setting lotion, hair nets or perming lotion. I used to sleep with my hair twisted in rags and even resorted to making skirts out of old curtains, like Scarlet O'Hara, though needlework was not my forté.

Cambridge   **November 22nd, 1941**

Fortunately I have found a free hour at last, and that is only because there weren't enough seats in Hall tonight. It's College Night, which means there are free drinks all round and speeches after 2nd Hall.

I read about the Anglo-Soviet Campaign which you mentioned. You seem to be impregnating my sister with seditious views, by the way. The Joan Beauchamp who spoke at the meeting is, I believe, a friend of Molly's.

I'm getting pretty fed up with Cambridge again, and this makes me all the more eager to be with you even though it will only be at home. I think I love you more with each day that passes. Life wouldn't be worth living if I didn't know that only a few weeks or days distant you would be there.

Perhaps I'll bring my Home Guard outfit home so that you can have the thrill of seeing your soldier boy in uniform.

Cambridge   **November 27th, 1941**

I am writing one or two letters, doing a little general reading, and blancoing and polishing my equipment – the last I can cordially recommend as a pleasant means of whiling away an idle hour. On December 6th I'm going on manoeuvres with the Home Guard around Cambridge. I don't know what their scope will be, and even if I did I should probably not be supposed to disclose it. As the soul-stirring poster says in Headquarters:

'Tell nobody — not even Her'. Anyway I do know that the local Hospital had quite a busy time after the last scouting expedition.

After the festivities on College Night I was out with a group of friends when we were stopped by the Proctors. I had no square (mortar-board) and so I was summoned to appear before one of the said gentlemen. But he let me off with only a caution.

Today we had another football match, but this time we only drew. Nevertheless we shall probably be the runners up in the College League table.

Before I lose all sense of space and time in recounting my unexciting adventures, let's talk about you. A compound of Marxism and highbrow music is hardly what could have interested you a few months ago. Evidently someone is going to explain to you the Marxian theory of value. If you can understand it and state it to me when I come back, I'll give you a kiss. You ask me also to tell you something about mechanistic determinism. Well, I do know a little more about that although it's very difficult to explain in everyday terms.

(1) Mechanistic determinism is a theory of history and a form of philosophy.

(2) A lot of people take up this attitude with regard to Socialism. They say that Socialism is inevitable, and that the attitude which you and I adopt doesn't really matter much. I've even heard Conservatives take up this point of view.

There follows two full pages of explanation

All this is frightfully intellectual and divorced from our immediate emotions — and our relationship is I think primarily emotional. Once I am back with you I hope to convince myself that I am essentially human.

We did manage to meet once during the Michaelmas term, on Sunday, 30th November, when we went to an afternoon concert at the Royal Albert Hall. The programme, which cost 6d, included works by Borodin, Beethoven, Dvorak and Sibelius. Basil Cameron conducted the Royal Philharmonic Orchestra with Pouishnoff as the soloist.

As Stanley was writing his next letter the Italians were surrendering to the British Forces in Ethiopia. Two days later Britain, Russia and the US held a three-power conference in Moscow.

Cambridge   **December 4th, 1941**

First let me say how sorry I was to hear of your uncle's sudden death. I had better defer tendering personal condolence until I return home.

All my lectures for this term are over now, and for the next two or three days most of my time will be spent in packing and at the Corps. There's this confounded exercise over this weekend. I sincerely hope that your presumption that "the manoeuvres are not mechanised" is correct. They go by the not very auspicious name of "the scorch".

The term has ended just at the stage when I am getting really interested in my work and fed up to the teeth with Cambridge: the two things never seem to coincide. Also I wound up the Undergraduate Council work. Our collection for the Medical Aid for Russia seems to have beaten all the other colleges.

Since I went to the concert with you I've been to see a couple of films. One of them starred Walter Winchell and various other smart guys. The other wasn't too good either. I believe it was called 'George and Margaret' – not meaning, of course, to decry our Youth Club production of the same name.

I'm glad you enjoyed our day in town last Sunday. One more thing before I close. Give my humblest apologies to my cousins, Marjorie and Sybil, for my failure to write to them. •I shall expect you to have them eating out of my hand by the time I get back.

December '41 began with the greatest set-back the Allies had yet experienced. On the 7th the Japanese attacked Pearl Harbour without warning and the next day occupied Thailand and invaded Malaya. A couple of days later the Axis declared war on the USA and the Germans sank The Prince of Wales and HMS Repulse. Though Repulse was old, the Prince of Wales was one of the latest and most powerful of British battleships and Churchill had sailed in her to the States two months previously.

We crowded around the wireless for every news broadcast but they seemed to get worse and worse. As Stanley was writing his last letter of 1941 the Japanese took Wake Island and on Christmas Day they invaded Hong Kong.

Cambridge   **undated 1941**

This is for your sixteenth birthday and for Christmas, too, if you like.

The book* is advanced and is difficult to read continuously, but I am assured by all the book reviews and by my scientific friends that nothing so good has been written on the subject. I hope you like it. All my love

*'The Social Function of Science' by J.D. Bernal, then Professor of Physics at Birkbeck College. I still have the book, inscribed and dated.

My mother also gave me a book for my sixteenth birthday called 'Science for the Citizen', by Lancelot Hogben. That, too, is inscribed and dated and in my possession.

Parental Problems

'The world is not made merely for the benefit of people who love each other'
January 13th 1942

1942 did not start well. In the first week of January the Germans pushed back the Russian parachutists who had landed in the Crimea. Manila was captured by the Japanese, Zagreb synagogue finally disappeared after being dismantled stone by stone by the Nazis, the Philippines were declared by General Marshall impossible to defend and the German's launched a major offensive against Tito's partisan forces in Yugoslavia.

On a personal level, too, difficulties had emerged which threatened our relationship. Stanley's parents, for whom he had great affection and respect as well as being financially totally dependant on them, had made it almost impossible for us to meet during the vacation by insisting on his fulfilling family commitments. Not unreasonably they argued he should devote the rest of his spare time to preparation for his law finals. His postponed call-up had given him this unwarranted opportunity when so many of his friends were already fighting and dying. Why was he wasting his time with girlfriends – particularly one so young?

My parents seemed to be in collusion with them though we did manage to see each other at the Club and in his cousins' house on a few occasions. I, too, had spent much of the Christmas holiday engaged in unpleasant arguments. My basic problem revolved around schooling – or rather the lack of it. My own school in Hampstead had stayed put, though it was operating on a 'mornings only' basis. The Grammar School I was now attending had been evacuated from London and the girls billeted with families in and around High Wycombe, whose population had already grown from thirty thousand to seventy thousand with other south-east evacuees. I was lucky, one of only two girls in the school living with her own family. Many less fortunate children suffered permanent mental scars from culture shock.

The families with whom they were billeted were often very different from their own in habits, family structure, wealth and expectations. It could be devastating to both the child and those taking them in and, of course, it worked both ways – for example, the rich child in the poor home and the poor child in the rich. But there were also numerous cases of people from totally different class backgrounds forming lifelong friendships.

The school I attended met mostly in a church hall, six classes in one room, and we devoted much of our time to singing and needlework. There were no science facilities available, no games or gym though we occasionally did PT, and no qualified maths teachers. A local school kindly provided classrooms on some days.

After eighteen months of this I was desperate. With Stanley's encouragement I read very widely and went to the local Technical School one evening a week. In London my closest friend, Margaret Pincus, persuaded her parents to allow me to share her room so that I could study with her for the matriculation exams at our old school in Hampstead. I begged, pleaded, cajoled and promised anything if only they would allow me to go back to my London school.

Margaret's family were Australian. Her father, Paul, a research dentist, had come to England to get another degree – he already had ten sets of letters after his name – and they were stranded here when war broke out. Paul served as a captain at the Army Dental School throughout the war. Her mother, Myrtle, seemed permanently occupied making chutneys and blackberry jam, fashioning rugs out of old silk stockings or crocheting squares for the largest table-cloth I had ever seen, intended for Margaret's trousseau.

John, Margaret's elder brother, became a great friend. He joined the RAF at seventeen and got his wings at Cranwell. At the time he was Britain's youngest pilot though he wore an Australia flash on his shoulder. Bobby, the youngest, looked after the animals, dogs, cats, goldfish and rabbits.

The bombing in London had quietened down though our own house had recently been damaged. We had returned for a weekend just before Christmas to collect some belongings but on the Sunday my mother said she suddenly felt ill at ease and insisted we must return to Wycombe immediately.

The lady next door had a similar premonition. All day a black crow had sat on their roof and that night, although there was no air raid warning, she persuaded her family to bed down in Hampstead Underground Station. At 1am on Monday morning their house received a direct hit and was obliterated, though fortunately the blast went the other way and our house suffered only superficial damage. But the same stick of bombs had caught the corner shop at the end of the road and all the occupants, who lived above, were killed.

Reluctantly my parents gave their permission for me to live with Margaret's family provided I did not see Stanley until the exams, his and mine, were over. I agreed to the embargo, though they later relented. I knew once I left Wycombe the opportunities for our meeting would be greatly reduced anyway.

On the day Stanley was due to return to Cambridge we had planned to travel as far as London together. Even this was nearly thwarted by his mother who was so annoyed with her son's refusal to give me up that she ignored my presence on the station platform. She even tried without success to put his luggage into a separate compartment. The journey took one hour to Paddington, the only hour we spent alone together that Christmas.

Not all the war news that week was gloomy. On January 1st in an historic declaration Churchill and Roosevelt, together with twenty-six other nations, vowed to devote their total resources to fighting the Axis. They called themselves 'the United Nations'. And at Bletchley British code breakers were at last deciphering some of the German Enigma messages, a breakthrough which played a vital part in the success of the invasion of Europe, in which Stanley took part, two years later. On January 5th 1942 two allied officers escaped from Colditz. One of them was Airey Neave, later to become Secretary of State for Northern Ireland, who was assassinated by the IRA.

In the second week in January the weather in Britain turned very cold, with severe frost and snow. On the Russian front the Soviet counter-offensive began in the bitterest conditions. German wounded froze to death as the temperature fell to minus forty degrees centigrade but Hitler refused to allow any withdrawal. The Japanese were nearing Singapore and were only a hundred and thirty miles from the island as Stanley wrote his first letter of 1942 to me.

Cambridge   *January 13th 1942*

My emotional stability seems to be rather shaken tonight and since you are the seat of the disturbance I must convey my thoughts to you by the only medium available. The events of the last twenty four hours have been very upsetting to me but they have principally had the effect of proving to me how intensely I really love you. My depression is due partly to the fact that I am leaving you for at least two months, partly to the fact that I have offended my parents but above all to the fact that I have had to acknowledge to myself the possibility of losing you altogether. The harm done can be tactfully repaired or at worst patched up and in the meantime we both have jobs to get on with.

But you must remember, as I must, that the world is not made merely for the benefit of people who love each other. Anyone who is to justify his existence at all must make whatever contribution lies within his or her power to further human happiness and progress, regardless of whether that involves a diminution of his private individual happiness. If either of us falls short of this standard, as we often do, we must learn from our mistakes and do our best to base our conduct on proper principles. I feel certain if we fail to do this it must in the long run be fatal to our relationship.

I love you very much but I must not allow my love for you to constitute an obsession which will prevent me fulfilling duties which are more important than you or I or anyone else. And you will take the same view, I am sure. To me this means WORK LIKE HELL! with useful political activity providing a constant background. To you I hope it'll mean "I've got to get Matric — French as well." In the meantime write to me regularly, won't you, darling. I worry about you being in London.

Re-reading this I know it sounds awfully pompous but I do really believe what I've written even though I haven't managed to express it very well.

I succeeded in losing my gas-mask in black 'leather' case apparently in the

taxi from Paddington to Liverpool Street. Would you get in touch with the
Paddington Street Lost Property Office and find out where it might have
ended up? As for you, I hope you got to your destination safely and cheaply.
PS How about trying to get that photo taken whilst you're in Town?

I could not make up my mind whether his sentiments about love owed more to Tolstoy's view that you can't build happiness on another's unhappiness or to Richard Lovelace, 'I could not love thee, Dear, so much, /Loved I not honour more.'

His request for a photograph was not easy to satisfy. Many professional photographers had been drafted into the forces or, if too old, were engaged on other military work. Rolls of film were difficult to get and most family cameras lay unused throughout the war. Appeals were made to the Ministry of Supply to release more film, by social workers amongst others. They claimed that photos of absent wives and children were necessary to maintain the morale of men in the fighting line.

A few months later a reverse appeal was made to the public to submit pre-war continental holiday snaps to the Admiralty. The planning of the invasion, though not to take place for another two years, had already begun and fine details of coastal areas and rivers, etc. were urgently needed.

Cambridge   Saturday, January 17th, 1942

You haven't replied to the letter which I posted on Wednesday morning. I've
a horrible suspicion that I sent it to the wrong address. If I did then it's just
too bad because it was to say the least a very emotional letter. It's hellish not
to see or hear from you for 6 whole days.

The weather is absolutely awful – very chilly – and my rooms
draughtier than I thought and I've got a bit of a cold. There's no fire in my
bedroom and last night I found ice in the bottom of my hot-water bottle. And
always when I wake up in the morning the tip of my nose is frozen. Added
to which the College's supply of firelighters has run out, so that it's very
difficult to get a fire to light now even in the sitting room.

I'll just have to forget my woes in hard work. Even if we can't meet you
can at any rate send me a photograph of yourself. Please! You don't seem to
realise how much I want one.

I sent him a snap-shot taken near the Rye in Wycombe, standing on a little bridge which we had walked over to the tennis courts the year we met. He carried this photo all through the war.

This morning at 8.30 I had the pleasure of going off to Corps, a mile from the College, in a snowstorm, enduring three and a half hours of lectures etc and then coming back in a hailstorm.

When I last wrote I don't think Professor Winfield had invited me to write up a long and important case for this year's Cambridge Law Journal. Well, he's just done so. In addition there's a devil of a lot of back work still to be made up. I have some questions to answer for supervision tomorrow morning. I was unhappily compelled to abstract a book from its proper place in the Library by dint of much stealth and cunning and now must needs peruse the said volume until the cock croweth on the morrow and thereafter return it to its appropriate abode.

You asked me about the importance of Disraeli. My answer is that unless he was the founder of Tory Democracy I don't know who really was. As far as I know he was the creator of modern Conservatism and based his political policies on a sort of romantic imperialism and social reform. He legalised peaceful picketing and other Trade Union practices during strikes by an Act of 1875.

I'm glad to say that I've re-established amicable relations with my parents. In fact the other day they sent me a very large parcel of warm clothing and various luxuries, such as chocolate, home-made marmalade and a new towel.

PS I have been informed by the Lambeth Lost Property Office that they have my gas mask. Just as well there's been no gas raids.

Professor Winfield was at that time Professor of English Law at Cambridge. Although getting old – he was born in 1878 – and rather deaf, he was a terror to his students but at the same time one whose lectures they could not afford to miss. He was the author of a standard work still much used known as 'Winfield on Tort' and he edited the Cambridge Law Journal for twenty years. In 1949 he was knighted and died four years later, aged 75.

I'm actually working hard now and am almost liking it so that I'm devoting as much time as possible to law while the spell lasts. If I appear less impassioned you can attribute it entirely to that.

'O never say that I was false of heart
Though absence seemed my flame to qualify'
A pretty thought – Shakespeare's I mean.

I had a letter from Natey yesterday and one from James today. Natey has invited me down to spend a weekend with him next vacation but I'm afraid there won't be much time for work or for home life next Vac as OTC camp is

*likely to take a good slice out of it. James had quite a good deal to say. He too
wants to meet me some time next Vac. He was very sympathetic about our
emotional entanglements. I'll quote his words ''God! I can sympathise with
any filial duty/love life dilemma. Yours is no special case: seems to be an
affliction of our generation.''*

*Sorry darling this is hardly suitable for parental perusal. Do you think it
would make any difference if I finished up 'yours affectionately'? But I don't
think I will. It wouldn't express my love for you adequately.*

My mother frequently asked to see Stanley's letters but I hid them away
among my school books, saying there was nothing interesting in them and
that I had torn them up.

The Japanese were now within fourteen miles of Singapore and had
landed in New Guinea. In the Middle East Benghazi changed hands for the
fourth time as Rommel pushed the British back towards Tobruk. 46 Allied
ships, nearly 200,000 tons, carrying vital supplies for the war effort had been
sunk off the coast of America. And in Germany a leading Nazi,
inappropriately named Martin Luther, was given the task of finding 'the
Final Solution to the Jewish Question'. In the House of Commons Balfour
urged 'Let there be justice'(for those who commit these crimes against
humanity) 'but let it be tempered with memory'.

Cambridge   **February 8th, 1942**

(The day the Japanese invaded Burma)
*When I get to a certain stage in preparing for an examination I find it
terribly difficult to sit down and write anything other than notes or essays.
Also there's this blasted article for the Law Journal. I had already drafted my
contribution when the case was reported in full on Saturday (yesterday).
The report was about four times as long as the one on which I had based my
note so I'll have to re-write it. Damn.*

*Your letters, far from boring me, are a major event in my life. But your
absence no less than your presence has a decidedly adverse effect upon my
powers of concentration. I'm glad to see you are not neglecting cultural
activities. But remember that political knowledge is every bit as important as
cultivating your personal tastes and engaging in social activities.*

Cambridge   **February 12th, 1942**

*I've handed in my article for the Cambridge Law Journal now.
Unfortunately there's still Cert A to prepare for and I seem to waste a
considerable part of most mornings by getting up at a very unsatisfactory*

hour. By the time you get this I shall probably have taken my Tests of Elementary Training in the rifle.

This coming Sunday I'm expecting a visit from my mother and possibly my father. It will be a welcome break in the monotony. James is also going to be in Cambridge though for sundry reasons I don't suppose I shall see much of him. It seems very probable I shall have to spend the first fortnight of the Vac up here, after all, but we must try and meet somehow.

To answer your query re Trade Unions, I'll just summarise how I think the subject might be treated:

(1) Combination Acts of 1789 and 1800 passed at the height of the reactionary periods following the French Revolution rendered Trade Unions illegal. (You haven't forgotten, have you, that we met over a discussion on this topic?)

(2) 1824. As a result of the agitation (n.b. Francis Place) TUs were legalised though their powers of lawful action were strictly limited by the Act of 1825.

(3)-(9)etc.................................

If you deal with these nine major landmarks in the suggested manner you should get a good mark. I hope this will be of some help to you, anyway.

This time Stanley's efforts were suitably rewarded and I received an A+ for 'our' essay.

Strikes virtually ceased during the First World War and though the intervening peace from 1918-1939 saw some of the most notable examples of working class solidarity in the face of increasing unemployment and depression, the outbreak of the Second World War brought the cessation of much, though not all, union activity for some time.

Patriotism, though less jingoistic than twenty-five years earlier, was the order of the day in the face of the horrors perpetrated by the enemy. Factory Acts were forgotten, pay bargaining was put in storage for the duration and the working week included all hours – usually at least 60 hours a week – one could give to help supply the armed forces.

On February 15th the Japanese captured Singapore. Of the 60,000 prisoners more than half died before the end of the war and there were horrifying tales of brutality. Sixty-five Australian nurses, of whom only one survived, were driven into the sea and shot. The Prime Minister of Australia was certain that Singapore was Australia's Dunkirk but Churchill was, as ever, more positive. 'Let us move forward steadfastly together into the storm and through the storm'.

Cambridge   **February 17th, 1942**

On Friday afternoon I took my tests in Rifle use and passed all that I went in for. I have still to pass my Bren Gun tests which are pretty formidable.

And then there's the dreaded Cert A. which will be on March 15th or 16th. Term ends on the 13th March. If I should happen to get Cert A I'll have to remain up here till 28th for an intensive short course. So you see my spare time will be terribly small. I don't like this at all.

On Saturday I was at last able to get a game of football – the first in nearly three months. But unfortunately the pitch was as slippery as ice and the match was in the first round of the inter-College Cup so that when the game ended with the score level we had to play extra time. CAT'S scored the winning goal but at the finish I could hardly stand. As I managed to stub my toe in the blackout that night my gait on Sunday was not exactly vigorous.

But Sunday was a pleasant day. My mother and father came down from Wycombe early in the morning and we all had a good time though I wasn't sure whether I was meant to be entertaining them or whether they were entertaining me. James was up here for the day, too. I was very glad to see him again and he and Molly had tea with myself and my parents. He's coming up again in the last week of Term when he's passed out from Sandhurst.

Tonight, after a cold afternoon's Corps, I've decided to confine my activities to letter-writing and to going to a talk in the college by Dr F.R. Leavis, who is one of the leading literary critics in the country. He's speaking on English Literature Between Two Wars.

PS Your new school uniform seems very intriguing: jumpers and white socks are a most pleasing combination.

On February 19th Darwin harbour was bombed by the Japanese who destroyed all the seventeen ships anchored there. Unfortunately the month brought many other shipping losses elsewhere. The Germans began successfully intercepting British naval signals whilst the advantage we held through cracking Enigma messages was temporarily lost as codes changed, a bitter blow to the code makers and breakers at Bletchley.

On a personal level I was beginning to find our separation very frustrating. There was no-one really to discuss my feelings with, as Margaret thought I should give less time to worrying about Stanley and more time to her brother, John. After all, she pointed out, John was in the Air Force and quite likely not to survive, whilst Stanley was skulking in Cambridge avoiding National Service.

Schoolwork, too, was proving excessively difficult, in spite of Stanley's help. I had missed so much and despaired of ever catching up. But I still found time to go with Margaret and her parents to see Ivor Novello in 'The Dancing Years'.

JOHN PINCUS, WITH HIS SPITFIRE 'J FOR JAKE'.

Cambridge   **February 24th, 1942**

You really mustn't get so depressed about things, darling. You know, don't you, that there's only one thing to do when two people are in our position – keep one's mind occupied with other important things. It was only by doing this that I converted myself last month from the embodiment of despondency into a more reasonable sort of person. You have a good excuse for feeling depressed over our position but all we can really do is pretend that things are – or will be sometime – better than they are right now.

Next weekend from 8pm on Saturday till 1pm on Sunday we have a Home Guard exercise. We have been warned that we can expect to march at least fifteen miles and that we should consider ourselves lucky if we are able to sleep in a barn! On March 13th there is another exercise and on the 16th there is the Cert A exam. So if you can manage any weekend before the end of term it would have to be the 7th/8th. If we can't meet then we'll just have to wait and hope that my military and domestic obligations – and your parents – will not make it impossible for us to see each other during the next Vacation. We weren't very fortunate over Christmas. You know how much I love you, darling, so you can imagine how much I am missing you.

Academic work unfortunately is taking a receding place in my order of priorities. I've lots of Corps to do. I've got to pass my Bren Gun tests and then there's this blasted exercise this weekend. On Thursday I'm having tea with Professor Winfield who edits the Cambridge Law Journal. In his lecture today he mentioned the case I am reviewing and that a gentleman in the room had kindly undertaken to annotate it for the CLJ and advised everyone to study with 'the greatest attention this learned note' when the Journal appears in April. Whereat the said learned gentleman was rather astonished and very elated. It surprised me because when he spoke at a meeting recently on '40 years in the Law Faculty' I told him how I thought the curriculum ought to be reformed. I thought that had cooked my goose but apparently not.

Many years later Stanley's career was to be linked with Professor Winfield's in a number of ways.

Law Finals

'Spring makes Cambridge beautiful'
May 10th, 1942

T hirty-one years after the publication of his first article in the Cambridge Law Journal, Stanley became the Editor of the Journal himself but I am sure that on that February day in 1942 such a thought never entered his mind.

At home our trivial difficulties in coping with life day-to-day were increased by the announcement that shops could no longer provide wrapping of any kind for goods. This meant among other things that we had to take our old newspapers – very valuable for making spills to light our meagre fires – to the fish and chip shop. It was announced that no white bread would be made from April and that by July the petrol ration would be cut to zero. Children's toes, it was reported, were being deformed by shoe rationing.

It was still possible to buy practically anything from black marketeers but they did not flourish in England and were vigorously prosecuted. In the streets of London white feathers, symbolising cowardice, were being handed to young men, such as Stanley, not in uniform. But often the gesture was grossly inappropriate as in the case of those invalided out of the services. Such things paled to insignificance beside the horrors of life in Europe. During February nearly fifty thousand Warsaw Jews and a hundred thousand Russians in the besieged city of Leningrad died of starvation. On the Eastern Front the temperature fell to minus 52 degrees Centigrade.

On March 6th General Alexander, the last man to leave the Dunkirk beaches, ordered Rangoon to be evacuated. A few days later the Japanese took both Rangoon and Java. In the North Sea the German battleship Tirpitz, whose location was monitored through Enigma signals, was attacked but not sunk. The British bombers were not much more successful in their first big raid against German industrial towns. The raids were designed to relieve the pressure on Russia by diverting German resources from the Eastern Front since the prospect of a Second Front in Europe in 1942 was no longer a realistic hope.

Cambridge   **March 3rd, 1942**

Many thanks for your letter and photo. I think it is a good one but not good enough. Anyway it's a very fine embellishment for my comparatively bare apartments. Unfortunately though it tends to make me think of you even more often than I normally do.

The Home Guard exercise which took place last weekend began at 8pm on

Saturday, continued through the night and concluded at about 11.30am on Sunday. I can solemnly assure you that we marched, at a conservative estimate, 25 miles in full equipment and greatcoats, with a rifle and Sunday's breakfast thrown in. Our Company was detailed to attack an aerodrome about ten miles from Cambridge. We got within half a mile of the place at about 3.30am, having overcome the opposition of the local Home Guard, when we decided to put up at an old farm until 6am when we were due to make a dawn attack. But after I had been asleep in the open for twenty minutes or so I was rudely awakened. I asked the intruder where he had come from and was told he was the first line of defence. Thus we were violated whilst we slept. When we were marched to the defenders' HQ they took about half-an hour finding their way into the 'drome and about twice as long to locate their own guard room. This was pretty awful and everyone's feet were raw and blistered after a few miles. It was really pitiable to see the creeping procession of cripples leaving Corps after we had been dismissed.

I didn't mention that I managed to wangle through some of my Bren Gun tests. If the instructors had insisted on the War office requirements being fulfilled I would still be taking them. The most advantageous thing I could do now would be to fail Cert A because I would probably escape the Cert B artillery course. But I suppose I have to make a reasonable effort to pass. Assuming, then, that I have to remain in Cambridge till the 29th March I shall have just under three weeks in which to revise my work, stay at home for a time and see you.

I had tea with Professor Winfield last week but found that he had made no alteration whatsoever in my write-up. So it's all my own work – due to appear in about six weeks time. There was also a joint meeting of the Liberal, Labour and Socialist Clubs to discuss the recent Government changes at which I made a short speech, my first this year.

I haven't heard from my favourite cousin, Marjorie, yet but I heard from Natey the other day. He's being shifted from Reading so I'm afraid I won't be able to stay with him after all next Vac. He's been drafted overseas and at the moment is probably on the ocean waves.

Cambridge   **March 11th, 1942**

Today we were knocked out of the Cup on the Varsity ground, losing 1-0. It was a good game though. Afterwards we had a photo taken of the team. If it seems respectable I'll let you have a copy if you like. Last night we had an amalgamated dinner of the Soccer and Rugger Clubs – four courses, quite liberal supplies of alcohol, and a long cigar to finish. No wonder our meals in Hall had been so frugal the previous week!

This is definitely the end-of-term atmosphere which makes the prospect of next weekend all the more depressing. If I fail Cert A I have no idea what the effect on my 'army career' will be. Anyway it means I won't be able to do Cert B which qualifies the holder for admission to OCTU (Officer Cadet Training Unit) this year.

Cambridge   **March 17th, 1942**

As you see I am still in Cambridge. Unfortunately this doesn't mean I have obtained Cert A. I'm afraid my forebodings about the Bren Gun tests were justified. I probably got through on tactics, map-reading and drilling a squad quite comfortably but when I tried to load a Bren Gun twice in succession without unloading after the first time that was that.

This was of course somewhat disgraceful and certainly disappointing. My disappointment was enhanced by the fact that not only did this prevent me from doing the Artillery Cert B course during this fortnight but I, and some sixty fellow military geniuses, are being compelled to do the Infantry Cert B course. Exactly what repercussions this will have on my army career I don't know yet. I'll be damn glad to get this week behind me though. There's far too much early-to-bed, early-to-rise about it. Far too much scrubbing gaiters and blanco-ing equipment, followed by disparaging kit inspections. Life in the PB Infantry undoubtedly has its good points, though they are hard to appreciate after an hour's precision drilling or when the Colonel's inspecting one's turn-out.

Did I mention James was up here last week? He has passed out of Sandhurst with an 'A', a considerable honour. He is now stationed at Thetford, Norfolk, and has been commissioned as a 2nd Lieutenant in the Royal Irish Fusiliers.

I see you'll be doing your mock Matric next week. I'm glad you have become engrossed in your work but you mustn't become muddled by trying to memorise too many facts. With subjects like History, Eng Lit, Geography and the theoretical parts of the science papers, what you require to get a high mark is not so much knowledge of a vast number of individual facts but a very clear idea of the proper sequence to maintain in drawing up your answers.

Apparently you break up on the 27th. That is the day when my intensive course ends as well as being my birthday. So I can go up to town on Saturday morning and stay somewhere until Sunday at least. This is a marvellous opportunity for seeing you.

We met in London over the weekend of the 28th/29th March and on the Saturday afternoon we went to see Richard Tauber in 'Blossom Time'. My parents, who had recently returned to our London home, invited Stanley to stay with us overnight. In the early hours of that Sunday morning St Nazaire, the only dock on the Atlantic coast capable of repairing large German battleships, such as the Tirpitz, was totally destroyed by a British commando raid. The news came through the same morning and I still recall the thrill it gave us. The next night British bombers destroyed Lubeck. But March ended sadly for the Navy. More Allied shipping had been lost than in any other month of the War.

High Wycombe   **April 1st, 1942**

Although things at home are quite harmonious now, I can't pretend that I didn't have a pretty tough time when I first got back. I guess I should have gone straight home and asked permission to stay with you. My mother was annoyed because she thought she had made it fairly plain to you that she wasn't at all keen on my going to your place.

Apparently your mother phoned her and said that she wasn't really inviting me but was just arranging to put me up for the weekend as one of your various boy-friends, since I was passing through London and would otherwise have to stay at a hotel. All this put both you and myself in a very difficult position for my parents knew nothing of my intention of staying in Town!

The result of this very unfortunate conversation was to leave my parents very offended about the whole affair and although I have managed to restore harmony my parents are likely to look even less favourably upon our relationship than before. You can't allow your parents to remain unaware for an indefinite period of how strongly we feel about each other. In an affair like this obviously one can't disclose everything but you must tell them as much of the truth as I have suggested, as gently, gradually and tactfully as possible, but as soon as possible.

The weather is pretty good and the countryside is of course lovely at this time of the year but Wycombe itself remains unchanged except for your absence. I hope to be seeing you again in Town in about a week's time. Then perhaps we can have a whole day together.

We spent Sunday, April 5th, at a concert given by the London Philharmonic Orchestra with Richard Tauber, not performing this time but conducting. Our meetings continued to be fraught with difficulties. His parents tried to occupy every minute he spent away from Cambridge whilst mine kept reminding me of my promise not to 'go out with him', as opposed to having a casual friendship, based on his helping me with my work.

Wycombe   **April 7th, 1942**

You know how much I should love to have you come up to Cambridge, darling. Even so I think it's best if you do come it should be behind a complete smoke-screen. My parents should know nothing of it though you had better get your parents' permission to visit some reliable friend. I don't like doing this but neither do I like the rows with them that ensue when I meet you. My mother seems to think you are a bad influence on me morally though if the truth were known the reverse is probably nearer the truth!

Whilst our romance was fighting for survival perhaps the most romantic city in the world was dying. Legend had it that Buddha stood on a green hill beneath a sky as blue as a water hyacinth and prophesied that one day a splendid city would arise there. From beginning to end it would only last a man's life span. The city was Mandalay. It came into its glory in the last quarter of the nineteenth century and on April 13th, 1942 Japanese bombers raided it, setting much of the city on fire and killing two thousand people. Only the red walls of the original city remain today and the large bronze figure of a Buddha.

In retaliation the US forces bombed Tokyo.

Cambridge   *April 16th, 1942*

Here I am back in College doing some work again at last. The weather is delightful and nearly all my friends are up here so I am far from being as depressed as I was at the beginning of last term. But the thought of examinations gives me the jitters in full measure. Though sad you couldn't arrange to come here it's just as well that I haven't access to the object of my passions for some time to come. I almost wish I could put you out of my thoughts, too. But there are limits to austerity.

Before I close down for the night, one more reminder about your French. You should try to get hold of a simple vocabulary book. It's far from pleasant learning things that way but at least it might prevent you mixing up déjà with maintenant. Remember I am expecting you to reach at least School Certificate standard in French.

PS James will probably be coming up again at the weekend so I expect I'll meet him.

Cambridge   *April 21st, 1942*

I'm afraid I've spent quite a lot of time strolling by the river which is very beautiful just now. I've also been twice to the pictures and once to the theatre. I saw 'Sante Fe Trail' and 'Femme du Boulanger' – dictionary, please – and 'The Importance of Being Ernest'. All very good.

Lectures begin on the 22nd and I have Corps parade on Friday. It has been rumoured that we'll have a Home Guard exercise every week which sounds almost too bad to be true. I've decided to cut out tennis but I hope you will find the opportunity to play, preferably with some experienced players, while I'm away.

The Cambridge Law Journal has just been published. My modest contribution looks quite good in print but unfortunately is marred by absurd misprints. One passage refers to 'the combinations causing the damage' instead of 'the combination causing....!

Marjorie wants to know when you are going to write to her. She would like to see you sometime and I think she might help to re-establish you in my family's affections.

PS It was rather a waste of paper to start a new page for these last few lines. My apologies to the War Effort! Tonight I have an all-night fire-watching duty. Wish you were here.

'Femme du Boulanger' was a rolicking French farce about a baker's wife whose infidelity so distresses her husband that his bread becomes leaden and lumpy. Because of this the villagers interfere and stop the liaison. Regarded by international critics, including Graham Greene, as a work of art, it entrenched the image of the naughty, bucolic pre-war French.

Bread in England was also undergoing a change. The National Loaf was now the only bread obtainable, although bread was not actually rationed till after the war, and the weekly corned beef allowance disappeared. Britons were still entitled to 1/– (equivalent to about 5p but worth much more today) of meat a week.

Unbeknown to the general public news had reached British Intelligence that the Germans had begun to work on the atom bomb. The heavy water necessary for the research was being produced in Norway and top secret plans began to be made to destroy the installation.

But news of other German war objectives could not be concealed. That week the Germans started to systematically bomb historic British cities. Exeter, Bath, Norwich and York all suffered terrible damage though Churchill ordered the BBC to play it down.

In the Far East the first naval air battle in history was being fought. None of the ships involved fired a single shot – only the planes they carried engaged in combat. It lasted four days. The US successfully prevented the Japanese invasion forces from crossing the Coral Sea and establishing a base in New Guinea, less than four hundred miles from Australia, though not without sustaining heavy losses. Later that month two midget Japanese submarines got into Sydney Harbour, the only time war physically touched mainland Australia.

The weather continued to be almost unbearably beautiful in contrast to the appalling winter that had just passed.

Cambridge   May 2nd, 1942

It's a good thing for you to have French coaching provided you don't go into the exam with an entirely defeatist attitude. I know getting only 26% in your mock matric wasn't very good but if you insist on saying 'I'll never speak French' you may as well not have any lessons at all! Remember, you can often benefit from the advice of your elders, my sweet. (I sound like my father, don't I? Sorry.)

I feel envious when you talk of spending three days dancing, going to concerts etc. I don't suppose I'll go to a dance or the pictures or the theatre until after my exams now. But this is really only a just retribution for my idleness and self-indulgence during the last Vac.

PS Glad you didn't think the photo too bad.

Cambridge   **May 10th, 1942**

My Finals begin on the 28th and I'm miles behind with my revision although I'm working reasonably hard in the evenings and going to bed at (on the average) 1am. Unfortunately I'm not doing enough work during the day-time: the weather's too fine, my friends are too near and I'm not over-enthusiastic at having to ram a vast multitude of facts forcibly into my unwilling brain. It seems a psychological impossibility for me to immerse myself in the study of law when so much is happening to the world, on a far more important scale.

Spring makes Cambridge beautiful, too, though its effect is perhaps less conspicuous than in Bucks. Last Sunday I was out in the country – on a Home Guard exercise. It involved scouting, patrolling, moving behind cover and eventually having a mock battle. But looked at as a whole it was very much like a game of hide-and-seek.

Next Saturday evening we have a full-scale Exercise like the one last term. This is extremely annoying inasmuch as it will interrupt my work (should I happen to be doing any) at a critical stage of my revision. I hope you (unlike me!) are really working hard now. I strongly advise you to begin your revision as early as possible, also to pick out probable questions in various subjects by referring to past papers.

This week I shall probably be having a couple of interviews which may help me to get a reasonable position in the Army – if any Army position can be found to suit my peculiar combination of talents.

I'm sorry to hear that Peter is thinking of joining the Oxford Group movement. Frankly I don't know much about its professed ideals, except that they consist largely in encouraging people to forget the unhappiness rampant in this world by (i) pretending that there is a genuine likelihood of solving the difficulties on a basis of brotherly love and (ii) by concentrating people's attention on spiritual things and other worlds instead of on the tremendous material problems that face us.

PS Another point: a few years ago Dr Buchman, boss of the Oxford Group, said 'Thank God for Hitler'!

Cambridge   **May 17th, 1942**

Between 3 and 11am this Sunday morning I was tramping around the countryside in one of our great Exercises. The entire University Home

Guard was turned out for the happy occasion and we were opposed by a Battalion of Welsh Fusiliers. We had a little sleep in the very uncomfortable grandstand at the University Football Ground but we were woken by the firing of blanks all over the place.

Our section sallied forth to find the foe but about half a mile from our HQ we were ambushed by a group of the Regulars with Tommy guns and rifles. Had this been in day-light with umpires present I suppose we should have been taken prisoner or 'wiped out' but no one was very anxious to play according to the rules and before long we were having a hell of a set-to with these fellows. I made rather a mistake by tackling two of them and after a somewhat vigorous tussle I was flat on my back. But it was so dark I slipped away and joined up with another section. Everyone thought 'My God. If this was a real invasion we'd never get back to Cambridge'.

Our Platoon Commander told me to jump into a passing car, get to a certain aircraft factory which was about half a mile away and which was occupied by the 'enemy' and do as much damage there as I could. Unfortunately after I had shot up the sentries and fired some imaginary bullets through the windows I discovered the factory was still controlled by our own troops.

Enough of this or I shall lose all credence in your eyes as a fighting man.

You mentioned you were wondering what to do after Matric. I should very strongly advise you to stay on at school for a couple more years. You will learn a great deal in that time about the subjects that really interest you whereas at present your knowledge of science, for example, is relatively elementary due to the ghastly Wycombe teaching. Every worthwhile technical position is held by a person who has a good general knowledge of scientific or engineering matters as well as a detailed knowledge of his (sic) particular speciality.

Congratulations on your French greetings, darling. Que je t'aime. Mais il faut concentrer sur mes devoirs pendant les dix jours prochains et il faudra t'oublier jusqu'a la fin de mes examens.

Be sure that you work systematically, allocating sufficient time to each subject. Try to spot likely questions and work them up.

It was very difficult to obey Stanley's exhortations to study because another slice was being taken out of my time by the requirement, under the Emergency Powers Act, that girls of sixteen and seventeen now had to register with the Labour Exchange. They were advised to join either the Air Cadets or the Girls' Training Corps. I joined the latter and rose to the exalted rank of corporal – I still have the two red stripes to prove it. We were never fortunate enough to go on the sort of fun exercises described by Stanley and spent most of our time drilling in the local park and learning First Aid in a sports hut.

On the 26th May, the day of the signing of the Anglo-Soviet Treaty, Rommel renewed his offensive in the desert. The month ended with the announcement of General Eisenhower's appointment as C-IN-C of the (then non-existent) Allied forces in Europe. And on 30th May more than a thousand British bombers flattened Cologne. William Joyce (Lord Haw-Haw) threatened 'hell repaid with interest' and the next night Canterbury was bombed – but so was Essen.

Lord Haw-Haw's comments on these raids and reprisals were reported in The Guernsey Star on June 4th. His strange, derogatory name was inspired by a journalist who said he spoke the English of the 'haw haw, dammit-get-out-of-my-way' variety. Although a term of abuse this apparently was not obvious to the Germans in control of the Channel Islands. Perhaps they thought he really was a lord. Under their very noses the English newspapers in Guernsey always used this disparaging title when reporting his broadcasts.

In Cambridge Stanley took two weeks off from letter writing to sit his Law Finals.

Graduation to Call-Up
'Every day I get more impatient to receive my call-up papers'
October 22nd, 1942

For the oppressed people in Europe June was a dreadful month. In reprisal for the assassination of Reinhart Heydrich the Czech village of Lidici was liquidated. One hundred and fifty thousand Jews were murdered in Poland and elsewhere and several hundred Russian agents were tortured and killed. The Germans tested out a twelve ton rocket with a range of 200 miles which became known as the dreaded V2.

At the beginning of June Japan was defeated in the Battle for Midway Island. The battle was fierce but their ploy – to draw American forces away from the area by landing on the Aleutian Islands – failed miserably.

As the decoders were listening in to the Japanese plans for invading Midway, Stanley resumed his letters from Cambridge.

Cambridge   **June 2nd, 1942**

The only time when I forgot you was when I was actually in the middle of my exams, which I have just finished. I'm afraid they weren't as good as I had hoped. I could have done better in a couple of the papers and after the second day I felt absolutely despondent. Still, I assume I have got either an upper or lower second. The results will be out in a couple of weeks.

Tonight I'm on all night duty again. I hope the RAF won't choose this for a reprisal visit to the Reich. Every night when these mass raids are on we hear vast numbers of bombers coming across the Town and it's difficult to get to sleep. But not as difficult as it is for the recipients. Of course the neighbourhood is full of aerodromes.

I suppose your exams will begin within a couple of weeks now. Thorough systematic revision is absolutely necessary. But finish as much as you possibly can before the night of the actual examination. For God's sake don't do what I had to – spend 30 hours out of 48 working solidly.

On Saturday I intend to travel down from Cambridge and will arrive at Liverpool Street at 3.30pm. Could you meet the train? I'm longing to be with you again, darling, and hope it will be OK. But you'd better not tell your parents you are going to meet me. I hope so very much to see you.

Cambridge   **June 11th, 1942**

We have Corps all day Friday and all day Saturday and then Cert A on Sunday. I shall be going down on Monday the 15th and coming up to take my degree (if any) on Tuesday 23rd. If I get Cert A and haven't been called up in the meantime I'll be back here for a three week course in July.

About the 24th June I may be going on a walking holiday with some friends so I won't be able to see you till after your oral exams at least. I expect you are going hell for leather at your work now. Keep at it; allow yourself no distractions whatsoever from now on − not even me.

But perhaps you will have time to fit me in one day before your written exams. I don't want to have to wait another two or three weeks till we meet.

A postcard, dated June 18th, 1942, told me that when Stanley arrived home he found a telegram waiting for him from a friend in Cambridge telling him that he had got a First. He also told Stanley that he had won the George Long Prize in Jurisprudence which was worth about nine pounds and was the only University Prize awarded in the examination.

The longest day dawned in Britain with the promise of perfect weather but in the Western Desert the day was marred by the fall of Tobruk to Rommel's forces.

Another postcard from High Wycombe arrived dated June 25th.

Just a short line to wish you the very best of luck for Matric.

On Tuesday I took my degree without incident. There was a lot of mumbo-jumbo and dressing up but not much else. The College, by the way, has given me £8 and elected me a Scholar.

The glorious weather continued into July as I sat sweating over exam papers that covered over two years work which I had tried to cram into six months. Different set books, different periods of history, different geographical areas, made it a daunting task. Fortunately during the Geography paper − after I had answered the only two questions out of the compulsory seven that I even vaguely understood − the air raid siren went. We spent five hours in the basement before the All Clear sounded and the exam was abandoned − marks to be awarded on a percentage basis on the work completed in the first half hour.

In spite of heroic resistance July brought news of defeat after defeat. The Germans reached El Alamein, crossed the Egyptian border and were only sixty miles west of Alexandria. On the Eastern front Sebastopol fell.

High Wycombe   **July 5th, 1942**

I was very disappointed to hear you weren't very satisfied with your French paper. I can only hope you haven't done as badly as you imagine.

But the best of luck with your Art and Physics.

My military arrangements have been altered somewhat. I shall not be going to Camp at Cambridge from July 6th-26th. Instead I shall be doing an Artillery Course in August and September up there. But I am going to Cambridge on Saturday next, July 11th, for the day. Could you possibly come with me? My parents are quite agreeable. The fare will, I think, be about 9/–: it may be as much as 12/– if there is no excursion that day but I have my prize money.

I heard from Natey last week. He's in Egypt, but I have no idea of his whereabouts. His letter was dated June 11th but the news since then has been bad.

Wycombe   **July 15th, 1942**

Percy came down for the day on Monday. They have had a wire from Natey saying he's OK but an elder brother of theirs is out in Egypt, God knows where, driving lorries and they haven't any news of him. Percy says his mother is going crazy with worry.

On Monday next I am due to start a fortnight's land work on a farm near Booker Aerodrome. But life here is quiet and uneventful – a sort of lull before the storm.

There is a Red Cross Lawn Tennis exhibition at Queen's Club on Saturday afternoon (July 18th) which will include a match between Jean Nicoll and Kay Stammers (two outstanding members of the British Women's Tennis Team). The admission charge will be about half-a-crown. Can you keep Saturday afternoon open? I'm sure you'd enjoy it. I'll let you know for certain on Friday.

Wycombe   **July 24th, 1942**

If these lines bear traces of the work of a horny hand, blame the good earth of Buckinghamshire. For the last few days I have been a very hard-worked and highly unskilled farmer's boy. The first thing I have to do in the morning, unless I manage to be far away at the time, is to clean out the cow-sheds. On Monday and Tuesday we were making silage – cattle food made of green corn and treacle – and then had to stamp it into a container for hours on end. Since then I've been cutting down rose-bushes, thistles and ragwort with a sickle and a chopper.

Whether I shall continue next week is extremely doubtful, especially as the farmer and his Mrs are anything but cordial folk and are unwilling to pay me the statutory wage-rate because of my inexperience. The other labourers – two men and a Land Girl, all authentically Bucks – are also pretty silent and undemonstrative towards strangers but I get on quite well with them.

It's amazing how far physical fatigue can sap your mental energies. On Tuesday evening, though, I had one of the German prisoners in for a couple of hours. He's a Socialist and formerly studied Law at the University. A most interesting fellow.

I expect to come up to Town on Saturday week to go to a cricket match so I hope very much to see you then. By the way, my cousin Harry Brown definitely seems to be going overseas this time – though one can never be sure.

Wycombe   **July 25th, 1942**

I've finished a week's farming at Booker and I'm now taking a couple of days' rest prior to doing some harvesting next week. The work was extremely hard, 8 hours a day with just an hour for lunch and no opportunity for taking a few minutes' break during the morning or afternoon. In conversation the farmer and his wife were abrupt to the point of rudeness. They didn't offer me as much as a cup of tea and I had to eat my lunch in an old barn as they wouldn't allow me to have it in their house. My propensity towards squeamishness has been decreased as a result of some of the less salubrious jobs they made me do.

Here in Wycombe life goes jogging along as usual. Several of the girls you knew have gone into the services or back to London and most of my father's family will be returning there in a few weeks' time.

London was returning to a semblance of normality as the raids decreased but the nightly ack-ack fire to keep the German planes at bay still rained down shrapnel into the streets. It was a common experience to be returning home in the dark and to see a red hot lump of metal land a few feet away from you. When they had cooled down they made excellent souvenirs though none of the pieces which embellished my study shelves for years remain today.

Many German bombers were diverted both from British targets and the Russian Front to help in the Western desert. General Auchinleck had begun to counter-attack and for the moment Rommel was halted.

At the beginning of the month two thousand partisans had been killed in Yugoslavia and mass deportations planned. Helping to calculate how many trucks etc. would be needed for this exercise was Lieutenant Kurt Waldheim. He was subsequently awarded the Silver Medal for his meticulous execution of these duties.

Stalingrad continued to be threatened and the Japanese succeeded in pushing the Australians back to Port Moresby in New Guinea. The Japanese had already begun work on the notorious Burma railway, an enterprise which cost the lives of fifteen thousand British POW's.

Wycombe   **August 6th, 1942**

It was wonderful seeing you on Bank Holiday Monday after all our attempts to do so in the last couple of months failed. But why does it always rain on Bank Holidays!

I missed the last train from Paddington but a Good Samaritan was standing by the ticket barrier. He was just about to drive home to Wycombe and offered me a lift thus warding off an untimely attack of apoplexy. This evening (Thursday) I am going to the Proms with Sylvia. She tells me that a friend of yours, Sylvia Loss, has been round to see her in Wycombe.

(Sylvia was the niece of Joe Loss, the war-time band leader, whose signature tune 'In The Mood' held the affection of an entire generation. Occasionally we were privileged to see the band performing live. We had been school-friends in London before the war and had recently met up again).

Meanwhile I have been round to see two farmers but they don't require unskilled labour at the moment (or maybe my reputation had gone before me). At other local farms the weather seems to have delayed the harvest. But I've plenty to keep me busy. Next week I may have to do some housework whilst Mabel's away on holiday. Also I am doing some reading: a couple of philosophical works, 'How to Ride a Motor-Cycle' and the juicier parts of the sixteenth century State Trials, eg the divorce of Catharine Howard.

On a more serious note, I was extremely disappointed with your attitude towards that part of your work which you dislike. That is exactly the part you should work hardest at. You know that Matric is the stepping stone to any worth-while career: you know that you owe it to yourself and to Society as a whole to give the utmost of which you are capable. Perhaps it is merely because you are so young and I expect too much of you. But I do take a matter like this very seriously indeed, so try your best, darling, if only for me.

I remember thinking that the last paragraph might have been written by my father!

August 7th, 1942, was the day that Klaus Fuchs, later to be convicted as a spy, took his oath of Allegiance to the Crown. Even then he was passing secrets about the atom bomb to the Russians. The Americans landed on Guadalcanal but met stiff resistance and it was to take them and the Australians six months of bitter fighting to drive the Japanese out. A few days later in Russia Churchill told Stalin there could be no Second Front in Europe in 1942 but promised the Allies would land in French North Africa.

By August 15th Stanley was back in Cambridge and reported to me that a quantity of articles, including some crockery and his army boots and gaiters, had disappeared from his rooms. But he had his suspicions and was hot on the trail of the offender. He also asked me if I knew anyone who could be persuaded to part with a second-hand bike – they were like gold dust since the basic petrol allowance had been withdrawn – and reminded me to persuade my father to allow me to stay on for a further year at school.

On the night of the 18th/19th August the famous British/Canadian commando raid on Dieppe took place. In spite of appalling losses Admiral Mountbatten later told Churchill that it had given the Allies the priceless secret of victory.

Cambridge   *August 21st, 1942*

I have found my army boots and recovered my crockery from the rooms of the unauthorised borrower thereof. I have written extremely fierce and menacing letters to this gentleman and to the fellow who occupied these rooms during my absence whilst engaged on important agricultural duties. I await their replies with interest.

The Artillery Course is certainly much more interesting than any of the military work I have done up to now. During the week we were changing our old ammunition for new and this involved loading and unloading quantities of cases of live shells. Up to now we have only handled blanks. A good deal is technical and requires the handling of complex scientific instruments and the manoeuvring of big guns. My chief handicap has been my usual strong inclination to drop off to sleep after lunch-time but I suppose this would not be so likely under enemy attack.

The next few days will probably be the toughest for me. We are being put through a hyper-intensive Motor Transport Course and we shall be expected to drive and maintain a motor-car, lorry and motor-cycle within 4 working days. This seems rather fantastic especially as we have been issued with a brief official pamphlet of six hundred pages on the subject.

You seem to be rather confused about the law of libel. There is no actionable libel unless the words are published. Publication may take place in various ways – eg by conversation – but it is assumed to have taken place if the defamatory words are written to anyone on a postcard – presumably the postman might read them. But these are curious possibilities which never seem to happen and I don't think any Court would allow 'justice' to be defeated by a technicality.

PS The withdrawal from Dieppe was a tremendous disappointment to me. I had hoped they would try to establish a bridgehead for the Second Front.

The country learned the tragic news of the accidental death of the Duke of Kent in an air crash in Scotland on August 26th. He was a very popular figure and one on whom the King relied to support him in the many onerous tasks that Royalty undertook during the war. The purpose of this particular flight was not revealed in the first reports but a photo of him with his baby son, Prince Michael, taken ten days previously by Cecil Beaton, appeared in some newspapers. It typified what was a frequent nightmare to many Britons – the fatherless next generation.

Cambridge   **August 30th, 1942**

I have just spent nearly three hours sticking the latest amendments into one of the War Office booklets which the Corps issues to us. I made a rather embarrassing start to this fascinating occupation: the lid of the glue-pot was stuck and came off suddenly, with the result that the contents were precipitated over and through my trousers.

The weather here has been extremely hot and on Friday afternoon it reached 87°F in the shade. Fortunately at that time we were relaxing in the shade watching the RAF Regiment pushing our guns about. Yesterday we had our first daylight raid for many a long day. A solitary plane dropped a solitary bomb in a solitary field, causing neither damage or casualties. The aircraft then turned round and flew off unmolested.

We have finished our MT course but as the instructor was here for less than the required four days we didn't learn to drive properly. However it's obviously a very simple business, much simpler than learning how the things work.

I have not recovered my property yet but I seem to have put the wind up the thief for he came all the way from London to see me last Sunday. Unfortunately a friend of his now has some of it.

Last Wednesday James came to see me. We went to a rather poor film, starring Carmen Miranda, and he stayed in College overnight.

It doesn't do any harm for you to discuss the Indian situation but I'm afraid it's too late for a settlement to be reached before the Japs march into the country. The news is certainly not very good. No Second Front. And then, as a crowning blow, comes the accident to the Duke of Kent!

Lord hast Thou forsaken us?

In the first week in September there was another raid on the Channel Islands. The Germans began their most determined effort to seize Stalingrad. On the 5th they entered the city but still the Russians would not surrender and bitter street fighting ensued.

CHAPTER 5

Cambridge   **September 9th, 1942**

Congratulations on your Matric results! I hope you are as pleased as I am. We had a spot of bother here last night: a few bombs, plenty of ack-ack fire and a raider shot down just outside the town by a night fighter.

I was more surprised than pleased about my exam results – a distinction in French, of all things, plus distinctions in Physics, Chemistry, Maths and Art. Thanks to Stanley's persistent encouragement and advice I also gained Matric level in seven other subjects, including Geography! Examiners must have been kinder in those days.

On the night Cambridge was attacked, Bremen was bombed by the RAF, making it the hundredth raid on a German industrial town.

Cambridge   **September 20th, 1942**

This morning we had three hours lectures and I had planned to work all afternoon and evening. But I suddenly found that I was mentally stale – browned off, in fact. So I went to the pictures in the afternoon. I don't think I shall be able to revise adequately for next Friday but I think I should have sufficient technical knowledge to scrape through. So much for Cert B.

Our captain has made enquiries of the War Office from which it has emerged that the fellows in our squad will probably be called up round about the middle of October – probably between the 10th and the 20th. I hope to see you again before then.

Last Tuesday I had a most unpleasant experience. I was cycling to Corps after lunch and was just slowing down at some traffic lights when there was a crash just ahead of me and something was flung through the air apparently from the back of a passing lorry. I suddenly realised it was a young woman; she had been knocked off her bike at the cross-roads by the lorry. It was the most startling thing imaginable: a crash, no cry, then silence. The girl was unconscious and had very severe head injuries. I and other people nearby couldn't do anything and after the ambulance came I continued to Corps. But I was frightfully upset to read in the next day's local paper that the poor girl had died that night. She was Czech and only eighteen.

By the 22nd of September German troops had reached the centre of Stalingrad but still the city did not fall. In America, in the greatest secrecy, Brigadier General Groves was appointed to oversee the making of the atom bomb whilst in Germany Werner von Braun's V2 was about to be successfully launched and put into production.

High Wycombe   **September 29th, 1942**

*Unless I write this belated letter right away I am in danger of falling
asleep again. So I herewith take a strong sniff of Benzadrine and fix my
mind firmly on the object of my affection.*

*I don't think I told you that I got through my Cert B. The next step is pre-
OCTU which is likely to be at Rootham (sic) in Kent. I shall then learn to
drive at last, I hope.*

*On the last night of my stay in CAT's I had dinner with the Chaplain –
the first time in my three years there. The previous day I went along to the
Poor Man's Lawyer run by Glanville Williams, where lawyers give
voluntary legal advice. Most people seeking help there seem to have
quantities of illegitimate children but I found it more interesting than
embarrassing.*

*(Glanville Williams was his mentor and friend who later also taught me
law.)*

*I was not sorry to leave Cambridge: during the last year or so I have seen
rather a lot of it. But after a few months in the forces I dare say I shall feel
very nostalgic.*

*PS My father has just bought me an extremely fine bookcase to house all
the volumes I shall have to remove from my rooms in Cambridge shortly.
You may borrow anything you want, of course, as I'm hardly likely to be
needing them in the Army.*

The bookcase had pride of place in his study for twenty years.

In the last week in September Renee Blum, the brother of the former
French premier, was gassed in Auschwitz together with 4000 other Jews.

But October began with excellent news. The Germans at Stalingrad had
at last been halted, though further attacks against the city were launched
later that month. Rommel was thwarted in his push towards Cairo by British
air supremacy. And a British commando raid was carried out on Sark. This
so annoyed Hitler that he ordered all British POW's to be shackled and
Britain responded by doing the same to German prisoners.

The importance of the Channel Islands – a comparatively small theatre
of war – was enhanced because they were the only British territory to be
occupied by the Germans during the Second World War.

Wycombe   **October 5th, 1942**

*When the weekends come round it seems I always have some obligation to
fulfil. Last Sunday I took Marjorie and Sybil to the Youth Club. Stifling and
rather sexy and full of Yanks, yobs and jitterbugs. Not what it used to be,
though you might have liked it more than I.*

But I haven't received my call-up notice yet so I may not have to go till the 20th. In that case perhaps I shall be able to see you the weekend after next.

I have been reading a book on Psychology and am now in the middle of Lord Samuel's 'Belief and Action' (quite good). I recommend you to read it when you have the time.

Wycombe   **October 12th, 1942**

Really I haven't very much to write about — this waiting is awful — but since I know you will simply wither away through anxiety unless you hear from me today I must wrack my brains for items of interest. On Sunday morning I played tennis. Sybil called round and told me she had been called up and is training for industrial work. You owe them a letter, by the way.

With regard to next weekend we will probably be able to meet as I haven't received any invitation to the party from the War Office yet.

Now to matters of weighty moment. I have been looking through my mountainous sources of information on the English Judicial System for you and am quite certain they include everything you will want for a paper on that subject. You should, I think, treat it like this:

1) General principles

2) Skeleton outline of system of Courts (I'll give you a plan of that)

3) Personnel of the Law: judges, JPs, barristers, solicitors, juries. I'll lend you my own note-book.

4) Are rich and poor treated alike? My notes, again.

PS On second thoughts, Saturday will probably be a better day than Sunday for us to meet. There's a football match I'd like to see. If you came with me I could kill two birds with one stone.... OK, OK, I'll see you on Sunday.

Wycombe   **October 22nd, 1942**

The call-up notice still has not arrived so that I know nothing at present which is likely to prevent me from meeting you on Sunday. But everyday I get more impatient to receive my call-up and get myself properly trained.

The only drawback is that if I am sent overseas quickly, or even if I'm posted to a remote corner of this blessed isle, the chances of our meeting will be even smaller. You will try to come and see me wherever I am for as long as possible, won't you? Lord knows just how many more times I shall see you but, if and when we succeed in this ghastly endeavour to beat the Madman of Munich (and, of course, if I come through it) we will have all the time in the world to make up for our lost years.

His eagerness to get his call-up papers was not shared by all those who had just reached their eighteenth birthdays. The call-up age had been eighteen and a half but with the losses that had been sustained at Dunkirk, in the Far East and in the Western Desert it was now necessary to lower the recruitment age. Many lads joined up voluntarily at seventeen and there were several cases reported of boys of sixteen who tried to volunteer. Some succeeded.

At home a big round up of tyres from laid-up cars was ordered. Railings were removed from the Royal Parks and melted down. The egg ration was reduced to one a month.

But at long last Montgomery launched his brilliant attack against the Germans in the Western Desert and on the 23rd of October, after five days of fierce fighting, El Alamein was recaptured. The opening barrage was so loud that an Artillery Officer, who had been through many battles, said he had never heard anything like it, before or since. He was counting shells at the time and when he had recovered from nearly jumping out of his skin he had to start all over again.

It was to be three more days before Stanley finally received his call-up papers.

Initiation into the Army

'Soon I shall be able to boast with pride that I have spent a Christmas in the Army'
Dec 21st, 1942

610499 Cadet de Smith, S.A.
"B" Battery Pool, RA Wing, E Camp
148 Training Brigade,
Wrotham, nr. Sevenoaks, Kent   *November 5th, 1942*

Darling
    As you will see from this remarkable address I have arrived. I can't say I'm really bursting with enthusiasm at the moment. It's pouring cats and dogs and the Camp is becoming a sea of mud. I can't tell you much about the size of the Camp but as far as I know it is the only pre-OCTU (Officer Cadet Training Unit) in England and comprises seven different units. The artillery wing alone houses an extremely large number of cadets. The chief trouble is the black-out: in the dark you think you have strayed into a maze of pathways, trees and mud.
    We don't begin our course till Monday. In the meantime we are being issued with loads of equipment, standing around, and doing fatigues. The Sergeant-Major has promised us this afternoon we can do some fencing; not with swords, but with axes, hammers and nails. Life alternates between wild scrambles and waiting for something to happen.
    The environment is very different from what I've been accustomed to; but it could be a lot worse. I am definitely lucky in that the fellows here are a very good crowd. It seems that I shall have to stay here for eight weeks at least. This came as an unpleasant surprise to me but it appears they have formed a pretty poor opinion of Cambridge blokes. What worries me is that we must go before a War Office Selection Board. This is said to be a pretty grim affair by those who have been through it.
    Leave will not be plentiful. I can get a pass for one Sunday but only if I don't go through London. The Camp isn't very far from Maidstone so if you could come down there that would be just fine.

Whilst Stanley was settling in, the news came through that the Americans had successfully landed in North Africa and taken Algiers and the British had regained Sidi Birani. It was the occasion for another cautionary Churchillian remark: 'This is not the beginning of the end but the end of the beginning.'

Wrotham *November 10th, 1942*

I don't think I've told you much about the Camp yet. It's set in a fine position on the North Downs, but it's about four miles to the nearest Railway Station, Snodland, which is five miles distant from Maidstone. I can get into Maidstone in just over an hour.

If I get a few days off for Christmas I'll definitely want to see you. I shall certainly still be at Wrotham then. This is a notoriously difficult place where almost everything is done at the double and where reveille is at 6am. Today we had intelligence tests for the War Office Selection Board. In a few weeks we will have the physical tests which are plenty tough.

As for the gloves I am awaiting them with pleasurable anticipation. We have already been issued with mittens.

What do you think of the news? Very fine, I think: the best possible substitute for a real second Front. Things are looking up at last.

The good news that he referred to was that the British forces had entered Libya. But the Germans now moved in and occupied Vichy France which had until then been under the direct control of Petain.

Wrotham *November 14th, 1942*

I acknowledge gratefully receipt of gloves. They suit me fine, and I believe your knitting is nearly as good as your mathematics.

You ask me for more details concerning the way things are here. This is a brand new, very large and incredibly muddy camp. We live in Nissen huts where we all catch each others' colds. The food is good enough, and we have a NAAFI where we can supplement the meals if we wait an hour but the facilities for washing up are not good.

The actual training is decidedly rigorous and so far not very interesting. We push guns (new 25 pdr field guns) around the atrocious gun park and have occasional lectures on regimental organisation and applied trigonometry to fill in the time. But the PT is pretty good stuff and we had a 3 hours "toughening tour" on Wednesday running up hill and down dale, followed by 15 minutes hard marching drill.

The chief trouble is that we have so much cleaning and tidying to do that we hardly have time for study. Fortunately we do get some time for sport and tomorrow I am due to play soccer for the Battery.

You asked me about the intelligence tests. First we had a simple paper of ninety-eight questions, with certain possible answers numbered. We had to write down as many as possible in twenty minutes. I did ninety-two. Then we had to complete squares − rather hard − and patterns − fairly easy. We finished by writing out a very personal questionnaire, for the benefit of a psychiatrist who will interview us later. At the end we had to write out a description of our own characters a) as if by our best friend, b) as if by our worst enemy. This gave me the opportunity for being facetious.

I mentioned that I was with a decent crowd of fellows. Amongst them is "Billy" Hughes, who is the peace time secretary of the Fabian Society.

My parents want to come down to Maidstone one Sunday but they haven't specified any date. I think I could say pretty definitely that I could meet you next Sunday. How about it?

The Russian counter-offensive began on November 19th and within three days they had encircled a quarter of a million Germans around Stalingrad in a noose which gradually strangled the invaders.

Wrotham   **November 20th, 1942**

Our letters seem to cascade to and fro these days. Congratulations to your brother on his promotion. Peter's a long way senior to me, I can assure you.

I was, of course, very surprised and disappointed to receive your latest. You must have expected me positively to have seethed with rage. Why upset yourself so much because you had to break the arrangements? Now I'm beginning to imagine myself as the inquisitive psychiatrist who interviewed me yesterday. In the circumstances you couldn't do anything else. We can only look forward to another day. In any case I have had several of my fellow-sufferers' colds.

PS I'm not sure what leave I'll get over Christmas.

Wrotham   **Saturday, November 21st, 1942**

I phoned you this afternoon. Your mother made it pretty plain that she didn't think much of the idea of you coming down to this part of the world. Wycombe was different, she said. Well. maybe she's right: you are only 16.

PS I haven't heard from the WOSB (War Office Selection Board) yet. No news is good news, because those who pass are not notified.

Wrotham   **November 26th, 1942**

As you see I have not yet been slung out of this joint, and it seems rather as though the Selection Board approved of me. But I don't want to count my chickens prematurely.

For the first fortnight the emphasis has been on gun-drill. The curriculum is now more varied with less enthusiasm for violent physical activities. However we still have to double almost everywhere. Yesterday we had a forced march of 8 miles or so. On the way we saw a 3" mortar firing live shells and actually saw the projectiles in their line of flight from the barrel.

We get a remarkable quantity of meat. As for comfort this Camp hasn't a distinguished reputation. We have few fires and no radio, except in the NAAFI. But we do have a theatre in which they present ENSA shows and films. Also religious services are conducted there.

I received an airgraph from Natey today. He seems very browned off with the location of his Camp and the monotony of his work.

The most cheering thing these days is the news:

a) I have been told that the Cambridge thief has at last coughed up ten bob for the missing equipment.

b) There is certainly no doubt that Hitler is in a hell of a mess at the present moment.

The theatre at Wrotham Camp was named the Erskine Theatre after Brigadier (later General) Erskine and until a few years ago served as a meeting hall for the post-war village of Vigo, which eventually arose on the site of the Camp.

There were many interesting people at Wrotham during the war. The Commander of "A" Camp was 'Fruity' Metcalfe, the Aide-de-Camp to the Duke of Windsor at the time of the Abdication. Sir Robin Day spent several weeks at Wrotham and claims that the nearest he came to violent death during his Army service was whilst learning to ride a motor-cycle there at high speed. The son of the Labour MP Manny Shinwell, ('Father of the House' after Lord Boothby retired) also did his officer training course at Wrotham.

Wrotham   *December 1st, 1942*

Your letter was today's silver lining. The very best of luck in your exams.

We, too, had a Maths test the other day. The type of problems we have to solve aren't very profound; the elements of trigonometry, how to use log tables intelligently, a certain number of formulae, the standard form for setting out our calculations. In the test eighty-five marks were awarded for the mathematics and fifteen for the lay-out. I got sixty-seven for the maths, zero for the lay-out.

A good deal of my time is taken up with eating, queueing and cleaning my clothing. But I do try to spend a little time each day reading. I've borrowed the recently published selection from James Joyce's writings, edited by T. S. Eliot. I am also reading snatches of the new Penguin books by Liddell Hart and Tom Wintringham – both on military strategy.

Then there's the weekly publication of the Army Bureau of Public Affairs. We spend an hour every week discussing the current number and this has given me the opportunity for greater distinction than I have yet achieved –

or am ever likely to – on the gun-park. Today we went over the assault course. It involves a good deal of climbing & rope-walking, which all takes place near the top of a steep hill. It all looks rather grim.

I haven't heard from WOSB since I took the tests so it seems they liked me. I'm afraid there'll be no leave after all till shortly after Xmas. Unless I get sent to a Training Regiment beforehand I won't finish here till at least January 12th and the Forces mustn't travel between December 21st and 29th.

I wasn't surprised to learn that you found Harold Laski's drawl almost paralysing. But the content of what he says is usually first-rate, and his argument is always difficult to counter because he expresses himself with such a bewildering fluency. He can also put over an anecdote extremely well.

Before I wind up I have a humble confession to make. I've lost one of your gloves. They were both found where I left them but the person who took charge of them lost one.

PS The glove I lost appears to have been the left one.

The day I received this letter the first controlled nuclear chain reaction took place in America, which confirmed the feasibility of producing an atom bomb.

Wrotham   **December 6th, 1942**

I have to blanco some equipment and read up some notes so I don't expect to go out today. Yesterday I went into Maidstone and bought you the little artillery brooch I have enclosed. You will see it is inscribed 'Ubique' (means 'everywhere').

We haven't had many severe fogs here, but there have been plenty of ground mists in the valley below the Camp. Yesterday morning, just before PT, there was a torrential downpour of rain and hail. So we had to plunge into the icy hell and do PT bare-backed. I have never been keen on cold showers and this experience has not w(h)etted my enthusiasm.

We start a fortnight of weapon training this week: Rifle, Bren Gun, Pistol, Tommy Gun, Anti-tank Rifle and Grenades. We also have to go through the notorious Battle Course.

I have only read the outlines of the Beveridge Report but it is certainly an historic document. If accepted as it stands it will constitute the biggest dose of social reform which a capitalist society has ever been able to administer. Up to now it has been surprisingly well received by all parties: but there is no immediate likelihood that its proposals will be translated into legislation.

The big insurance companies are almost certainly represented in the House – they won't like his proposals at all – but I don't expect strong opposition from the Trade Unions. There is bound to be a serious economic situation in this country after the War: we have lost huge foreign investments, many export markets and have subordinated the requirements of peace-time and post-war industries to those of the war industry.

This means it will be very difficult and probably impossible for Britain to recover her pre-war world position or to return immediately to her old standard of living. The problems of demobilisation will be difficult, too, I fear. We shall have to retain some unproductive war industries. Then there is the problem of the reconstruction of the devastated areas so it will be necessary to maintain taxation at a high level.

I am not an economist and I have not studied the question deeply. But what views I have formed lead me to conclude that it will probably be impossible for a capitalist system to go on functioning properly while supporting at the same time the heavy expenditure on social reform which the Beveridge Plan would demand.

Whilst on the subject of benefits I must return to the gloves. Picture me – if you dare – with my left hand welded solidly to the handle-bars of a motor cycle round about Christmas time.

PS My parents did come down to see me last weekend and a pleasant time was had by all.

Wrotham   *December 12th, 1942*

Many thanks for your long letter and for the glove. You must have done some amazingly energetic plains and pearls, or whatever you specialise in, to finish the glove so quickly. The difference in colour is insignificant. I almost wish it were cold enough for me to wear them.

We do a good deal of route-finding by maps, and on one expedition I took a wrong turning on my bicycle and became detached from the main party, with the result that I had to push my bike up an extremely steep hill with all my equipment on and my rifle and map-reading instruments over my shoulders.

Later in the week we had to do route-finding by night, on foot and in syndicates. Our syndicate found only two of the five rendezvous and after two and a half hours adjourned to the local pub for consolation.

We have had some quite good fun weapon training. I have fired the Rifle, Bren Gun and Tommy Gun on our ranges. Twice during this coming week we shall be going to Gravesend to fire up there. We also take the battle-course in our manly stride. Your strong rough soldier isn't a bit frightened at the prospect. In fact, he's scared stiff.

Yesterday I went to Chatham. There was nothing of much interest except the vast numbers of loose women. On this coming Thursday I shall probably be going to Maidstone for a "farewell" dinner. We are inviting the Troop Officers and Sergt. Instructors to a party at a hotel. 7/6d a head.

(Worth about 30p in today's money but quite expensive then. Restaurants were banned early in the war from serving meals costing more than 5/– a head, excluding drinks.)

I've had very little spare time to read the papers this week and I have heard nothing on the wireless either. Cadets are not permitted the necessities of life.

Going back to Beveridge, the worthy Sir William is open to criticism by the Left on the grounds that he seems to expect Want to be abolished without the overthrow of the present economic system i.e. he does not envisage Socialism as being the essential preliminary to the cure of social and economic disorders. Hence his plan may prove to be the salvation of the Tory Party. But if mass unemployment returns the rulers of industry will be unable to afford their contributions. That is why I think the Plan cannot solve all economic problems and is a potentially dangerous political weapon.

Stanley also felt that it would be impossible to fund such social services solely from income tax, despite the fact that the level of personal taxation had risen to 50% in 1941.

The Allies were at last turning to the offensive on several fronts. In the Western Desert they drove the Germans out of El Agheila and, around Stalingrad, General von Paulus with his crack German troops was trapped inside the noose. Rather to the relief of the Allies, Admiral Darlan was murdered. Although he had refused to hand over the French Navy to the Germans he was still considered anti-British.

Wrotham   *December 21st, 1942*

Soon I shall be able to boast with pride that I have spent a Christmas in the Army.

I managed to contract a septic heel at the beginning of last week which prevented me from doing PT or the Battle Course. So my baptism of fire will be delayed till I reach OCTU. However I had a very pleasant time watching the other blokes sweating. (Sorry about the scribble but this is being written in a NAAFI queue.)

Now we have begun the Motor Transport course. For five days we toured Kent in 30 cwt trucks for about six hours each day. Two fellows are allotted to each truck with a driving instructor. As you can imagine we have a remarkably fine time compared with what we had a month ago.

Driving is easy enough, apart from the Army system of gear-changing, which is rather awkward. They made us drive from the very first lesson, and I must say I was rather surprised to find myself bowling along casually at 25mph after a few minutes of instruction. Fortunately the instructor knew the sequence of stopping.

I was interested to hear news of your activities. GTC, art and nursing babies should equip you well for wifely duties and motherhood. But I hope you won't disdain academic work which is at least as important as anything else.

Xmas won't be too bad. Even Army life has certain merits. After sharing a

Nissen hut for a month or so with the same crowd one develops a certain affection for one's comrades in distress.

―――――――――

Now that Matriculation was behind me I had a little more time to spend on other activities. I wanted to learn more about Art and for a year I went to Hornsey Art College as a weekend student. Margaret was already there full-time, studying commercial art, and among my fellow weekenders was Hoffnung. He was always getting into trouble for fooling around and drawing cartoons. Herbert Read was the head of the College in those days and the standard was very high.

But both Margaret and myself felt that during the vacations we should also try to do something useful so we became volunteer assistants at a war nursery. Babies from the age of six months were left there, often for days at a time, whilst their mothers worked in nearby factories, frequently on night-shift. A popular song of 1942 extolled the women's importance:

'It's the girl that makes the thing that holds the oil that oils the ring that works the thingummybob that's going to win the war'.

In our nursery most of the mothers were employed by de Havillands, making plane parts. But the effect on some of the children was heart-breaking. It was the first time I had seen young children rocking themselves continuously to and fro in misery and it is a picture I have never forgotten.

On Christmas Eve, in Germany, the first flying bomb was tested. But at home our attention was dominated by food news. Rommel reportedly got a pound of captured British coffee as a present. Apples and oranges, but not bananas, appeared in the shops and long queues formed. (Bananas were an unknown pre-war luxury to the toddlers of the day and were only imported on rare mercy flights for children suffering from coeliac disease.)

Mincemeat, it was recommended, could be made satisfactorily with currants, preserved eggs, chopped oranges and liquid paraffin, the last ingredient replacing the meagre weekly ration of cooking fat. Eating out helped save coupons but even a rabbit sandwich with tea and bun, costing 6d, was quite expensive.

Toys were renovated and re-painted for younger brothers and sisters. Americans sent luxury food parcels containing chocolates and cigarettes and everyone shared and swopped to celebrate Christmas.

I spent that Christmas Eve with Margaret, at the Forces Canteen in Australia House, helping to make sandwiches. They had mountains of Australian butter and ham and the temptation to have the odd nibble proved too much for us.

On my seventeenth birthday, December 27th, 1942, Hitler at last listened to the advice of his generals and began to withdraw from the Russian Front.

I shall be able to see you within a week providing I pass the motor-cycling tests. I'm far from optimistic about this matter, because they have just raised the standard somewhat considerably and 50% have failed during the past two weeks. I have found truck-driving very pleasant indeed. I and a friend of mine took turns at driving our 30cwt lorry over the circuit which took us to within 14 miles of Charing Cross. We used to stop for lunch at roadside cafes, and take it easy in general.

The motor bike, however, is in a rather different category. In my hands it is an equally dangerous weapon, but unfortunately the danger is mine. The weather, too, is much colder. Snow is in the air today and we have to do some cross country motor-cycling, which under present conditions seems to be merely an ingenious method of committing suicide.

I shall get away not later than Saturday week and shall certainly spend a day in Town. After that I hope to go on to the OCTU which will be either Catterick (Yorks) or Alton Towers (Staffs) where the course will last about four months with a week's leave in the middle.

I don't think I have told you how we spent Christmas here. On the 23rd the Cadets put on a Concert Party, produced and written by Jeremy Hawk, a cadet who is a young West End actor. It was an absolutely first-rate show. We were also regaled with three film shows and an ENSA Concert Party. We had a special Xmas Day dinner served up by the officers. The only dissonant note was struck by some bright spark who organised a regimental "treasure hunt" on Boxing Day morning. The clues were in some cases completely erroneous, and the only treasure our group found was when we adjourned to the "White Horse" for refreshments.

On Sunday I met my parents in Maidstone again, passed a few pleasant hours, and returned laden with a cake, cigars, biscuits and chocolate. I finished by covering the three and a half miles to Camp from Snodland Station, up the long hill and carrying a suitcase, in forty-five minutes.

I haven't much personal news, except that Marjorie and Sybil will very probably be returning to Bath Road, Chiswick, early in the New Year. Marjorie looks like being called up soon. Sybil is doing part-time work in the Forces Canteen at Wycombe.

I'm pretty sure James Clarke is fighting in Tunisia with the 8th Army.

The last night of 1942 the RAF bombed Dusseldorf. They were trying out a new British invention for accurate bombing of cities obscured by cloud. Known as OBOE it used a radio beam to locate its targets. The trial was a success and greatly reduced the effect of weather conditions on the task of deliberate destruction from the air.

The New Year opened badly for the Germans. In North Africa the Allies were ready to strike and Rommel knew it. On January 8th von Paulus, trapped near Stalingrad, was issued with an ultimatum by the Russians but fear of disobeying Hitler's orders to fight to the last drop of German blood, made him refuse to surrender. A few days later the Russians broke the siege of Leningrad and set up an overland supply route to the beleaguered city, though it was to be another year before the city was finally liberated.

In the Far East the Japanese were not doing very well, either, and at the beginning of the year decided to abandon Guadalcanal.

Troop A2, ''A'' Battery, Wrotham   *January 3rd 1943*

You will see that my address has changed. I have to do the second week of 'motor-bikes' in company with about half of B12. It was quite a strain to be on some of the roads last week. However, adverse weather conditions are not permitted to prevent the completion of our training.

There is very little danger except in the middle of traffic. Although accidents are fairly frequent, it's amazing what one can plough through and bump over on a motor-bike and still remain in the saddle. If you had seen our cross-country course you might have thought this impossible. It presented an absolutely fiendish succession of obstacles set remarkably close together. And the weather was really shocking on the day we went through it.

In the actual test I had the honour of stalling the engine in a pond. So I had to wade through shoving the machine in my boots and gaiters. On the way back home my machine wouldn't start, so I had to return on the instructor's machine. This broke down, too. When I got back to the Camp I was able fully to appreciate for the first time the inestimable value of a pair of dry socks.

I hope you are looking forward to seeing me again as much as I am to seeing you.

Stanley passed his motor-cycle test at the second attempt having discovered in the meantime that the secret of success was to tip the examining sergeant five shillings.

Wrotham   *January 7th, 1943*

This is just to let you know that I am going on leave on Saturday afternoon (the 9th January). I have to report at the OCTU at Alton Towers on Friday next.
All my love,

This extract from the last letter that Stanley wrote from his first Army training camp, the Wrotham Pre-OCTU known as Vigo Camp to the locals, gives no indication of his relief in getting away.

His eight weeks in a Nissen hut, among the woods and copses in what was once the grounds of a stately home, during one of the bitterest winters of the War, remained in his memory for many years as 'a most gruesome experience'. Not even the comforts of the Vigo public house, (used until recently by the local rugby side for changing rooms as they had no club-house), the White Horse (for many years a ruin but now refurbished), or the Cricketers at Meopham could compensate for the mud, lack of heating and hot water, and the rigorous training in full kit up and down the North Downs escarpment.

Had Stanley been at Wrotham a few months later, like Alan Wilkinson who now lives in Sevenoaks, he would have had pleasanter memories. In a letter to his parents dated 20th May '43, Cadet Wilkinson wrote from Camp B Wrotham:

'It is truly an exceptionally beautiful camp, built in the middle of a forest of silver birch extending for several miles. The floor of the forest is bright blue being carpeted almost entirely of bluebells. One side there is a massive escarpment from which there is a magnificent view across miles and miles of meadows and hop fields.'

Immediately after the War the Army Nissen huts were occupied by squatters bombed out from the East End of London. As the war had progressed the Camp had become better organised and to the squatters it was like paradise having roads, drains and electricity. When they were eventually re-housed the Camp lay rusting and idle until the planners settled their differences.

The assault course now lies within the boundaries of Trosley Country Park on the edge of the new village of Vigo. The paths which wander up and down the escarpment lead through the war-time training grounds – signs of which can still be seen.

The old trees and overgrown coppices contain yews, beeches and stumps of hazelnut and chestnut. Oaks, birch and hawthorn can be found, as well as hornbeam, ash and sallow. Travellers joy, willow herb, deadly nightshade and burdock are among some of the countless flowers that cover the clearings. Bird songs fill the air and even the nightingale can be heard there sometimes. The countryside lies peaceful again as it did before the Army occupied this corner of Kent.

OCTU

'made to feel we are more than halfway to our commissions already'
January 23rd, 1943

As far as I know Stanley never re-visited the site of his first Army Camp although we frequently drove within a few miles of Trottiscliffe and the North Downs escarpment when travelling to and from the Continent via Dover.

Wrotham Camp was the main topic of conversation when we met on Thursday, 14th January. At the time I wondered how on earth he was going to cope with the rest of his training let alone the experience of living under battle conditions. Till then he had been so protected, first by his family and then by the artificial atmosphere of Cambridge.

I have a clear recollection of that meeting – we sat talking for hours over tea at the Marble Arch Corner House – whilst I tried to explain to him the mathematics of a shell trajectory, by drawing parabolas on paper serviettes. His excellent arithmetical ability surprisingly did not extend to mathematics generally. It was probably the only time during our courtship that I was conscious of knowing more about a subject than he did.

Fortunately, now that I was back at my Hampstead school, the school day ended at 1pm, though I sometimes had to go in for games on Saturdays. Meeting Stanley in the afternoon in central London was safe and convenient, if not very exciting. It meant we could both be home before the evening raids started and without the necessity of saying where (or with whom) we had been.

But that evening we stayed in the West End and went to see 'Arsenic and Old Lace' at the Strand theatre. Lillian Braithwaite, Frank Pettingall and Naunton Wayne were in the cast. There was a raid during the performance but nearly everyone remained in their seats after the sirens sounded and the play carried on. We both agreed it was an excellent performance though at times we could hardly hear the actors for the noise of bombs exploding and anti-aircraft fire outside.

Exciting things were happening elsewhere that day. In Casablanca a momentous conference was taking place between Churchill and Roosevelt. Stalin was invited, too, but he was tied up directing the Russian offensive. The Conference lasted ten days and it was there that the two civilian leaders planned the campaign to overthrow the Axis.

First, North Africa was to be conquered: the preparations for the invasion of France to be begun at once for implementation in 1944: Sicily to be invaded as soon as possible: and, finally, unconditional surrender only to be accepted.

It became known as the 'Unconditional Surrender' meeting.

On the 16th January Iraq declared war on the Axis, thus becoming our ally. On the 18th, five Englishmen planning the destruction of the heavy water plant in Norway were shot. Deaths were occurring elsewhere in the world which were totally unrelated to the war. In Argentina, on January 15th, fifteen hundred people died in an earthquake. Perhaps it was taken as a sinister omen for two weeks later Argentina changed sides and broke with the Axis.

610499 Cadet de Smith, S.A.
Squad 77, ''A'' Battery, 121 OCTU (RA) HAC
Alton Towers, Staffs   *January 17th, 1943*

I arrived here yesterday and I must say I was most pleasantly surprised. This is a remarkable Camp — unlike any that I imagined. It is situated entirely within this massive and fantastic mansion. The barrack-rooms have brick walls and resemble large dormitories. Washing facilities are under the same roof. The rest rooms and NAAFI are very good, too, and the meals are served by some very charming ATS girls. And what is even better they do all the washing up. The Towers, a well known beauty spot in peace-time, dominates the quiet village and the valley below. I hope to get a week's leave after two months here so it shouldn't be very long before I see you again.

We are expected to do a tremendous amount of work in a relatively short space of time. But whereas at Wrotham we were made to feel that we belonged to the lowest known species of animal life, here we are treated with almost absurd deference by the NCO's. So you are likely to hear at any time of the day: ''What the *!*!*! do you think you are doing .... Sir?'' I expect to enjoy it a good deal more than Wrotham.

But I enjoyed my leave more than anything the Army could ever provide. This was largely due to the very happy day I spent with you.

The following day broke with the news that Eighth Army was on the move and that Rommel's Army was retreating into Tunisia. A few days later Tripoli fell.

In Europe the bombing raids on major cities continued. Both sides regularly lost planes in spite of fighter cover. On the night of 17th/18th January twenty-two British planes were lost over Berlin whilst the Germans lost ten over Britain. In London on 23rd January an elementary (primary) school was hit in a daylight raid, killing five teachers and over forty children.

Alton Towers   *January 23rd, 1943*

I should have gone out today to Derby or Stoke but I had to have two inoculations after lunch so I'm stopping in as a safety precaution. My arms are pretty stiff but apart from that there are no ill effects. In a fortnight's time I have another inoculation and also a vaccination. God knows where they are thinking of sending us with all this stuff pumped into our veins.

Three weeks from now there is Battle School in North Wales. In preparation we are having a good deal of Infantry training and Assault courses, and other diverting little novelties. We cover an extremely wide field from telephony to map-reading, from mathematics to gunnery.

On the whole it's enjoyable — quite interesting work and good living conditions. We wear a collar and tie and a full white hat-band. We are made to feel that we are more than half-way to our commissions already. But I expect it's just to instil us with the appropriate zest for the awfulness ahead.

I was quite alarmed after reading about the result of the recent daylight raid on a London school so I was relieved to hear from you. But no wonder you were distraught by the strain of sitting in an air-raid shelter all that time.

I hope you still find life drawing fascinating but you are extraordinarily unlikely ever to have the opportunity of painting my torso in oils.

Re: the present I promised you, I asked my mother to find a powder bowl but she says they are virtually unobtainable. What else would you like? I could get you a slide rule but don't ask for silk stockings!

On 25th January the Russians recaptured Voronezh, a sixteenth century city which, in the eighteenth century, had nearly been destroyed by fire three times. In the twentieth century, when the Russians at last re-entered the gates, it must have looked rather similar to the aftermath of those infernos.

Two days later the United States Air Force carried out its first raid on German territory, attacking Wilhelmshaven in broad daylight.

Alton Towers   January 30th, 1943

This Saturday morning we were given a cross-country outing on motor-bikes. Unfortunately there were two downpours and I finished with my bike completely bogged down, more than ankle-deep in mud, sweating and shoving. We also had to do map-reading and produce a representation of Alton Park with its correct contours without the use of any instruments. My effort would not have qualified for admission to the Royal Academy.

I shan't be commissioned till the end of May at the earliest. I'm looking forward very much to that but I mustn't look too often because every time I look I see the Battle School looming in between.

Last weekend whilst recuperating from my inoculations I read two full-length books in just over twenty-four hours: 'Education for Death', a very glum picture of Nazi education and its products, and 'Fiesta' by Ernest Hemingway. Both very readable and interesting. Now I'm on to a couple more: one on the last war by Liddell Hart and one entitled 'Russia Fights On'. Well, what else could she do?

ALTON TOWERS TODAY.

Certainly the Russians fighting on was producing results. On January 30th von Paulus was captured, the day after Hitler had made him a Field Marshal. By February 2nd, with the capture of sixteen other German Generals, he offered the complete surrender of Stalingrad.

In North Africa the Eighth Army were pursuing Rommel and on the 4th February they crossed into Tunisia. Eisenhower was made C-IN-C of the whole of North Africa.

Alton Towers   February 6th, 1943

Today I managed to get into the Major's bad books over my kit lay-out. What I heard was hardly encouraging though I fail to see how it affects one's ability as an Officer, particularly under fire. These peace-time Sandhurst products ....Ah, well.

Needless to say I have no objection to your going dancing provided you don't become enamoured of your partners. Were I in a position to I would love to take you myself so long as you don't expect me to jitterbug. Perhaps you'd better stick to your netball and cycling – you're less likely to be tempted away from the straight and narrow. And it might give you more time for writing to me. PLEASE make your letters a little longer.

Margaret and I sometimes went to Covent Garden, not to listen to opera since that had ceased at the outbreak of the war. The stalls of the Opera House had been covered with a dance floor and refreshments were served in the first row of boxes. There was a large, revolving, mirrored globe suspended from where the great chandelier used to hang, a novelty in those far-off days before 'Come Dancing'.

To us it had lost none of its elegance but ghosts of the opera must have shuddered at the noise made by the big bands who played there. It was always packed with soldiers, sailors and airmen of various nations on leave, out for a good time, and Stanley's worries were not without foundation. However, Margaret and I never used our real names and invariably managed to slip away if we suspected someone might be troublesome. We liked it best when Margaret's brother, John, was on leave as he often accompanied us with friends of his.

The minor irritations of life in England at that time continued. On 17th February a ban was placed on transporting flowers by rail or post. This angered florists who said that relatives of Canadians, wounded at Dieppe and now in hospital, were always sending cables requesting flowers be sent to them. For a time the flower sellers, both outside the hospitals and in Piccadilly Circus, disappeared.

On February 9th the Americans finally cleared Guadalcanal of the last remaining Japanese. Because they refused all offers to surrender it had cost over fifty thousand Japanese lives as well as some eight hundred Japanese planes. The American losses, made unnecessarily heavy by the Japanese stand, amounted to some sixteen hundred soldiers killed and another four and a half thousand wounded.

But the sacrifice made by the five Englishmen, murdered by the Germans in Norway the previous month, was about to be rewarded. On February 16th six Norwegians flew in and landed near the heavy water plant. Together with four men from the earlier mission they carefully re-planned, and eventually executed, its destruction.

Alton Towers   February 21st, 1943

This is being written on the train as I come back from Battle School at Penmaenmawr between Llandudno and Bangor. This was the place where the two little twins were lost a few weeks ago and from the newspaper reports I had come to expect to find a remote mountain village. But it's actually a pleasant little sea-side resort, with a very mountainous hinterland. We were billeted in a small holiday camp on the sea-front. The food was by far the best I've had since I've been in the Army but I don't think I'll volunteer to go again.

The Army food obviously compared very favourably with the weekly rations which civilians were entitled to at that time: 1oz lard (three farthings worth), 1oz butter, 2oz each of margarine, bacon, sugar and tea, plus 1/4d worth of meat.

Stanley continued with a diary of his week:

Monday. *Two hours lectures on explosives then up the mountain to handle the real thing. We threw live grenades and blew things up. One* *instructor (who was standing beside me at the time) got a piece of a grenade in his throat.*

Tuesday. *We fired almost every type of Infantry weapon. My ears are still ringing slightly from the noise.*

Wednesday. *This was Battle Inoculation Day. We were brought under fire and had grenades, thunderflashes and other nasties thrown at us. I felt little sense of danger and shan't mind if I never have to undergo anything more unpleasant during the war.*

Thursday. *We finished with a trip down the 'Fairy Glen'. A notice-board proclaimed that admission to the public cost 4d but we were granted the privilege gratuitously. We were also permitted to wade through the stream at the bottom for a mile or so carrying kit, weapons and accessories. It wasn't too bad except at the waterfalls where we had to jump into icy cold water which swirled around our chests. Several blokes lost their footing and equipment.*

In the evening we had a night exercise which proved a complete farce. However we had good fun blacking our faces and singing negro spirituals.

Friday. *This was Austerity Day – we went without lunch and tea. I was presented with a Bren Gun to wrap around my neck and before reaching the top of the mountain I died about fifty deaths. We arrived at our bivouacking area late in the afternoon and at 7.30pm settled down to sleep in the open. It was so unpleasant that we weren't even sorry when we were awakened by thunderflashes and Verey lights. So we picked up our blankets and groundsheets and marched ten miles back to Camp, arriving at 3am.*

I hope there is a letter from you when I get back. When I last heard I had almost given up wondering when you would write and started worrying if you would write. Try to write at least once a week – never mind the literary qualities. Letters mean a hell of a lot – especially yours – when I am separated for so long from the persons and things I love.

I am looking forward to seeing you again more than ever before, if that is possible. I hope the abolition of physical distance between us will help to eliminate any other gap which exists or which you still seem to think exists. I know things become exaggerated by pondering over them too much but that is the trouble with Army life. Long periods of intense physical activity punctuated by unutterable boredom and it's likely to be much the same when we're actually under enemy fire.

There was plenty of enemy fire for the Australians and Americans to face in the Bismarck Sea area, off New Guinea. The Japanese were desperately trying to maintain a foothold which meant supplying New Guinea by convoy. At the beginning of March, when the Bismarck Sea massacre took place, three thousand Japanese died as their convoy was attacked by RAF Beaufighters and American torpedo boats. Still the Japanese did not give up.

In London a terrible accident occurred during an air raid, which somehow shocked the country more deeply than the loss of life by enemy action. As people had poured down the stairs into Bethnal Green tube station, after the Alert sounded, a woman tripped. Nearly two hundred people died in the resulting crush.

Churchill had been reported as unwell and by the end of February it was confirmed that he had pneumonia.

Alton Towers   March 3rd, 1943

This time I am the one who has been slow to write. Even so I can't muster a fountain pen, and I'm beginning to believe it has gone where all good fountain pens go. Why, oh, why am I always losing things?

This week we are on MT again and, though I hate to admit it, you were right about the sparking plug gaps being 18 thous. I believe it is a thing called a contact breaker which has a gap of 12-15 thous.

Alton Towers   March 10th, 1943

I note that you have strayed from the narrow path of duty in connection with the GTC. Take care: many a fallen woman took the first step on the downward path by missing her parades.

My fate — though I haven't missed any parades — hangs in the balance. I have to go back to Battle School though I can't think why. Meanwhile I'm Cadet Subaltern for the next three days. I have to march my half of the squad about, see that everyone (including myself) is on parade at the right time and place, provide ample chalk for lecturers and generally hold the baby if anything goes wrong. It will.

As for leave, assuming that I pass through into the next Battery, it may come at an awkward moment. It would be from Saturday, April 10th to Sunday, April 18th and I think this clashes with your 'Council for Education in World Citizenship' week at Cheltenham. Naturally I'd like it immensely if you could come to Wycombe while I am on leave. There seems to be this awful yawning chasm between us so much of the time.

In a broadcast to the nation Churchill outlined a four-year post-war reconstruction plan which included compulsory National Insurance covering everyone from the cradle to the grave. He had recovered from his attack of pneumonia but his voice sounded even gruffer than usual. In one way his illness had been a blessing in disguise. Because he had derived so much pleasure from the flowers he had received from well-wishers, he partially lifted the ban on the transport of flowers that he had imposed the previous month.

In Germany, although it was not generally known till after the war, a serious attempt was made on Hitler's life on March 13th. There had been one previously – at a beer hall in November 1939 – but this one seemed foolproof. The bomb was concealed in a bottle which was to be given as a present by Hitler to a general he was visiting. Unfortunately the fuse was defective and failed to go off whilst both Hitler and the bottle were travelling by plane to the meeting. The culprits were never discovered and no one was arrested.

121 OCTU Battle School, Pilkingtons Camp, Penmaenmawr   March 20th, 1943

Still haven't heard from you so I may as well update you on this week. It's Saturday evening and I'm doing picquet duty as a kind-hearted stand-in for the said duty officer who is going out with a woman. It will keep me out of mischief.

Although I didn't enjoy it, I weathered this week better than last time. We had quite a few casualties – two of them hospital cases – and several fellows fell sick.

When we next met he told me that one of the casualties was an Instructor who had almost lost his life trying to save a cadet. The cadet had pulled a pin out of a hand grenade, then dropped it. As it rolled down the mountainside towards another cadet the Instructor had flung himself on it. The cadet who had dropped it was only slightly wounded but the Instructor had his right hand blown off and received serious wounds to other parts of his body. Miraculously he survived but his army career was at an end.

The most perilous day was Wednesday when as luck would have it I was detailed as Commander of the Section which led the advance to the battle area. The Platoon came under fire from several machine guns raking the ground half a dozen yards in front of me. The instructors assisted us as usual by tossing thunderflashes in our direction and exploding anti-personnel mines all round us.

I decided that discretion was the better part of valour and took to ground. Dear God, what will I do in the real thing? Everybody thought the attack was a very good one. I, on the other hand, thought our part in it wasn't exactly brilliant – in fact it seemed one hell of a muddle – but who am I to quibble?

Now in the glimmer of the rising sun we must leave Hawaii – I mean Penmaenmawr and Llanfairfechan...... These little seaside towns are really extremely pleasant places. I shouldn't at all mind spending my next leave with you at Colwyn Bay. But that sort of thing will, I'm afraid, have to remain a dream.

Did I tell you about my last month's report? It was remarkably satisfactory – even flattering. I got 90% in the exam and finished second. (Actually it was 88% but the examiner couldn't add up.) On this basis I applied for an interview with an Intelligence Board but all they did was vaccinate me again.

I've just had an airgraph from Natey. He's still in Iraq or Persia and tells me that Percy is in the same part of the world.

On March 21st another unsuccessful attempt was made on Hitler's life. This time a General planned to sacrifice his own life by carrying a bomb in his pocket and detonating it as Hitler passed by him whilst reviewing troops. He failed because he couldn't find a bomb with a short enough time fuse – ten minutes was the longest delay he dared have between sighting the Fuhrer and priming the bomb.

In Tunisia a week-long battle for the Mareth Line, comparable with the battle for El Alamein which lasted from 23rd October-5th November, 1942, was brought to a successful conclusion on March 29th. James Clarke was fighting with the Eighth Army at the time, but it is another friend who was there serving in a field artillery regiment, Captain Geoffrey Harris, who gave me the following account of the campaign.

'With the German decision to withdraw, exploiting the advantage of shortened lines of communication and a reduced area of territory to be defended, the Allies faced a new aspect of the enemy's efficiency – the establishment of fortified lines of defence to which they would retreat after thorough preparation, always selecting mountainous terrain with observation posts commanding flat open plains.

From then on, the course of the war was phased into major offensive operations to breach a series of such lines through Tunisia, Sicily and Italy, firstly on the River Sangro and, most formidable of all, which ran through Cassino eastwards to the Adriatic Coast.

In the four months after the breakthrough at El Alamein, the Eighth Army advanced twelve hundred miles westward capturing Tobruk, Benghazi, El Agheila and Tripoli, reaching Medenine in Tunisia on 24th February, 1943. There they met the first of these major defences at the Mareth Line. So formidable were these defences that General Montgomery was not prepared to risk the heavy casualties that would have been incurred by frontal attack. A landing behind the Mareth Line by sea was out of the question because the German and Italian Navies at that time had complete control of the Mediterranean. (All the Eighth Army's supplies of personnel, rations, ammunition, fuel and equipment came via South Africa, the Indian Ocean and the Red Sea.)

Monty recognised that throughout the entire campaign both sides had been confined to a narrow coastal strip, where the sand was compacted, whereas further inland the terrain was rugged with deep sand dunes and generally impassable for a mobile army. A small reconnaissance group was despatched and reported back with maps showing the 'going' for two or four wheel-drive vehicles, tanks and tracked vehicles. A possible but difficult route, from which to attack with a 'Left Hook', was planned.

On 14th March a small force set out moving stealthily and often under cover of darkness. It was a week before they encountered any opposition and then strong reinforcements were brought in to complete the breakthough. The Left Hook was a major success and the Germans had to withdraw from the Mareth Line to a new defensive line surrounding Tunis.

In the Far East the last major naval battle to be fought solely with naval guns took place in the Aleutians. Although no capital ships were sunk the Japanese never again succeeded in reaching the islands.

Alton Towers   **March 25th, 1943**

When I came back from Battle School on Sunday evening I found your letter awaiting me. I probably won't write much in reply because I have so far taken thirty-seven pages of foolscap notes this week. After the strictly Trade Union conditions of Cambridge I find it most galling to be hounded in this way, with spit and polish and plenty of homework thrown in.

However, life is never without its compensations. On Tuesday we were given a privileged showing of 'Desert Victory', the film about the Eighth Army. Well worth seeing if only for the moment when the 25 pounders (my favourite guns) opened up on the night of the big barrage at El Alamein.

Marjorie is joining the Wrens next month so I don't suppose I shall see her when I'm next on leave. We'll drink her health in ginger ale, shall we?

PS Your new style Morse script is quite beyond me and I haven't deciphered it yet. For a would-be British agent this is admittedly pretty poor going.

'Desert Victory' – a combined effort by the Ministry of Information and the British Army Film Unit – is the classic war documentary, with no stars and only a few shots taken in the studio.

Alton Towers   **March 31st, 1943**

Thank you so much for the very fine present you sent me. It really was very sweet of you to spring such a pleasant surprise. I really didn't think anyone would remember my twenty-first. I'm not sure exactly what it's supposed to hold so I'm just calling it a hold-all.

But I'm sorry to see you have descended to cheap sarcasm at my expense. Do I feel like a man yet? I, who have been three years at Cambridge University, who have been through fire and under water – sorry, under fire and through water – at Battle School: I, the hoary veteran of a thousand experiences. What a question! The answer is NO. I feel precisely as I did a week ago, bemused and bewildered at what I am supposed to be doing in the Army.

PS It's only about twelve days now before I see you again, dear. Tuesday, 13th April, at Piccadilly Circus at 11am, bombs willing.

On his birthday, by a remarkable but unrelated piece of good fortune, British Intelligence learnt of the progress and plans for launching the V2. Hitler's 'secret weapon' was no longer secret due to a hidden microphone which overheard a revealing conversation taking place between two German generals who had recently been captured.

Best of all, as his twenty-first birthday dawned, England learned that the heavy water plant in Norway had finally been destroyed, thus ending the hopes of making a German atom bomb for years to come.

Commissioned at last

*'You haven't been in the forces so you don't
know how much letters mean'*
May 27th, 1943

A t the beginning of April, I spent a week at Cheltenham Ladies
College. A conference had been organised there by the Council
for Education in World Citizenship which was aimed at problems
which would face children all over the world in the future. How
were the victorious Allies, when the day eventually came, going to cope with
the inevitable division between the conquered and unconquered without
sowing the seeds of a Third World War? The conference was specifically
aimed at the problems of under-nourishment, lack of education and the
orphaned, stateless condition of millions of innocent children, whether
enemy or otherwise.

To date, amongst the British Forces alone, 39,000 soldiers, 30,000 sailors
and 24,000 airmen had been killed, leaving countless children fatherless.
In addition 45,000 civilians had lost their lives. But there was an optimistic
mood in the country, as reports came in from all Fronts of Allied successes.

Although the war was far from won many people were already trying to
prepare for the aftermath of victory. The factory run by the Blind Institution
in London, for example, was reputed to be making two hundred thousand
enormous wicker baskets, each capable of holding a half a ton of food, which
were to be dropped on occupied territories immediately hostilities ceased.

Budget Day, 1943, brought no relief from the financial restrictions we all
lived under. There were higher taxes on beer, tobacco, wines, entertainments
and non essential goods like jewellery. In other words, it was a normal
budget.

Alton Towers   **April 7th, 1943**

*I'm glad you're liking it at Cheltenham and hope you enjoy the rest of the
Conference. It should leave you refreshed for next week. Is 11 o'clock on
Tuesday still OK? Apparently I am having some sort of ersatz twenty-first
party on Sunday when I arrive home. My mother has asked whether you
could come, so things must be improving. But I had to tell her this was
pretty well impossible as you would be travelling back from Cheltenham that
evening.*

*Last Sunday our Squad played a game of soccer, the first since I've been
here. We beat 81 Squad 4-0. I scored the first goal playing inside right and
the general impression was that I did OK. Possibly I shall try and get a
game with Wycombe Wanderers whilst I am on leave. Who knows, I may
end up as a professional football player.*

I certainly won't end up as an artist. One afternoon last week we were detailed to draw another military panorama and my picture was returned with a single comment: ''Lousy''.

We met on Tuesday, April 13th, as arranged and in the evening went to see Bernard Shaw's 'Heartbreak House' at the Cambridge Theatre. It was a fine performance, with Deborah Kerr, Isobel Jeans and Edith Evans, and ran for some thirty weeks, a long run in war-time for a straight play.

That day the Germans claimed that mass graves of ten thousand Polish Officers had been found in Katyn Forest near Smolensk. They had apparently been killed in the Spring of 1940 when the Russians, then Hitler's allies, controlled the area. When Sikorski, the Polish Prime Minister in exile, asked for a Red Cross inquiry the news so infuriated Stalin that he broke off communications with him. Even today the subject of Katyn is one of bitter controversy between Poles, Russians and Germans, though the Russians have recently admitted that they were to blame.

April 13th was also the day that the Allies learnt, through decrypting a Japanese message, that their Commander in Chief of the Combined Fleet, Admiral Yamamoto, would be making a visit by plane to Japanese bases in the Solomon Islands. On April 18th the Americans successfully intercepted the plane and shot it down, killing the most charismatic of Japan's war leaders.

Alton Towers   **April 27th, 1943**

Your letter was a very charming one. I'm glad you enjoyed my leave. I felt the same way – and about you. But I feel very much under a cloud at the moment. On the way back to Alton I left a number of my belongings on the train. I'm worried no end about it and I was too ashamed to write home till yesterday. I went to Derby to investigate but the only remaining source of hope was closed for Easter. So I went to see Abbott and Costello instead to cheer myself up.

On the bright side is the fact that I am still with the Squad though three other fellows have been dropped. We had one of the three principal RA bands to play for the Passing Out parade on Good Friday, which was attended by no lesser personages than two Brigadiers.

Today (Tuesday) we went on a Drill Order in which we did everything except actually fire the guns. I was a signaller (telephone) and had quite a pleasant time lying on my stomach whilst establishing communications. The drawback was that our Squad Officer then cut the line and his little joke wasn't detected for about 15 minutes during which I was giving elaborate orders to fire to no-one.

PS I heard from Marjorie today. She's doing OK in the Wrens and expects to be transferred to a port as a Pay Writer pretty soon.

On April 20th the RAF paid Berlin a visit to celebrate Hitler's fifty-fourth birthday and so did the Russian Air Force. Another unwelcome birthday present for Hitler was the news that Turkey was no longer neutral but now considered herself 'pro-Allies'. The success of the Soviet forces in the Crimea undoubtedly influenced Turkey's decision to change her allegiance.

In England it was announced that the ban on bell-ringing in church – introduced so that bell-ringing could be used if necessary as a warning of invasion – was to be lifted from Easter Sunday. Unfortunately there was such a severe shortage of bell-ringers that few churches could take advantage of it.

Other warning systems, too, were in the news. On that warm and sunny Easter Day, April 26th, an All Clear sounded without there having been a previous Alert – someone had dusted a switch too thoroughly.

At the end of the first week in May, Tunis and then Bizerta fell to the British and Americans respectively. The British tanks rolled in to a welcome of flowers and hugs. Tunis, a city probably older than Carthage, had been occupied by the French since the end of the nineteenth century. But the German invaders had been far from popular and the stragglers from Hitler's famous Africa Corps received no help from the populace. Fifty thousand German prisoners were taken. By May 12th General Alexander claimed 'We are masters of the North African shores'.

Alton Towers   *May 10th, 1943*

My case with all my belongings has come back. You can imagine how pleased I am.

On Wednesday I'm going to be Cadet Orderly Officer. It is also the day when we have gas practice on parade and I'm waiting with some apprehension for the moment when I'll have to bellow "Battery 'Shun!" from inside a gas mask.

Your letter has given me plenty to think about in the meantime. The most helpful book on the topic of Parliamentary Government is by W. Ivor Jennings who is a very great lawyer and political scientist. Until recently, (dare I say with uncustomary lack of modesty) perhaps the best lawyer my old college has produced.

But now listen to the current expert.......

1. The duty of the Government is to govern. Parliament must therefore be incapable of imposing too many barriers to strong action by the Executive. A weak Executive means it will be impossible to put through progressive legislation.

Most writers are biased in favour of a strong Parliament to control the wild excesses of the despotic Executive and the Civil Servants behind it. That is, the more discussion, the less action.

In France the Executive was weak and Parliament a mass of warring factions. In the US the value of Congress is exaggerated. Investigations by Congressional committees usurp the powers of the Cabinet and the

President's policies are often hamstrung.

2. Can we devise a fairer system of Representation?

Distribution of constituencies has not kept pace with movements of population. Double franchises are inequitable. Proportional representation would lead to a multiplicity of parties and therefore unstable government.

A better proposal is the alternative vote system.

3. Status of MPs

They should be compelled to present themselves for re-election if either they change their party or more than half their electorate require it. They should also be required to attend Parliament for a certain proportion of their time.

4. Why two Houses?

In any form the Second Chamber is meant to act as a brake. A Second Chamber of 'experts' would only be a research body. Any form of sectional representation is essentially anti-democratic and is found in all the corporate fascist states.

(My summary of Stanley's nine-page letter on the subject.)

Them's my ideas in a nutshell but if you can obtain Jennings you'll get a much better mark.

There was great excitement in England when the news broke on the 18th May that three enormous dams in the Rhine and the Ruhr had been blown up. Two of these seemingly impregnable structures had been breached by a brilliant British invention, the bouncing bomb. Developed by Barnes Wallis and delivered by Lancaster bombers they caused immense flooding and loss of life. Eight of the Lancasters were lost with their crews, almost half the force that had set out. Barnes Wallis said afterwards that if he had known the likely toll he would never have started the project.

Britain was increasingly successful on another watery front, the North Atlantic. Now that she had mastered the German naval Enigma codes, Hitler's U-boats were taking a severe beating. Thirty-two were sunk in the first three weeks of May and on May 24th, after two more U-boats were destroyed, Admiral Donitz ordered their withdrawal from the North Atlantic convoy routes.

In the middle of May, Churchill and Roosevelt decided that the cross-channel invasion of Europe must on no account be delayed later than May 1st, 1944, just under a year away. They also decided to share all information on the development of atomic warfare.

Whilst the Allies were discussing the progress of the deadliest weapon mankind had ever tried to develop, the Germans at Peenemunde were approving the production of two deadly weapons of their own: the V1 or pilotless plane and the V2, the rocket bomb. Both were long range missiles aimed at bringing the civilian population to its knees.

Three days later, in Germany, the civilian population of Wuppertal were reeling from the shock of a British raid on the city which resulted in a firestorm – 2500 killed and over 100,000 homeless.

Troop I 1/2, 123 OCTU, Bourlon Lines, Catterick   May 27th, 1943

Why don't you write more often? I simply can't understand it. You haven't been in the Forces so you don't know from experience how much letters mean. You can go to umpteen dances but you can't spare an hour in eight days to write to me.

Stanley was not the only member of the Forces complaining about my poor showing as a correspondent but on this occasion I had written to him – he had forgotten to warn me of his change of address. At the same time I was being inundated with letters in rhyme from John Pincus begging me to write to him.

Contrary to Stanley's accusation I spent much more time going to films than I did dancing. Two films which I remember impressed me very much around that time were 'Pygmalion' and 'Gone with the Wind'. Both starred Leslie Howard, one of my favourite actors.

On June 3rd a British airliner was shot down over the Bay of Biscay with the loss of all passengers. Aboard was Leslie Howard, as well as several children, evacuees who were returning from Canada. The Nazis had mistakenly thought Churchill was a passenger. And again I wondered if I might have been one of those children had I gone to Canada, as planned, on the ill-fated 'City of Benares' in 1940.

Catterick   June 5th, 1943

Forgive me. Thank you so much for your letter. It went to my old address and I was so fed up with this place I just let rip.

I could write a small book about my experiences here but it would include rather a lot of rude words, I am afraid. The Unit is permeated with regimentation and spit and polish. We queue for everything; for shaving, eating and every other necessary function. However, I have survived and managed to steer well clear of trouble up to now.

But again there is a ray of sun-shine. The other day I had to fill up a form as S. A. de Smith, 2nd Lt RA – which sounds rather conclusive. My uniform in its final shape should arrive this Tuesday but I don't know yet what posting they'll give me. I've applied for Medium Artillery and Eastern Command but the War Office may have other ideas.

Naval Artillery was playing a vital role in preparing for the Allied invasion of Italy. For ten days, together with air bombardment, the naval guns hammered three islands between Tunisia and Sicily and by June 13th all three were in British hands after the Italians in the islands surrendered unconditionally.

Catterick   **June 12th, 1943**

Everyone has become completely browned off by now. The Squad is really falling to pieces. We had our final Drill Order on Tuesday and it was an absolute shambles. The signalling truck lost a D V Telephone (£6/3/–) and I contrived to drop – and lose – a small pivot pin from one of the instruments on the gun. We are all having to share the cost.

Talking of cost, this Monday we do actually fire our guns and I am one of the ten fellows selected to direct fire from an OP. I'm not looking forward to shouting "1 Round Gunfire" and seeing 4 shells (=£13) crashing miles off target.

I'm beginning to think that too much training has a reverse effect on both efficiency and enthusiasm. And unfortunately it will be my turn to be Troop Officer on the ceremonial passing out parade. Just pray for me. I would never have won the Sword of Honour as the best cadet at Sandhurst.

The following day, Whit Sunday, was bright and sunny. We had a visit from friends of my parents, who were technically enemy aliens but who had volunteered for the Pioneer Corps. They told us that a new ruling now permitted them to change their names to anglicised versions – the first step to integration in their new homeland. Should they or shouldn't they? They were worried about loss of identity.

I remember it well because I was thinking quite a lot about the effect of changing my surname some day – from Natley to de Smith – although marriage had never been discussed between us. Nevertheless, I filled pages of my last school rough-note book trying out new signatures for this awkward name, when I should have been using it for revision. One of the versions is the signature I still use today on all formal documents.

No. 4 PC Battery,
Trawsfynydd, Merioneth, N. Wales   **June 20th, 1943**

I'm writing now, in an antiquated tea-shop full of aspidistras and Victorian pictures, in this unpronounceable place. It's been enjoyable here on the whole. After Catterick we are not hard to please.

We have even been complimented on the show we have put up – probably the first time on record that this has happened. But needless to say there have been one or two unfortunate incidents. On Monday our gun demolished a few telephone wires much to the annoyance of the locals and on

Tuesday a smoke shell (luckily not high explosive) exploded just outside the muzzle. I can hear very little now except the sound of Bow Bells. However I dare say I shall be able to hear your sweet murmurs of love.

We will be firing armour-piercing shot against tanks over at Harlech and then we return to Catterick on Thursday, after which I go on leave. I must see you next week. You must be able to get some time off when you're not actually sitting the exams. Just let me know and I'll be there. My leave will end the next Friday.

PS Note that I've found my fountain pen at long last.

The day Stanley wrote this letter Operation Bellicose, the first shuttle bombing raid of the war, was launched. Lancaster bombers bombed Friedrichshafen, where a production line for V2s was being set up, and then flew on to North Africa. There they reloaded and refuelled, bombing Spezia on the way home. Another raid on Hamburg at the same time resulted in a firestorm, in which three thousand German civilians were killed, more than in the whole of the Blitz. It looked as if the war might be over before Stanley was commissioned. But then his next letter arrived.

Knaresborough, Yorks   **July 4th, 1943**

I am writing this in the Officers Mess on rather pretentious regimental note-paper. Medium Regiment means medium sized artillery and DLOY stands for The Duke of Lancaster's Own Yeomanry. So I more or less got what I had hoped for, though a bit more westerly than I wished

The Colonel bears a close facial resemblance to der Führer though he appears very reasonable on the whole. But he has already informed me that as a very junior subaltern I must say "Sir" much more frequently to the Adjutant. And I thought one could be very familiar with the said officer.

The surroundings are very pleasant and the place itself is conveniently situated. One half of the Unit is in the town itself and the other half is up here on the hill. I have comfortable quarters and a batman all to myself. So there is some hope that I may not lose so many things in future.

One of the men who served in the Duke of Lancaster's Own Yeomanry was Arthur Lowe, later to become famous as an actor through his roles in 'Coronation Street' and as the officer in charge of 'Dad's Army'.

Arthur Lowe was Stores Officer in the 77th and, according to Sergeant-Major Wilson who served with Stanley throughout the war, Arthur Lowe was a stickler for formalities. It was exceedingly difficult to get anything at all out of stores, in spite of having documents in triplicate, signed and counter-signed by all and sundry.

First foothold in Europe
'I haven't done anything yet for which I can be court-martialled'
July 9th, 1943

Sadly, at the beginning of July there was a mysterious plane crash in Gibraltar. On board was General Sikorski, the Polish leader, who only a couple of months before had been devastated by the news of the murder of so many of his people in Katyn Forest.

A few days later Cologne was bombed though fortunately the Cathedral escaped serious damage. The Nazis condemnation of Allied wickedness was loud. Churchill was unmoved. He had recently proclaimed that bombing was the weapon the Axis had chosen to destroy Pearl Harbour. The deadly day and night raids against Germany were no more than poetic justice.

The build-up of such over-powering military strength was not without cost. At home there were further reductions in clothes coupons and old dresses were made into pyjamas for the children. Tomatoes disappeared from London shops, peas went up to 1/– a lb, and tennis balls, if obtainable, were second-hand and pre-war. But it still only cost 3d to send an airgraph to the Forces overseas, a halfpenny more than inland mail.

Knaresborough   July 9th, 1943

Thank you very much for your letter and the enclosed diary. It will be extremely useful to me — if I don't lose it.

On Wednesday I was given the job of troop leader of A-Troop on an all-day scheme. I had visions of leading eight guns and their massive tractors up some narrow lanes and then finding that I had taken the wrong turning. However, I didn't in fact do anything for which I can be court-martialled, though my consumption of alcohol has risen rather steeply in the last few days.

This is a very charming part of the country. It's rather like Marlow, though more hilly and picturesque. There is the river and crowds of pubs, which all need sampling. I hope I am here long enough to try them all.

PS Next week we are off to Firing Camp.

The invasion of Sicily began on July 10th and that night British troops occupied Syracuse, the first Italian city to fall into Allied hands. But the fighting for possession of the island was not going to be as easy as

Montgomery and Patton had hoped. It continued for another four weeks, during which time the Axis managed to evacuate most of their troops and materials to the mainland.

The invasion was not without its lighter side. One ship-load of British soldiers arrived on the Sicilian beaches only to find they were missing a vital piece of equipment. A volunteer rushed back for it as the boats were pulling away. It was a football.

Churchill and Roosevelt issued an appeal to the Italian people: 'Do you want to die for Mussolini and Hitler or live for Italy and civilisation?' It was only a couple of weeks before their answer was made known in dramatic form. Meanwhile Rome – 'the soft under-belly of the Axis' – was bombed.

In Malta at long last the siege ended and it became known how bad conditions had been. Food had been provided by Victory kitchens and all-day queues formed early in the morning. All the island's goats had been eaten. Eggs were 15/– a dozen when obtainable, rabbits were 17/6d. Light was provided by old shoe-laces stuck in a little paraffin in potted meat jars.

At home J. B. Priestly wrote a piece in 'The Listener' in which he praised all those people who would never receive medals but who were making tremendous sacrifices – the retired doctors, waiters, civil servants, old actors and actresses. He praised the switch board girls who stayed at their posts under enemy bombing, the light-house keepers, the postmen. 'We are in truth one people, completely dependent on each other.'

Otterburn Camp, nr. Newcastle upon Tyne   *July 18th, 1943*

All yesterday afternoon I was helping to camouflage our tanks for the firing camp. In the evening I packed and rose at 4am for the journey here. I rode on a motor-bike from Knaresborough to Darlington and from Newcastle to Otterburn without even stalling or coming off so I must be improving. I'm hoping the shooting won't increase my deafness. But I may be lucky as the 5.5" has a less sharp detonation than the 25pdrs. I may even have the pleasure of firing 100lb shells.

My aunt, Marjorie and Sybil's mother, is getting married again next weekend and my father has the privilege of giving her away. The girls will be bridesmaids and my father tried to persuade Cyril Brown (another cousin of Stanley's who later became a leading crystallographer) to be page-boy. Fortunately for him he refused and for me my presence at Firing Camp will prevent my attending this happy ceremony.

Sorry about my lapse into pencil – no, I haven't lost my fountain pen again but they don't seem to stock ink in this Camp.

Have you heard from LSE yet? How did you manage to talk to your father into letting you go? Perhaps he was worried you might finish up as a squadron leader. Your GTC visit to Hendon ought to be interesting. I quote from your last letter: 'We are going to be taking over Hendon aerodrome'!

Although originally I had wanted to read medicine at University, sixth form work had increased my interest in political and economic affairs. There was no likelihood, anyway, of my being accepted at Medical School as I hadn't done any Latin since the first year of the war. Latin continued to be a requirement for entrance to medical schools up to the 1960's. But the major problem lay in persuading my parents that I should go to University at all.

My father considered it unthinkable that I should ever work for a living. In due course I would marry a suitable young man, settle down and have children and live the sort of life my parents had. Unfortunately, though, the war had prevented them sending me abroad to finish my education according to plan so I had been allowed to stay on at my London school as second best.

Stanley gave me continuous encouragement and advice on how to handle them. My brother, Peter, was in the Air Force having shown no interest or ability in further study. He was a natural musician – jazz piano – with perfect pitch and was busy entertaining the RAF though not officially in ENSA. Why, I argued, not let me take the University place my brother didn't want? Economics, after all, wasn't likely to lead to a career and could be useful in running a home.

After long discussions with my teachers they reluctantly agreed to let me go to the London School of Economics. The operative word was 'London' since I could continue to live at home. The necessary application forms, etc were signed. I was accepted. Then, and only then, I told them that LSE was in Cambridge for the duration of the war.

Otterburn   *July 27th, 1943*

> *I was very glad to hear about LSE. It will be useful for you to be in touch with Molly, so I shall drop her a line soon. I know she will give you good advice about books etc. and help you to settle down in Cambridge. How did you finally pull it off?*
> *Those last words were written in the fading light of my tent at Otterburn. Since then we have travelled many a mile and have taken part in a big three-day exercise with infantry, tanks and aircraft. For one reason or another it is going to be very difficult for officers to get leave after the next few weeks. I can't say why nor even that I wish you were with me now. It's too bloody uncomfortable.*
>
> *Although the last two weeks have been hectic, just now things are fairly quiet. I sometimes find it desperately hard to find something to do – or even to look as though I am trying to find something to do. The trouble is we have too many officers in the Battery. As the least experienced I am rather expecting to be posted before we go into action. If I do get posted I might be able to have a crack at the Intelligence Corps.*
>
> *PS What do you think of the news about Mussolini?*

On July 24th King Victor Emanuel was asked by the Fascist Grand Council to assume effective command of the Italian forces. The next day Mussolini was told that the King had become Commander-in-Chief and had appointed Marshall Badoglio to run Italy but that they would still fight on the side of the Axis. Both the new leaders were over seventy but many in England remembered Badoglio as the man who had used poison gas against the Abyssinians in 1935.

Mussolini was to leave Rome for a place of safety. On the 27th of July, as Stanley was rejoicing in Il Duce's downfall, Hitler decided to 'liberate' Mussolini though it was another six weeks before his plan succeeded.

August Bank Holiday weekend promised to be a scorcher. In spite of the radio warnings against travelling, thousands stood in queues all night long to get away to those parts of the coast which were not barred to the public. Travelling by road had its problems, though. All road signs had been removed in 1940 after Dunkirk and were not replaced until March 1944. Along the Southern coast, which was again off bounds to the public, thousands of Canadian tank troops and British commandos gathered.

Knaresborough   August 11th, 1943

I am writing this in the Adjutant's office. No, they haven't appointed me Adjutant. I just happen to be the Orderly Officer tonight and so I have the privilege of sleeping in his office and turning out the guard at some time during the small hours. Both the CO and the BC are on leave but when I shall get any is impossible to forecast. I'm hoping for the weekend of 21st/22nd August.

In the meantime I've seen a couple of films, 'Yankee Doodle Dandy' and 'Algiers'. The first film, with James Cagney, was based on the life of a music hall artist and I enjoyed it very much. The other one which starred Charles Boyer and Hedy Lamarr was pure Hollywood nonsense.

On Thursday our lads played an RAF side at soccer and gave them a good run although the opposition included two internationals. I also played in a tennis match with two socialite land-girls. Quite pleasant and no hanky-panky.

I hope you are taking life rather more seriously than I am. At Cambridge you may not find it too easy to work and even if you do, lectures move forward at a remarkable pace. If you show me a copy of your reading list I'll try to advise you so that you are well equipped before you begin.

Are you looking forward as much as I am to our next meeting? If you are you must love me much more than I deserve.

On August 13th Churchill and Roosevelt signed an agreement never to use the atom bomb against each other's country.

High Wycombe   **August 14th, 1943**

I have been offered nine days leave commencing on August 25th and now I learn from your letter that you are going to camp in Hereford at midnight next Sunday, the 22nd. When will you be returning? I don't think I can get the leave rota changed now. What are we going to do about it? Please, please reply straight away.

On August 17th British bombers carried out a massive raid on Peenemunde, where the rocket and flying bombs were being constructed. During the raid one hundred and thirty German scientists were killed deliberately by bombing their homes. Some six hundred foreign workers also died.

Also on August 17th, thirty-nine days after landing on the island, US forces entered Medina and the whole of Sicily was in Allied hands. Southern Europe could be seen, only three miles away, by the soldiers who crowded the cliffs. But Montgomery was cautious and did not want to invade the mainland too soon.

Roosevelt and Churchill had agreed that Germany was to be defeated before Japan and had settled on May 1st 1944 as D-day for the cross-channel invasion. There was still eight months in hand to mop up Italy before leading the troops in Northern Europe towards victory.

The campaign on the Eastern Front to regain all lost Russian territory and to drive the Germans out of the country was also going well. Kharkov was retaken on the 22nd and the Russians pushed on towards the River Dnieper.

FARM CAMP ADVERTISEMENT, RADIO TIMES, 1943.

By the morning of the 23rd August, the date of Stanley's next letter which reached me at camp, both the Russians and the Americans were a thousand miles either side of Berlin.

I had planned to take a holiday working at a Volunteer Agricultural Camp before going up to Cambridge. The work was not particularly heavy – hoeing, planting, weeding, harvesting and picking vegetables. Margaret and I stayed at the camp which cost 28/– a week and took our own crockery, cutlery, towels and linen. We earned 10d an hour though men got 1/– an hour. As we were only in camp for a week I was able to reassure Stanley that I would be back in plenty of time to meet up with him.

While we were there a Spitfire performed a double loop-the-loop, then dived very low over the camp and dropped letters, weighted with pennies, for Margaret and me. The pilot was her brother, John, who was stationed at RAF Rednal, near Oswestry in Shropshire. He ran out of fuel on the way back to base and landed in a field. But such was the shortage of fighter pilots that he got away with only a reprimand.

Knaresborough   August 23rd, 1943

I caught an early train to London on Sunday with a special 48 hour pass so I could see you before you went to camp only to discover that you had already left for Hereford on an earlier train than planned. Why, oh why, is fate always against us?

It's conceivable that this forty-eight hours may be my last leave. We seem to be kept permanently on alert, which confuses us more than the enemy. Anyway I am keeping my fingers crossed that I shall still get the remaining seven days leave starting next Friday and that you will be back in time.

At the end of August Lord Mountbatten was appointed Commander-in-Chief of South-East Asia. He began to plan offensives to re-establish Allied power in Burma. But the news was dominated by the death of the King of Bulgaria at the age of forty-nine. He was the only King who was a member of a Trade Union – the Bulgarian Railwaymen's Union had made him a life member as a wedding present. His death was surrounded in mystery, especially as he had visited Hitler a few days previously.

Other European royalty was in the news. The King of Denmark refused German demands to his Government to discourage the widespread strikes and resistance. On August 29th the Germans re-occupied Copenhagen, disarming the Danish army and confining the King to his palace.

In England King George V1 asked that September 3rd, the fourth anniversary of the outbreak of the war, should be a National Day of Prayer. And indeed when it dawned it seemed as if our prayers were already being answered as the news came through that General Montgomery's troops, the 5th British and the 1st Canadian Divisions of the Eighth Army, had landed on the toe of Italy.

The invasion of the Italian mainland was preceded by a huge artillery barrage from Messina across the Straights, in preparation for which the Gunners had sweated blood, humping thousands of rounds of ammunition by night, so as not to be seen. Following the barrage the invasion forces landed around Reggio di Calabria, entirely unopposed. The Germans had withdrawn from the toe of Italy to prepare defensive positions along the River Sangro.

There was no Italian resistance, in accordance with the armistice conditions that had been agreed two days earlier with King Victor Emanuel but kept secret from the Germans.

The Kings of Europe seemed united in their dislike of Nazism.

Knaresborough   **Sunday, September 5th, 1943**

I hope you enjoyed last week as much as I did. We were lucky to get tickets for the first night of 'Uncle Vanya'. And on the last night of my leave, too.

We'll be changing camps on Wednesday but before then I have to arrange soccer, cross-country and tug-of-war matches with a battery some 25 miles away. I'm half hoping that the other crowd won't be able to play.

Italy capitulated on the 8th September and Badoglio called on the Italians to free their soil from the Germans. In response Hitler ordered the immediate German occupation of Italy. Alexander reported that Reggio, where Montgomery had landed, was more like a regatta in peace-time than a serious operation of war. The Italian navy set sail for Allied ports or scuttled themselves to avoid capture by the Germans.

c/o GPO Retford, Notts   **September 9th, 1943**

When we arrived at our new location the first news that greeted us was that Italy had surrendered. We heard it on ear-phones on one of our ordinary RA sets. On the surface this seems to be the best news of the war though many things may happen to alter this estimate. Anyway, we haven't decided to cancel out training programmes and go for a holiday at Blackpool.

There's a hell of a lot to be done to make this Camp decently habitable for the men. The officers and sergeants are inside a disused country house which is very comfortable though slightly dilapidated, but most of the men are under canvas — four in each small tent. We haven't even got a NAAFI. It won't be too pleasant if we have to spend the whole winter here.

I've had some stomach trouble which has forced me to take things easy. I couldn't ride a motor-bike today, so I drove one of the trucks. I was very apprehensive going through Doncaster but no casualties were sustained except to the gear-box.

As well as being in charge of about forty men in new billets I've been appointed Battery Sports Officer. We have no sports ground, no fixtures and no equipment so I've plenty to do. But not today as it has rained incessantly. In this sort of weather the pleasures of rustic solitude become rather obscure.

So when I come on leave I naturally want to make the most of things in the shortest possible time. Were I leading a sober suburban life I don't suppose I should want to go to a couple of shows a week or have my meals in hotels and Soho restaurants. As it is I am trying to cram a lot into what may be a short life.

I don't like parties much. This is partly because I'm naturally rather uncommunicative – except with you – partly because I am watching what is going on all around but mainly because I am disinclined to bore people by talking about myself and airing my knowledge. But when I'm alone with you in quiet surroundings – that's a different matter.

Don't think I am abnormally indifferent to other women these days, though I suppose my enthusiasm for the chase has waned somewhat. All I meant was that I am not disposed to treat other women seriously.

Talking of serious women, I have written to Molly, mentioned your plans and given her your address. I think you had better contact LSE again and get that book list. I see you have taken to 'lazing around and reading odd bits from various books'. I spent the better part of three years at Cambridge doing just that but it was the two or three months of sweat and tears at the end that really counted. It is so easy to be wise after the event.

On the streets of Rome there was bitter fighting as the Italians tried to harass the Germans who were taking over the city. The Nazis were now in control of North Italy and had evacuated fifty thousand Allied prisoners of war to Germany. But the Allies had invaded and captured Taranto and Salerno. The following day, September 12th, the Germans launched a counter-offensive against Salerno but on the island of Capri the German garrison surrendered without firing a shot. Douglas Fairbanks Jr., then a United States naval officer, was awarded the Silver Star for his part in this operation.

For the Germans the loss of Capri was more than offset by a daring commando-type adventure – the seizure of Mussolini from a hotel in the Abruzzi mountains where he was being held. He was flown to meet Hitler but never regained control of even a part of his country.

On the Russian front the Red Army had success after success: on the 17th September they took Bryansk, on the 25th, Smolensk, and on November 6th Kiev fell.

At home milk zoning began with only two milk firms allowed to deliver in each road.

It is now hoped to get all the men inside the Hall. Unfortunately this means that the officers have to move up to the neighbouring vicarage. This is the most frightful Victorian building in a state of wretched disrepair, cluttered up with piles of dusty old junk. The Vicar is a down-at-heel fellow who talks incessantly and has the typical forced laugh of some of the minor clergy. Dickens could have easily written one of his more depressing descriptive chapters about the place.

On Wednesday I ran a three-mile cross country with the men and then went 'swimming' (I had one foot on the bottom). The next day I played in the Troop soccer team. My stomach ache gave place to pains elsewhere.

I'm glad you've had news at last from LSE. You won't be able to pick and choose your rooms so, providing they're not too bad, I think you should take the ones at 35/– a week if it includes breakfast.

My father had asked Stanley on his last leave how much allowance he should give me. The reply, which was confirmed in his letter above, was: 'I found I needed £6 a week whilst living in Cambridge so I think £3 would be the right amount for her.' Perhaps he thought I should have to spend less money on food and entertainment than him as it was unheard of then for girls to pay for themselves when taken out. There were no facilities for cooking in the proposed digs, so hot meals had to be obtained in the college buttery or in one of the many cafes in the town.

The food minister, Lord Woolton, announced that we would soon taste some of the fruits of victory – literally. He had bought large quantities of lemons, oranges and onions from Mediterranean countries. The war-time diet – which though quite healthy was extremely monotonous – was being improved by the arrival of Lease-Lend foods from the States. Canned luncheon meat, ham loaves, dried eggs and more cheese, though they were all still rationed, were at least more readily available in the shops.

September had been a good month militarily. As well as the Russian advances, the clean-up operations in the Far East were going well. New Guinea was gradually being reconquered. On September the 19th the Allied forces pushing north from the toe of Italy linked up with the Salerno beachhead. And in Norway the Tirpitz was so badly damaged in a midget submarine attack that it was put out of action for six months. Two of the submarine commanders were awarded the VC.

It was announced that since the beginning of the war up to the end of August the Germans had lost approximately half a million dead and two million wounded.

Your letter reached me during this 'campaign'. Unfortunately I can't mention any details but it has been my sole pre-occupation. But when will we put what we are learning into practice?

Your sole pre-occupation must be going up to Cambridge. I shall always remember my first week or two there. I really did find it wonderful and ever since I've always felt some enchanting attraction towards Cambridge. Even a stroll around the book-shops gave me a pleasure keener than any other I had felt up to then. Naturally Cambridge will have an even greater attraction for me now.

I am glad you are going to see Molly. She should be very useful to you. I heard from her a week ago and she told me that James was making a remarkable recovery.

Don't buy too many books – especially new ones – until you are quite sure what is really essential. Don't rush into too many things and commit yourself too deeply. And, most important of all, don't forget me.

James had been quite badly wounded in Sicily and was in hospital.

To celebrate my success in getting into Cambridge, John Pincus, who was home on leave, took me to see 'A Month in the Country' by Turghenev at the St James' Theatre. Produced by Emlyn Williams it starred Michael Redgrave amongst others. John told me afterwards that he was being sent overseas for a short time, to Iceland of all places.

Regimental routine and training

'I spent some time in the Battery Office pretending to be busy'
November 7th, 1943

At the beginning of October I went up to Cambridge to start reading for my degree in Economics. It was a strange 'town and gown' that met me.

The town was full of servicemen and evacuees. Accommodation was very difficult to obtain and neither the LSE billeting officer nor I were amused when my mother said, 'I hope you have found somewhere really suitable for her. It is the first time the little bird has flown the nest'. It wasn't true, of course, as I had lived with the Pincus' for several months in 1942. In the end I was billeted on a policeman's household and since it was against police regulations to have strangers in the house I had to pretend I was his cousin.

'Gown' was even odder. At that time women could not be members of the University and the two women's colleges, Girton and Newnham, ran their own affairs and awarded their own degrees. Their students all lived in college and were subject to the strictest control where men friends were concerned. The men's colleges were full of overseas students, some of whom had been caught there by the war and could not return home. Many English students had been called up or were doing war work of one kind or another, as were quite a few members of staff.

LSE was unique. We were given some facilities at Peterhouse College: in particular, we took over their student's social club, Grove Lodge. We also had access to the excellent University libraries, such as the Squire Law Library and the Marshall Library, and lectures were held in a variety of the University lecture halls. We were even able to attend lectures given by Cambridge academics though the majority of our courses were run by LSE staff, which included Professor Harold Laski and Professor Hayek. Our Director was Sir William Beveridge.

But the LSE students were not subject to the controls placed on Cambridge students. We did not, for example, have to wear gowns. We did not have to be in our rooms by 10pm, we were not answerable to the proctors. In other words, as women we had the best of both worlds and even our fellow male students led a much freer existence than their Cambridge contemporaries.

The beginning of October saw no let up in the Nazis' relentless grip on Europe. Though Naples had risen against the Germans they fought savagely to regain control. In Denmark they threatened to arrest all seven thousand Danish Jews, who were only saved by the Swedish fishing fleet in a remarkable cloak and dagger rescue. One of those saved was Niels Bohr, the atomic scientist.

In Greece all Athenian Jews were made to register and the local population gave shelter to some three thousand of them. One such sanctuary was provided by Princess Andrew of Greece, whose son, Prince Philip, was then serving in the British navy.

Grove Hall, Retford   October 8th, 1943

If only you were at Grove Hall instead of Grove Lodge! From the description you gave me the digs don't seem a very suitable place to work though I am glad you get on well with the two small boys. The Histon road area is also rather a long way from Grove Lodge. Perhaps you'll be able to change at the end of term if it is too inconvenient.

I was pleased, though, to learn how much you like Cambridge. I am quite sure you will enjoy yourself immensely. But you must work at least 6 hours a day. And you must try to lift your work to a much higher plane. It's insufficient merely to digest the very large mass of facts that will be pushed at you; you will be expected to look at the facts with an inquiring mind and a critical eye.

I'll come down to visit you as soon as I can but you know we've been very busy with this secret exercise. I don't think I told you how I was caught, literally, with my trousers down. The guns had come into position the previous night when it was teeming with rain: my trousers were soaked so I got into bed without them. At 5am the CO, impatient and ratty as usual, arrived at my tent and ordered me to look at some faulty camouflage immediately. So I had to leap out in my great-coat and short pants. Everyone in the Command Post thought it extremely funny but even now I can only laugh at it half-heartedly.

PS I'm glad you met Molly.

Molly was very helpful to me. She had already got her degree and was working in Cambridge. I admired her greatly because she not only knew the price of a cabbage – which I did not – but also how that price was made up: so much for the seed, so much for farm labour, so much for transport, etc. But she did not agree with the views of Ernest Bevin, then Labour Minister, on domestic help.

The 'domestic problem' was one of the minor irritations suffered by the middle classes during the war. Although it was still possible to get domestic help, they usually only wanted to work from 9.30-12.30 and not at all on Sundays. What was worse, domestic help for three hours a day, six days a week, had gone up to £1. Bevin wanted to make domestic service a craft, to be available to all classes and to provide regular and congenial employment after the war for thousands of women who had got used to working in factories. Molly had other ideas about the role of women in post-war Britain.

And in Germany Himmler had other ideas about women, too. Jewish women, that is. On October 6th he spoke about the mass killing of Jewish men. 'What about the women?' he continued. 'I do not feel justified in exterminating the men while allowing avengers in the form of their offspring to grow up in the midst of our sons and grandsons.'

The Allies were by now only ninety miles from Rome. By contrast with most of Germany, in Rome thousands of Jews were given shelter in monasteries and private homes and nearly five hundred more lived within the Vatican walls. Knowledge of the atrocities, committed both by the Germans throughout Europe and by the Japanese in the Far East, not only against Jews but against many groups such as Gypsies, the mentally handicapped, religious sects, prisoners of war, etc., led to the setting up by the Allies on October 20th of the War Crimes Commission.

Portugal decided it was time to come down on the side of the Allies and agreed to allow the Azores to be used as a mid-Atlantic re-fuelling base.

Retford   **October 19th, 1943**

I was Orderly Officer on Saturday and had to take the battery team to Ramskill to play the local Lunatic Asylum. This is a rather fine place, with commodious modern premises and excellent recreational facilities. Our opponents were mainly members of the staff. I say mainly because we discovered after the match that three of them were inmates.

The left half, who was marking me, was apparently a sex maniac. He paid me every attention — during the match. Just before the game began an enormous column of inmates filed in and took up positions along the touch-line. They were very orderly and in fact at times I wondered who were the lunatics.

Unfortunately the referee should certainly have been amongst them. He had an insufficient knowledge of the rules and appeared to be suffering from senility. Eventually we lost 5-1 after we had conceded yet another unfair penalty and our Captain had been ordered off the field. Our one goal was cheered tremendously by the spectators and every time one of the staff missed an opportunity they jeered and booed. They were completely browned off by the result and as I walked off one of them said to me ''Hi, mate, is this your first team?''

I imagine the twenty-first party you are going to in London over the weekend is Peter's. If you're not leaving till Saturday morning I could probably get to Cambridge for the day on Friday as I am due a 24 hr pass. The Brigadier was so pleased at a recent inspection (especially of the Sports Stores, note) that he's given us all a day's holiday. I could look up some old friends whilst you're at lectures and perhaps we could go to a show in the evening.

PS This is a reply to both of your letters — sweet, undoubtedly, but rather short.

We met on Friday afternoon, 22nd October, and in the evening went to see 'This Time It's Love', with Charles Heslop and Ernest Thesiger, at the Arts Theatre, Cambridge. Stanley stayed at his old college overnight and in the morning I went down to London.

My brother Peter was by now a corporal in the RAF, stationed at Scampton, near Lincoln. He had been refused transfer to ENSA on the grounds that he was too physically fit but he was still graded as 'part-time musician'. He wore a harp insignia on his sleeve to indicate this status, often referred to as 'my passport to heaven'.

At the party there was a wireless-operator/air gunner who used to unwind on his return from thousand-bomber raids by drinking mugs of hot chocolate with Peter – both of them were teetotallers. Thirty years later, whilst playing with Sid Phillip's band in Lincoln, Peter recognized him as the Commissionaire on the theatre door. On the night of Saturday, October 23rd, as Peter's party was in full swing, the industrial city of Kassel was targeted by a force which included bombers from their station. The ensuing firestorm caused the death of 5,300 people and also resulted in the destruction of aircraft and rocket manufacturing facilities.

Retford   **_October 26th, 1943_**

I arrived back at camp exhausted and was yanked out of bed at dawn to go on two days shooting. We were firing with 75mm guns to conserve our own ammunition. The shells weigh under 12lbs and are naturally referred to as pea-shooters. The target was on the sky-line but I knocked it out in just over five minutes.

After the day's shooting we went in a couple of trucks to the outskirts of Sheffield to an amazing working-men's club, Dial House. There were about eight hundred members present and concerts were in progress in two large rooms. The turns were quite good though the songs and jokes hackneyed but that didn't worry the audience. I've never met such friendliness and hospitality anywhere. It was Yorkshire at its very best. The Chairman made complimentary remarks about the 'guests' and we departed with a photograph of the Concert Hall, signed by all the committee members.

I haven't said how much I enjoyed last weekend. I think I managed to crowd into twenty-four hours most of the pleasures of a seven days leave. Unfortunately the College Porter was extremely snooty because I didn't get in till nearly 12.15am. I decided not to emulate some poor chap who recently tried to climb in after hours. He slipped and became impaled on the fifteen foot high college gates. In future I shall have to abide by college regulations.

___

The papers were full of headlines such as 'Russians Cut German Front to Pieces', 'Bombs Sapping Nazi Will to Fight', 'Peace by Christmas'. But for some that would already be too late. In Burma the Railway of Death had been completed at the cost of 16,500 Allied POW lives, to say nothing of the 50,000 Burmese who also died.

In the Aegean a British ship, trying to re-enforce Samos and Leros, was dive-bombed with the loss of forty-three sailors. The shattered, torn-off limbs were strewn about the deck and in the rigging. Among the officers responsible for clearing up the pieces of human flesh was Kenneth More, the actor.

The first exchange of prisoners from Germany took place through the Swedish Red Cross after two years of bitter haggling. The returning soldiers were desperate for news of how the war was going. They reported that the food they had in Germany was so bad that, without the Red Cross parcels, many of them would have died. But one of the returning prisoners said that perhaps it would ease the minds of relatives to know that he had not seen any signs of active ill-treatment during his internment.

Tackling starvation was the first priority of Lord Wavell, the newly appointed Viceroy of India. Vast areas of the country were stricken by famine and he used the Army to distribute food.

In Russia the battle for Kiev, their third largest city, took place at the beginning of November. By the 6th, the city was in the hands of the Red Army and victory against the hated invader at last seemed attainable.

Retford   *November 7th, 1943*

I'm sorry to hear you have flu. You should wear more clothes. (I say that as a concerned adviser, not as a Puritan.) Only once was I brought to bed at Cambridge and that was when I had unpatriotic German measles. It was freezing and when I finally felt well enough to get out of bed to wash, my flannel, frozen solid, broke in half.

Of course, when I got your message on Friday evening it made rather a mess of my rapidly constructed plans for the weekend. I didn't approach the BC about changing the 36 hr pass because, although he's quite a nice bloke, he doesn't seem to approve of leave.

I've been instructing our NCO's in map-reading and the engagement of targets and I've attended a regimental sports conference where the most ambitious schemes for inter-Battery and inter-Troop matches were adopted. It is difficult to keep the men from getting bored. I spent some time in the Battery Office pretending to be busy because I don't want to follow one of the officers from the other Battery who has been unwillingly transferred.

They are conscripting officers for the Infantry so it would be impolitic to appear idle or even over-anxious to get into the Intelligence Corps. Regimental loyalty is all and certainly I am not unhappy here.

On November 8th, the day after Stanley wrote, British Intelligence was trying to decide whether or not the Germans had actually succeeded in

FL LT HARRY EVANS – UNWITTING PHOTOGRAPHER OF ROCKET LAUNCH SITES.

making a rocket or flying bomb. They had two very important clues. One was the set of drawings of new installations on the coast that a British agent, Michel Hollard, had smuggled out a month previously; the other was a set of photographs which had been taken fortuitously by a navigator/photographer named Harry Evans.

On 14th October, 1942, Harry Evans, who is now my accountant, had left his camera running after a daylight photographic reconnaissance over the Polish coast covering Danzig, Gdynia, Hela and Swinemunde. The plates when developed showed strange and, at the time, unidentifiable markings. It was as a result of that chance reconnaissance that Peenemunde, the rocket research station, had been very badly damaged in the spectacular bombing raid carried out on the night of August 17th. It was now decided to send further reconnaissance planes to re-examine the so-called 'ski' sites.

Harry did not take part in these later sorties. He was shot down on 14th May, 1943 near Alsace whilst on a daylight reconaissance flight to Pilsen, and hidden by local people. His pilot was killed. Eventually, after several adventures, the French smuggled him across to Switzerland from where he returned to England.

Retford   *November 12th, 1943*

The Regimental Sports Officer is going on a tank course for a month and I have been appointed to take his place. So I now have to deal with matches at a far higher level and correspond with exalted personages in the military hierarchy. As I have to stay behind this Sunday to deal with these sports arrangements, whilst the Battery goes off to Sheffield again, I shall have the opportunity on Monday for my first flight. One of the Air OP's (Observation Posts) is visiting the Battery so I shan't have to motor-bike all the way there.

Subject to the CO's approval I might wangle some leave at the end of the month and would like to spend a few days in Cambridge. Whether your people would take exception or not, I don't know. But if your friend, John Pincus, stayed there for a week I don't see how they could reasonably object.

PS I note that you find LSE very free from the usual moral conventions whereas I am rapidly succumbing to middle-aged respectability.

A future Prime Minister flew into England on the night of November 15th, 1943. For a year Francois Mitterand had been secretly liaising with French POW's, having himself escaped from a POW camp in Germany in 1940. Within two months of arriving in England he was back on French soil organising a resistance group.

The following night, November 16th, American bombers dealt a final blow to the Norwegian heavy water factory. All production ceased and it was decided to send the existing stocks that had escaped the raid to Germany as soon as possible. But plans were immediately made by Norwegian saboteurs to stop it leaving the country.

London was full of weighty pronouncements that week;

Mr Churchill at the Mansion House:

"Next year will see the climax of the European war with costly battles and big sacrifices".

Dingle Foot in the House of Commons:

"The Government cannot agree to send food to occupied countries".

Sir Stafford Cripps (who was being tipped as a possible future Prime Minister) in the Times:

"I refuse to admit that it is only by bloodshed and revolution that changes can be brought about in our economic and social conditions. My guiding principles are those of the Christian ethic".

In London, as if to emphasise the last statement, Sir Oswald and Lady Mosley were released but to much criticism and many protests. Brotherly or any other sort of love was also noticeably absent from Stanley's next letter.

Retford   **November 19th, 1943**

I received your letter this afternoon. I have already written one reply but I decided not to send it. All the same it would be an understatement to say that I am just about completely browned off. Your curt note, for which I had waited all week, wasn't exactly calculated to raise my spirits. If there is anything wrong between us I must know and know immediately.

You know there is nothing I want more than to be with you in Cambridge — and these are not just fair words — but there is no point in my coming if you are so busy with your new friends that I shall hardly be able to see you.

Cambridge, the prize which Stanley had been so keen for me to achieve, was proving a double-edged sword. Whilst I appreciated to the full the wonderful opportunities offered to me on the academic side, I had also become aware for the first time of personal freedom. I had made many friends, both male and female, and I no longer felt as tied to or as reliant on Stanley as I had been for the last three years.

There were many people who wanted my company, to go out to dinner, to discuss politics, to go dancing or to the theatre. There were many interesting characters around at whose feet I would sit and listen whilst they expounded on the way to cure all the problems of the world. Where before Stanley had been unique, now there seemed to be equally brilliant minds to dazzle me.

Emotionally I was still very involved with him but even there gradually other men began to interest me. I tried in my next letter both to explain this and to reassure him of my friendship and genuine affection. If only, I thought, he would loosen the reins so that I might have a little gallop I would probably return to the paddock of my own free will!

Somehow the war seemed very remote in Cambridge though we heard the bombers every night on their way to raid German cities. And often we were awakened early by the sound of spluttering engines as some of them limped their way home at dawn. Berlin was so heavily bombed on the nights of the 22nd and 23rd November that the asphalt pavements caught fire.

Wycombe   *November 24th, 1943*

Thank you for your letter. I do try to understand and I am pleased you are so frank about it. Complete honesty between us is absolutely essential. At the same time I am afraid of losing you and I do not know how I could cope with this mad army life if it were not for your love.

I shall expect to arrive some time around midday Saturday and visit my friends before having dinner in Hall. Then I shall stay till Monday morning so we can spend all Sunday together. The rest of the week I'll be in Wycombe.

Good luck for the netball match and enjoy the party Saturday night.

High Wycombe   *November 30th, 1943*

Yesterday I had lunch with my parents and tomorrow I hope to meet Molly for a meal. Thursday I have to devote to relatives. Do you realise I haven't seen Piccadilly Circus this leave let alone smelt Soho or been to a show.

Wycombe is as monotonous as usual. I'm cheesed off with the place though I am very comfortable at home. This consoles me somewhat for having left part of myself behind in Cambridge. Anyway I've never had a happier weekend than I did with you.

You know now just how much I love you. If you feel even partly in love with me, don't forget I love the postal orderly almost as much. (Don't get me wrong!)

The end of November brought news of the meeting in Teheran between Churchill, Roosevelt and Stalin. Churchill told Stalin that the plans for a Second Front were dependent on the strength at the time of German forces in France. Stalin promised that as soon as the war with Germany was over he would declare war on Japan.

Neither told the other party what they knew about the atom bomb. Work on the atom bomb had reached a crucial stage where the means of delivering it were being finalised, but Stalin was not informed that a B29 was being modified for this purpose. He was soon acquainted with this development, however, when Klaus Fuchs was sent to join the American atomic team in the States four days later. The public statement issued from Teheran ended with the affirmation:

'We leave here friends; in fact, in spirit and in purpose. Signed: Roosevelt, Stalin, Churchill.'

Meanwhile another unsuccessful attempt on Hitler's life had been made. In a suicidal plan a German Officer offered to model a new army greatcoat for Hitler, carrying a bomb in his pocket, which would kill both himself and the Fuhrer. Unfortunately the prototypes of the overcoat were destroyed in one of the November air raids on Berlin.

The Russians were now less than four hundred miles from Hitler's headquarters in Rastenburg and in Italy Montgomery had broken through the German lines.

In England a mild form of flu was raging which luckily only seemed to last about two days. More serious was the incidence of nervous disorders amongst night bomber crews. They were advised by an article in the British Medical Journal that fear was a healthy emotion which sharpened judgement and that they should 'fear the worst but hope for the best'.

Retford   *December 6th, 1943*

I have a new job — Assistant Adjutant or the CO's stooge. This is not a coveted post and one which carries very awkward responsibilities. The regular Assistant Adjutant is down with flu. So is the Adjutant and the Battery Commander. Our transfer to Scarborough, by the way, has been postponed till after Christmas.

Molly thought I seemed older — she should see me now in my new job. What do you think? She told me that James has been promoted Major which is pretty amazing, isn't it?

Glad you are having a good time at LSE. I note you are Publicity Officer for SOCSOC. (the Socialist Society). No doubt you will retain the job as long as you toe the party line — on that basis I give you about a month. As for Dick X — he always seemed a rather unsavoury type to me. If your women friends want to get mixed up with him that's their concern. If you do it's very definitely mine.

We've just got back from Firing Camp. There were no untoward incidents apart from one of the Heavy Regiment's guns exploding. We are now more than ever the CAGRA's blue-eyed boys. The CO has the Brigadier absolutely in his pocket. As Assistant Adjutant I hadn't very much to do apart from helping the CO with his overcoat. The weather has been extremely good but I still think Otterburn's about the worst place in England. We had one quite heavy fall of snow.

It seems certain that we shall still be here for Christmas as Scarborough has been postponed again. When do you go back to Cambridge? I note you are violently impatient with bourgeois family life now that you're at home. Very much like me in my first year. But don't let the intoxication of Cambridge lead you to look at things in a false light and exaggerate trivialities. Keep a sense of proportion and try to tolerate the habits and prejudices of other people even if you can't agree with them. However much you dislike it and think it is hypocritical, we all have to live in society.

Your letter interested me in other ways, too. I'm glad you are not sleeping with anyone even though I had hoped to persuade you to make an exception in my case before I am sent abroad. However, I suppose I had better practise what I preach or you won't believe me about anything else.

In London I went to a carol service at the Albert Hall, conducted by Sir Malcolm Sargent. The following day his eighteen year old daughter died of infantile paralysis, a disease for which there was then no known cure or method of prevention. Churchill had pneumonia again and was treated with the new wonder drug, M & B 693, which had proved so effective when he had had pneumonia at the beginning of the year. The same drug was used on my brother, Peter, when he contracted meningitis a few months earlier in the summer of 1943.

Christmas 1943 did not lessen the fierceness of Allied raids on the enemy. On Christmas Eve we bombed Berlin. On Christmas Day twenty-four flying bomb sites in Northern France were attacked by the Americans. On Boxing Day American troops launched a new offensive in the Pacific. And on my eighteenth birthday, December 27th, the great German battleship, Scharnhorst, was sunk.

By the time you receive this you will have had a merry Christmas so I shall confine myself to wishing you a Happy Birthday and Peace in 1944.

I'm afraid I rather overstepped the mark on Christmas Eve when I quaffed seven gin and limes in a row. I felt really shocking. The following day we played our annual soccer match against the sergeants. As there are only eleven officers in the Battery I didn't have to worry about who to put in the team. We lost.

Then we had the privilege of serving the men with their Christmas dinner, followed by a first-class meal ourselves complete with Scots piper for the pudding.

Tomorrow is typhus inoculation day and next weekend we move out from here. But not to Scarborough. We are going to Southwell, near Newark, and I hope very much you will be able to visit me there. We shall get at the most two weekend leaves before we depart — who knows where? — and I shall be expected to spend them at home.

I become entitled to my second 'pip' today, subject to recommendation. The Battery Commander told me that I would have to wait until the announcement appeared in Regimental Orders before putting up the second 'pip'. So I am still 2nd/Lt de Smith in name if not in fact.

My swimming progress is slow but perceptible. Today I managed about twelve yards. In God's good time I may even swim the length of the bath. It looks as though I may have to swim for it before long as Monty may have sallied forth on the Second Front before I am twenty-two. If that is so then the War in Europe should be over before next Christmas. But then I've never been a great optimist so let's say
'before 1945'.

To me the end of the war means being with you. The vision is so delightful to contemplate and yet so elusive that I prefer not to think too much about it to avoid becoming depressed.

Cooling off

'I am too young to sit down and revise my sense of values'
March 17th, 1944

By the end of 1943 I had settled in well at Cambridge, made many friends and become involved in several societies. I was playing both netball and hockey for college, had started riding regularly and was generally enjoying university life to the full.

Christmas at home, too, had been very pleasant. It was the quietest we had had since the beginning of the war. Even the telephone was silent as the public had been asked not to use the telephone network over the holiday period. We listened to the King's Christmas Day broadcast:

"As we were not cast down by defeat, we are not unduly exalted by victory. No experience can be too strange and no task too formidable if a man can link it up with what he knows and loves".

The words seemed to have a special meaning for me. Love was very much on my mind. Now that I had reached my eighteenth birthday I thought parental restrictions would become less exacting. In some ways this increased the dilemma I found myself in. I could no longer use them as readily as an excuse for not seeing Stanley. There was no doubt that my feelings towards him had cooled. The difficulty lay in getting him to accept this state of affairs. I had tried gently telling him. I had cut down the frequency of my letters. I was omitting the affectionate terms I usually used. But still he persisted.

It seemed that he was very dependent on my maintaining the relationship. I was fully aware that he was likely to go overseas at any time and that each meeting might be our last, at least for many months if not years. I knew that I was enormously in his debt and I had to face the fact that he might never return. And so I continued writing spasmodically and even agreed to visit him, on my terms, at his new location.

Lt S.A. de Smith, 103 Medium Battery RA,
Maythorn Mill, Southwell, Notts   **(undated) 1944**

I'm glad you enjoyed your New Year's Eve. We spent the day moving here. The mill, where most of the men are billeted, is a huge ramshackle building with several families living in it. We've managed to get nearly two hundred men inside.

The Officers Mess is about two miles away on the opposite side of the town and I am billeted midway between the two, in an unfurnished old house with other junior subalterns and two or three batmen. The town itself is nothing more than an overgrown village and rather a drab one but it boasts a Norman Cathedral which gives the place a certain quaintness and charm.

I am now full-time instructor in the young Acks class (an abbreviation for assistant). It means a Gunner or NCO who assists officers in performance of their technical duties in gunnery and deployment e.g. selecting gun positions, getting the guns parallel and on the right bearing, plotting positions, taking shoots from the Observation Post (OP) etc. They only have a month's course and I've already come to appreciate the disadvantage of setting them mathematical problems: I have to work the answers out every time myself.

As yet I haven't investigated connections to Cambridge but this time I think you will have to make the journey instead of me. There's a very good hotel here, called the Saracen's Head, only about a quarter of a mile from my billet. Please come.

New Year's Eve had seen the launch of a major offensive by the Americans against Cassino but the German forces could not be dislodged. Further assaults on Cassino on January 12th and 17th led to the same impasse. But the planning for the Anzio beach-head, by-passing the German line of defence across Italy and thus gaining access to Rome, was well under way. In the early hours of January 22nd the first British and American troops landed at Anzio.

The US had by then over a million and a half service people ready to be used in Europe and nearly two million more dedicated to fighting against Japan. The country had confidently elected Franklin D. Roosevelt as President of the United States for the fourth time and the inauguration ceremony took place on January 20th.

On Sunday, 2nd January, set aside as an American Day of Prayer, there was a large but unprofitable raid on Berlin by the British. Out of some four hundred bombers twenty-eight were shot down and one hundrd and sixty-eight crewmen killed for the loss of very few Berliners' lives. A similar raid with a similar outcome took place the following night.

But there was news in the papers of a great new RAF invention, the jet plane. What was not known at that time was that the Germans were more advanced in jet development than the Allies. Other RAF planes were dropping arms and supplies to resistance forces all over Europe in preparation for the invasion.

On the Eastern Front, by the 3rd of January, the Russians were only ten miles from the old Polish border and to the north, by 15th January, the Red Army had broken the ring of German forces surrounding Leningrad. The siege of nearly nine hundred days was over at last.

As Leningrad citizens loosened their belts, we in Britain were tightening them a little. Odd shortages appeared. Milk deliveries were cut from seven days a week to five, dried milk and dried fruit disappeared from the shops, leather was unobtainable. A ship carrying Spanish oranges to Britain was blown up by delayed action bombs concealed in the cargo. And there were no torch batteries, due, the papers said, to the impending invasion.

Personal doubts about my continuing to see Stanley, who would undoubtedly be taking part in that invasion, were not made easier by the similar, though less intense, situation that was arising with John Pincus. Indeed, if anything, I felt more guilty about John since I knew he was engaged in fighting the enemy in the skies, and I feared for him every day. Another of his letters in rhyme written on January 21st, 1944, arrived just before Stanley's next letter.

POEM BY JOHN PINCUS, 1944.

Southwell   *January 25th, 1944*

I went home on a 36 hour pass but most of the time was spent travelling, with a nine mile walk at the end of it back to my billet, where I arrived at 4.20am. I've been very busy with the Acks and now Officers training has reached a new high-pressure level. We work in this regiment on Saturday and Sunday mornings, but I know I shouldn't complain. Compared to the lads in the field and the RAF crews it's a piece of cake.

About your projected weekend – you know I'll be delighted to see you whatever the circumstances. If this opportunity is wasted we might not have another. Don't delay till the very last moment before mentioning the matter to your parents: that would be rather transparent. If it will please you I will write to them myself. I have booked you a single room at the Saracen's Head. It's quite attractive though not modern. I hope you like it. Till Friday.

PS I see you have ascended the academic ladder of late. I never managed to obtain such a distinction as a political tea-party with Professor Laski. Has he attempted to seduce you?

The same day as Stanley's letter arrived I received the following letter (abbreviated) from my mother:

London   *January 25th, 1944*

'I have not time to discuss anything except the matter of your going to Southwell. Of course you know my views. While I have every confidence in both you and Stanley I do not approve of what you want to do. I know the circumstances and quite appreciate it would be nice for you to be together but I am rather surprised Stanley suggested it. Do you think the de Smiths would approve if they knew?

I don't like the idea of your being in a small hotel by yourself, the travelling is not good and a thousand other things go through my mind. We are proud of you – don't let us down. You are not engaged to Stanley unless there is anything definitely understood between you.

If the circumstances were the same about John P. I would say NO definitely with no explanation. Please do not lose your temper when you get this letter.

Your loving mother.'

Ignoring her advice, the following day I went to Southwell. Whilst I appreciated her concern, I knew that Stanley would never behave dishonourably and I was quite sure that my own reservations about the relationship were sufficient to prevent her 'worst fears' materialising. After the visit I was able to reassure her and it in no way affected her loving attitude towards me. In later years I came to appreciate the worries of parents and consider I was extremely fortunate in mine.

Apart from some slight embarrassment on Stanley's part – the hotel had allocated me the most beautiful room with a large four-poster bed which Stanley insisted was not the one he had booked – the weekend went very well. I dined in the Officer's mess, the only female present, and was charmed by his fellow officers whom I had not previously met.

Saturday evening there was a dance in a local Hall and on the Sunday morning I attended church parade, watching Stanley give orders to his men for the first time. Southwell Cathedral was beautiful, unadorned and gracious and the service was simple yet touching.

I was glad that I had decided to visit him though in his presence it was more difficult to resist his demands for a greater commitment on my part. What I felt might not be love, I thought, but he still meant a great deal to me.

Southwell   **February 5th, 1944**

Your letter saying you were happy to be down here last weekend was very charming – I shall keep it.

You must have got on well with the acting CO. On Monday morning he told me that I was henceforth Troop leader of 'A' Troop. This puts me back on War Establishment and I supersede a subaltern senior to myself.

Today, Saturday, I went swimming and managed to do about fifteen yards. On the way a tragedy occurred. We were taking a 3-ton truck (George Amman driving) when a puppy ran out in front of the vehicle. He was hit by the back wheel and died instantly. Everything was in order except that George had no authority to drive the truck and we were doing over 40mph.

Next Tuesday the Regiment is to have the pleasure of travelling eighty-five miles by road to attend an address by Montgomery. The pantomime will be attended by five thousand troops and probably the same number of cameramen.

Montgomery knew when he talked to the troops there was little he could say about the true plans being laid for the invasion. The operational radius of a Spitfire had been used to delimit the possible invasion zone. It extended from the Pas de Calais to the Cotentin peninsula. An elaborate attempt at deceiving the Germans was then under way, with the artificial creation of the non-existent Twelfth British Army alongside FUSAG – the First United States Army Group – which also did not exist. The deception plans included proposed landings in Calais, Norway, South of France, Spain and Rumania. The Germans swallowed the bait and diluted their forces in attempt to cover all possible sites of invasion.

But at Anzio the invading British forces had been pinned down. There was fierce fighting but by the end of the first fortnight of February the news had improved somewhat. Around Monte Cassino there was still no breakthrough and reluctantly the orders were given, after due warning to the inhabitants, to destroy the monastery totally.

February 14th, 1944

We are now on Exercise Eagle and are technically, if not literally, in the field. My mind is occupied by purely selfish apprehensions of acute discomfort but it's a change from the humdrum life we lead for so much of the time.

We have a pretty large contingent of officers here – two Light AA and one RAF pilot as spectators, apart from the War Establishment officers. It's all rough and ready but quite good fun. Postal services won't function as normally so your letter may chase me all over the countryside.

Equipment Wing, School of Artillery, Larkhill, nr Amesbury, Wilts
February 18th, 1944

I am up here on an enemy military equipment course, about my weakest gunnery subject. The room I am writing in would not disgrace the Ritz Hotel. This can't be the Army – not even a Hollywood version of it.

Last week I was very miserable and I make no apology for that. The week began with a depressing letter from you. Then I was confined to barracks with three other officers – yes, officers! – for going out on Saturday afternoon without informing the Troop Commander where I was going. This left me almost speechless.

On Tuesday I was just about 100% browned off. That evening, when I was doing a job as Orderly Officer, I drove my truck down to the gun park and on the way back drove past a halt sign and crashed into a Humber Snipe (belonging to a Colonel) together with ATS driver, to say nothing of my own truck. The AT was merely shaken but the Snipe has been completely written off and so has the poor old truck. I suppose I did about £800 worth of damage apart from making myself something of a laughing stock.

The CO, though, didn't take a too serious view of it and I got off with a £2 fine and no questions asked. However, the week finished in a blaze of glory with another letter from you.

This evening I walked out to Stonehenge. An absolutely amazing sight. It was a cool evening and for a moment I lived in the prehistoric past. Last week I visited Salisbury Cathedral which also affected me quite strongly.

I am planning to get to Cambridge within the next couple of weeks. Even if the prospect of meeting me doesn't make you gush with enthusiasm, I hope so much to see you. There's always the chance you will change your mind and our relationship will return to what it was a year ago.

In the event he was unable to come to Cambridge so once more I postponed defining the limits of our relationship. I could not do so by letter but I felt that it was unfair to continue to buoy up his hopes when I was becoming increasingly doubtful, as he had been three years earlier, about the meaning of love.

At the beginning of March, whilst the USAF were carrying out their first day-time raid on Berlin, the raids on London intensified though relatively few German planes managed to get through. German planes were dropping black and silver strips of paper to jam our radar systems – a method the RAF had used months earlier – but fighters from the south-east aerodromes were still intercepting them successfully. I worried a great deal about my family and, feeling responsible for bringing them back to the city, tried to persuade them to leave London again, at least for a rest. The noise from the big anti-aircraft guns on Hampstead Heath made sleeping very difficult.

Sleep must have been impossible for the residents of the German towns which were now subject to the Anglo-American 'Big Week' raids – a week-long series of massive raids on German industrial and port facilities. Leipzig was struck by eight hundred British bombers on February 19th followed by an American daylight raid on the same town. But the death toll was unacceptably high for the crews of the bombers – in that double raid alone nearly four hundred Allied airmen were killed.

In California a mock-up of an atomic bomb was dropped which, had it been real, would have been capable of killing four thousand times that number of people. It was the first of a series of dummy drops in preparation for the real thing.

And as Stanley was writing his next letter – he had been moved again – news came through that the RAF had dropped their biggest bombs ever, weighing five and a half tons each.

c/o GPO Patrington, nr. Hull, E. Yorks   *March 4th, 1944*

I've travelled through the muddiest parts of Yorkshire to arrive finally at this mud-heap to out-mud all others. The exercise we have just finished was very important because it provided the last opportunity for the handling of very large formations. Conditions were just like those of actual warfare – absolute concealment, movement almost entirely by night. The big schemes are always monotonous – like 90% of warfare – and while I was on the gun position things moved slowly.

Then I was detailed to act as relief at the OP. The OP officer uses one of those small tracked Bren carriers, an armoured vehicle with an open top. We were supporting the leading armoured regiment in an Armoured Division. Every man had a tank except me. I moved off with the carrier revving its guts out trying to keep up with them and although I dropped behind I caught up with them on a ridge by taking a short cut.

In the distance I saw a formation of enemy tanks and was just going to call for a regimental concentration over the air when an umpire (a Guards Lt

*Col) informed me that my truck was out of action, the Ack killed, the
signaller minus an arm and the driver's jaw broken – the result of being hit
by a 25pdr whilst taking the short cut.*

*Well, I couldn't waste time taking the appropriate action so I gracefully
withdrew from the battle and hied to the nearest pub. I nearly won a free
double whisky on Thursday offered by the BC to the first OP to cross the
Derwent, but the bridges had been blown and you know what my swimming
is like!*

*The same night we moved to our new billets, a journey of forty to fifty
miles. It took ten hours during which time I was standing in an open truck.
This nightmare journey was worse than anything else in the exercise,
including a motor-bike ride on a moonless night with almost continuous
sleet.*

*But we did pretty well on the whole – perhaps too well, because we look
like becoming permanent members of an Armoured Division.*

*There have been a spate of conferences over the scheme. First the RA
brigadiers: we, the junior officers, arrived two minutes too late to take part.
Then our CO and BC arrived too late for the next one at Bridlington. The
last one took place at Doncaster yesterday when the Corps Commander – Lt
General O'Connor who escaped from Italy – talked to the officers of the
Corps Artillery. I missed that because I was busy having two breakfasts.*

*Sorry about this military recital but eight pages are something of an
achievement. As for Patrington, it's a lifeless village in a remote part of the
country, between Hull and Spurn Head. You wouldn't like it. I'm hoping to
get some more leave at the end of March and will travel south. Like always
it may be our last meeting, so please...?*

A large Army operation was taking place for real in Burma. Wingate's
second Chindit Expedition parachuted several thousand British, Indian and
Ghurka soldiers more than a hundred miles behind the Japanese lines. But,
before the end of March, Wingate himself was tragically killed in an air crash.

In Europe bombing of French railway depots near Paris began in
preparation for the invasion. In the middle of the month another
unsuccessful attempt to take Cassino was launched and Alexander's forces
had no greater luck trying to break out of the Anzio beach head. But in
Eastern Europe the Red Army was nearing the Hungarian borders causing
Hitler to invade the country to protect his oil supplies. By the end of March
his troops had also invaded Rumania.

There was one item of domestic news on March 4th that doesn't often get
mentioned in the standard war histories. Ninety thousand Welsh miners
went on strike. It may have been partly due to the allocation, a month
previously, of the first Bevin Boys (named after Ernest Bevin, the Labour
Minister) to the pits. These were eighteen-year olds selected from all classes
– public schools, state schools and boys who had been working for some

years – for training as coal-miners. The miners felt that jobs in the pits were handed on from father to son and resented the interlopers.

But the main reason was undoubtedly money. In January 1944 a national minimum wage of £6 a week for underground miners was agreed. Unfortunately, no agreement was reached on who should pay for it, the mine owners, the consumers through higher prices, or a Government subsidy. And nobody picked up the bill. The strikes began in February and two million tons of coal were lost before the end of March. Finally both the Government and the consumers had to pay up.

In fact strikes were not as uncommon throughout the war as many people would like to believe and there are many references to them in contemporary newspapers.

Stanley managed to do some effective bargaining on his own account.

Patrington   **March 17th, 1944**

I've managed to change my leave so that it would coincide with your vacation though I've heard nothing from you recently. It will now start on April 3rd. I was, of course, most bitterly disappointed by our last telephone conversation. I think I made my feelings pretty clear.

It is hard for me to know how literally to take what you said. I am too young to sit down and 'revise my sense of values'. And so are you. Need I say you hurt me intensely? We have been extremely happy together, particularly when you came down that weekend to the Saracen's Head. Whatever you may eventually come to feel I have absolutely no interest in any girl but you and probably never will have now. I can't think of myself apart from you.

One thing is certain. I must see you as soon as I get home, on April 4th at the latest. Please write as soon as you get this. I shall be at Firing Camp in Dumfriesshire (c/o GPO Parkgate) until March 29th and after that at c/o Staging Camp, Jaffa Lines, Catterick, Yorks.

It would be difficult to imagine a more unsatisfactory camp than Patrington and I have come to the conclusion that no ordinary man can stand more than three months of Army life without a rest.

Once again my resolve weakened. When Stanley came home on what was, in effect, embarkation leave we went out together as if no change had taken place in our relationship. It made me feel very guilty and uncomfortable because now I was deceiving two people – Stanley and the man I had fallen in love with in Cambridge.

Preparation for overlord

'all our mail is subject to censorship'
April 13th, 1944

At the end of March the Japanese crossed the Burma/India border and began the siege of Imphal, a siege which was to last three months. But by 18th April an airlift operation was in full swing, supplying food, men and materials to the beleaguered city.

As spring returned to Eastern Europe the Russians reached the Polish and Rumanian frontiers and by April 8th they had begun the attack on the German Army in the Crimea, the last of Russia's territory still under Axis control. By 16th April they had recaptured Yalta.

In England preparations for the invasion of Northern Europe were gathering momentum but bombing was carried out over a wide area to keep the Germans guessing. On April 3rd the German battleship, Tirpitz, was again attacked as she lay in a Norwegian fjord. Still she would not sink but the damage was enough to stop her sailing again.

Bombing was extensive, too, in Eastern Germany, aimed at I.G. Farben factories producing synthetic oil and rubber. A reconnaissance plane flying over the German/Polish border on April 4th, to check the damage caused by the raid, unknowingly took the first ever aerial photos of huts at Auschwitz but their dreadful purpose was not realised.

And, of course, heavy bombing raids were carried out along the Normandy coast where the invasion was going to take place but their intent was concealed by even heavier raids in the Pas de Calais area. Speculation was rife at home. Would the invasion take place this month? Next month? In the Low Countries? Scandinavia? France?

Certainly when I received Stanley's next letter I knew something was afoot but that was all.

77th (DLOY) Medium Regt., 103 Medium Battery, RA,
Army Post Office, England   *April 13th, 1944*

You will notice the new form of address. It means:
1. All our mail is subject to censorship
2. I cannot discuss questions of location or training or
anything of a general military character
   I could write so much more but I can't. For now I just want to thank you for the very happy leave I spent. It was really delightful and I shall always look back on it with affection. It may recede into the past but it will remain in my memory. I may not have many outstanding things to remember from now on but I shall not forget my brief days with you.

In England soft April rain was falling. Daffodils were in bloom all around in the woods of Dogmersfield, near where Stanley was camped, as I later found out.

I haven't heard from you since we parted last Tuesday because censored letters have been held up en route. In fact nobody in the Battery has been receiving mail at this address.

I've been acting Troop Commander as the BC is ill and another officer away but I've not been playing soccer because I've injured my toe. It also stopped me doing myself justice at the Battery dance at XXXXXX, (censored by me) which was rather like a rugger match, where unfortunately I became inebriated. But so did Bill Bailey whom you met in Southwell. He tugged at my greatcoat belt so hard that my coat almost split in two. When I woke up in the morning I found a strange dog curled up beside my bed – yes, really!

Letters are twice as valuable these waiting days and there's the added inducement that you can write to me for a penny-ha'penny: postcards 1d. Parcels permitted but not registered letters.

PS I drove a truck through a pond which conked out half-way across. Result – a very wet bottom.

Stanley's letters were now all censored with the censoring officer's signature at the bottom – S.A de Smith. It was a job he later told me that he hated as he found it very embarrassing. The content of most of his men's letters was so forlorn. Hardly any talked of 'death or glory' or even fear and most were concerned with mundane domestic matters and the discomfort of their present conditions.

Everyone was trying to forecast when the invasion would take place. Everywhere in the South there were scenes of military and air activity. The Downs near Worthing were taken over by the military and the public were forbidden to walk there but all Allied Expeditionary Force vehicles were easily recognisable as they carried a large, white, five-pointed star. In many places there were broken paving stone kerbs and walls – sure signs that tanks had passed that way.

An armada filled all available natural anchorages: Chichester, Portsmouth, Southampton, Poole, Portland, Plymouth, Falmouth and even as far away as south Wales and East Anglia. April 23rd was a popular guess for D-day as the tides and weather were both favourable. But the Germans were convinced it would be May 25th.

Turkey had decided to switch her stance from neutral to pro-Allied but she still did not declare war on the Axis. However, her change of heart meant one more avenue of supply was closed to Germany.

APO Sunday   **April 23rd, 1944**

I see you are pessimistic about your work. Well, I was always pessimistic before an exam so maybe it's a good sign. It's my conviction that anyone who is of reasonable intelligence and does an average amount of work can obtain a pass in any University examination. Examiners aren't all that unfair.

But I should be very careful about using caffeine citrate. I used it and it was effective more often than not; but it mustn't be taken regularly and it's supposed to affect the heart in time.

I reminded him years later of his comments about the fairness of examiners when he was marking exam papers himself. He often took them with him to Lords to read in the duller moments of play. If the weather was fine and England was doing well, then he was in a generous mood. If not, how could he be sure his disappointment was not reflected in the marks he awarded? He gave up taking the exam papers with him.

As had been forecast April 24th, 1944 was a particularly lovely day, though there was no cricket to watch. Overhead, in southern England, the bombers droned on their way to destroy the railway system in Northern France. The Americans bombed the marshalling yards in Rouen in daylight, killing some four hundred of the inhabitants, and causing the resistance leaders to appeal for more care lest the population be antagonised. But the raids went on regardless.

There was some concern about the build up of German divisions in the region – if a certain limit was reached, Churchill had told Montgomery, the invasion would be called off. But the preparations for Overlord went on. On the south coast landings were practised on the beaches but not without the loss of some craft torpedoed by German submarines. Aboard one of the ships sunk were ten officers who had some details of the proposed invasion landing areas. Strenuous and successful efforts were made to account for their bodies in order to ensure that they had not been picked up alive and interrogated by the Germans.

A daring adventure took place in Crete that week aimed at capturing and interrogating the German General commanding the island. Two British officers landed in Crete and with the help of some Greek partisans ambushed the General, marched him seventy-five miles across the island and then took him by boat to Mersah Matruh in North Africa. They were both awarded the DSO for their part in this remarkable exercise.

May came and went and still there was no invasion. But elsewhere there was plenty of action. On May 7th Sebastopol was 'evacuated' by the Germans and by the 10th the Russians were in complete control of the city.

On May 11th two thousand Allied guns opened fire all along the Italian front from Monte Cassino to the sea and a week later the six month old battle for the monastery was over. By the 23rd May the Anzio troops were no longer confined to their beach-head and two days later they linked up with the other British forces who were by now only 25 miles from Rome.

It was now the turn of the French airfields to reel under the weight of the bombs dropped by the British and Americans. The RAF also set about destroying as many rocket launch sites as they could find. The Germans were still unaware of exactly which part of the French coast the Allies were planning to invade. But they did mine the Bay of Biscay and reinforce an area of the Cotentin Peninsula where the Americans had planned to send in paratroopers. Fortunately, through decrypting a series of messages in the last week of May, the Bletchley decoders were able to warn the Americans who changed their 'drop' area.

APO England   May 5th. 1944

My physical position is rather peculiar. I am sitting on my bed surrounded by snoring, grunting, coughing bodies. But in actual fact I am sitting on the edge of a volcano whlst you are leading a remote and largely unnatural existence in Cambridge.

Things, though, far more important than you or I are going on all round me. I suppose I'm lucky to be able to play an active, if somewhat inglorious, part in them. The main result has been to raise my liquor consumption by at least 100% in the last couple of weeks now that the effects of my leave have worn off. And I doubt if it has passed its nauseating peak yet.

The barrack room seems to deaden my emotional faculties as well as the intellectual. A couple of hours ago I could have expresed myself more fully but I can tell you this: I can wangle a 24 hr pass one day in the next couple of weeks and I want to see you for a few hours. I can't guarantee that it'll come off, but if you want to see me just tell me where and when. I'll do anything to be with you.

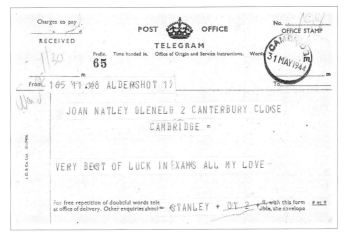

REVEALING TELEGRAM SENT BY STANLEY TO AUTHOR, 31ST MAY, 1944.

For some reason Stanley wrote only one letter to me during the whole of the month of May – or else I lost the others. And the elusive 24 hr pass never materialised. But he did send me a telegram to wish me luck in my first year exams. Which was how, contrary to all the top secret security arrangements in force, I knew exactly where he was stationed.

His next letter was written on the day the decision was taken by Eisenhower to invade Normandy on June 5th, more than a month after the latest date decided on by Churchill and Roosevelt in May 1943.

APO England   **June 2nd, 1944**

I dare say you will be in the thick of your exams when you read this. Don't let the unnatural concentration on study get you down. It's an unfortunate necessity of certain periods of University life but it's worth making a supreme effort for short bursts.

Unfortunately I can't assist you except by my best wishes and love. As you haven't seen me in Cambridge yet you have probably surmised – and correctly – that I can't get up there. All the same I am still hoping to see you some day, though only God knows how far away that will be.

The weather has been very hot here this last week or so – just what we need for an invasion and it has also meant that we've had plenty of sport to keep everyone's mind off what lies ahead. The climate has been an eye opener for the Northerners in the Regiment and we're all looking sun-burnt and fit and ready for pretty well anything.

The 'ready for anything' has included instruction on how to avoid, or failing that, deal with unmentionable diseases one might contract in Europe. However my first 'dose' for a long time has been of nothing more dangerous than culture. I went to a local piano recital. My appetite for music seems to have flagged though it can still put my thoughts and emotions into full circulation. If you are living the life of a nun at the moment, I certainly live the life of a monk – and not of the Rabelasian variety.

I hope this letter hasn't bored you. You will never bore me, though you may exasperate me at times. Thank you for your last letter – it was much pleasanter than the previous two – and I shall open the next one without that sinking feeling in the pit of my stomach.

It was some time before I wrote my next letter. The exams lasted two weeks and by the time they were over the Allies had entered Rome. In Northern Europe the invasion of France had been postponed from June 5th because of bad weather, but only for twenty-four hours. Operation Overlord was under way at last.

France at Last

'Every night beetles of diverse species hold a picnic in our dug-outs.'
July 20th, 1944

The invasion of Europe, code-named 'Overlord', was an exercise in logistics on a scale never before conceived and inevitably there were minor hitches, though the operation as a whole went like clockwork. Four thousand ships took part and many thousand smaller vessels. The enemy coastal defences were attacked by the RAF who dropped over five thousand tons of bombs. In the twenty-four hours of D-Day, June 6th, 1944, they flew over fourteen and a half thousand sorties.

At the same time airborne divisions, both British and American, were dropped in Normandy: the former to seize the vitally important bridges over the River Orne and its canal, and to capture the high ground to the east: the latter to cut off the Cotentin Peninsula with its vital port of Cherbourg.

Churchill announced that the first landings had been successful but, although he wanted to go and see for himself, he was dissuaded. By midnight of D-Day the Americans and British had each lost about a thousand men out of the one hundred and fifty-five thousand already ashore. But Montgomery's main objective for the day, Caen, had not been reached and was to resist capture for another two months.

On June 6th Stanley's Unit, 77th Medium Artillery, RA, were told that the invasion had begun and that orders to proceed to the marshalling area would follow shortly. At that time the Regiment had twenty-seven officers and five hundred and thirty eight men. It was divided into two Batteries, the 103rd and the 104th, each of which had two Troops – 'A' and 'B', 'C' and 'D' respectively. Each Troop was equipped with four 5.5-inch guns. Stanley was the Troop Leader of 'A' Troop in 103 Battery. The Regiment was commanded by Colonel F.G. Wintle.

They were well-trained, well-equipped, well-briefed and raring to go.

APO, England   **June 8th, 1944**

I expect you are in the thick of your exams and only hope your pessimism will prove to be as unjustified as mine used to be, and as yours was when you took Matric. My wire was a bit premature but anyway it arrived – or did it? But I thought I might not have the opportunity later though as you can see we are still here.

To us this is D + 2 rather than Thursday – the address above is only temporary. We are all tied up and just waiting for the word "GO". It's amazing how much we do know but of course I can't tell you anything. My

*chief worry at the moment is that I don't have to use the full complement of
vomit bags with which I am issued for the voyage.*

*I've just heard from Marjorie that Peter got married last week.
Extraordinary you not telling me, or are you off marriage? If he is still with
the RAF I should imagine he'll be lucky to work in a full honeymoon. I
haven't written to Marjorie for almost a year but I sent her a few lines
yesterday. Then out of the blue today I had a letter from her postmarked
Alexandria. She mentioned that I was a poor correspondent! The biter bit.*

*There's a hell of a lot going on and it is difficult to write. I suppose this is
the time when I should make some momentous remark, but I can't think of
anything. Except, that is, do write, for God's sake. Even if you don't get a
reply.*

On the day Stanley wrote this letter a bridgehead of twenty-five miles wide
had already been established by the British and Canadians in Normandy.
General Eisenhower was visiting Montgomery who had set up his HQ there.
The Americans had suffered severely at their landing area, Omaha Beach,
where resistance had been heavy but that day the Americans and British
joined up on the beaches at Colville-sur-Mer and by 11th June formed a
continuous inland front. The inhabitants of the first French town to be
liberated by them, Bayeux, went wild with joy.

As Stanley was waiting for the word 'Go' on June 8th, their Regiment's
advance party was delayed at Aldershot for another twelve hours – then
another and another. It was 2pm on the 10th June before the Regiment were
to told to move to their designated marshalling area. At 3pm the order was
cancelled. Finally two days later (12th June) the Regiment moved towards
Marshalling Area A in Portsmouth. At 8am they were keyed up and
expecting to embark within a few hours.

At 11am they were told they were in the wrong place and should go to
Marshalling Area B at Tilbury. So the lorries turned back towards Aldershot
and then round London via the North Circular Road. That night they
collected their life-belts and emergency rations, then slept beside their
vehicles. The following day, June 13th, they were wakened at 4am by an air
raid over the docks but no bombs were dropped. The Regiment eventually
embarked at 3pm on two LSTs, (Landing Ship, Tank) no.s 238, carrying 104
Battery, and 322, carrying 103 Battery. These were the largest ships used for
transporting heavy equipment and resembled the modern cross-channel
car ferries. But they had very little keel and were designed to run in to the
shallow waters near the beaches, before lowering their ramps. Whilst still
in deep water two large anchors would be lowered aft so that the LSTs could
later be winched off the shallows.

Stanley was not a good sailor but he decided not to lie down and try to
get some sleep. Instead he stood on the deck of LST 322 taking a last look
at England in the fading midsummer light. It must have been a moving

coincidence for him that the LSTs rendezvoused that evening with their escort off Southend, where he had been born.

June 13th was the day an experimental German rocket, launched from Peenemunde, fell onto Swedish soil instead of into the Baltic Sea. Examined by British officers and later transported to England, the Allies at last had one of Hitler's secret weapons, the V2, in their hands.

By then the Normandy beachhead was sixty miles long and had been visited by Churchill and General Smuts, the South African Prime Minister. The fighting was bitter but nevertheless King George V1 visited the beaches on June 16th.

In Belgium their King had been removed for fear that he would rally his people if he stayed in the country. The Nazis were taking no chances as they were still uncertain that Normandy was the real invasion point and not just an attempt to blind them to a main invasion further east, for example, in the Pas de Calais region.

Rumours of a pilotless German aircraft, which crashed and exploded when it ran out of fuel, were beginning to circulate but soon they were no longer rumours. The first pilotless planes landed in Southern England on the night of June 12/13. Of the first ten that were fired five crashed in the vicinity of their launch pads. Another one probably fell into the Channel and four reached London. One of these exploded in East London, causing six casualties, though the V1s were also blamed for a number of other misfortunes. Dairy farmers in Surrey and Sussex attributed a drop in milk yield to them and owners of ducks connected them with the reduction in egg output.

Many V1s or 'doodle-bugs', as the flying bombs soon became known, were chased and shot down into the Channel by RAF fighters before reaching England. But it was a difficult task since the V1s flew at nearly 400 mph – almost the limit of speed for Hurricanes and Spitfires – and they were a small and dangerous target to hit. A favourite RAF pilots' trick was swoop down and tip one of their wings under the 'doodle-bug's' own wing, diverting the bomb back out to sea or causing it to crash prematurely.

Other V1s were shot down by anti-aircraft fire nearer to London but still wreaked havoc as they landed. Within a few days it was decided to move entire ack-ack batteries to the South Downs in order to intercept the V1s before they reached the densely populated areas.

Of two hundred and forty-four V1s launched on June 15th, forty-five crash-landed immediately, eight were shot down by fighters and twelve more were hit by ack-ack fire. Seventy-three actually reached London and killed more than fifty people. On Sunday June 18th, the Guards Chapel near Buckingham Palace received a direct hit by a flying bomb. About sixty guardsmen were killed and an equal number of civilians. There were also many wounded casualties.

But Stanley had left British soil by then. It was a beautiful evening as the armada of ships that had gathered at the mouth of the Thames sailed on June 14th for Normandy, a journey of over two hundred miles. The weather was still perfect when, twenty four hours later, they arrived at Graye-sur-Mer, near Courseilles and about ten miles west of the mouth of the River Orne.

The water was too deep to land – it was the day before the Mulberry harbour at Arromanches was completed – and they waited for the tide to change. The sandy beach appeared quiet enough in the summer twilight. At dawn the first man ashore was Colonel Wintle, the CO who was to lead the Regiment, throughout the campaign in Northern Europe, to the end of the War. All of 103 Battery disembarked without incident but 104, who were further along the beach, came in for some bombing.

On 16th June the 77th moved into action as part of the newly landed V111 Corps, whose badge was a white charging knight in armour on a red background. (V111 Corps, together with other British Corps and Canadian components were known as the British Second Army which, together with the American First Army, made up the Twenty-First Army Group commanded by Montgomery.)

But Stanley's Battery, a very small section of Montgomery's troops, fired no shells for the next four days.

On Active Service
APO England   **Sunday, June 18th, 1944**

Here is my first letter written on the other side – or rather this one. I'm hoping to receive a letter from you in the next day or so but we've had no mail yet.

From the time we embarked till we set foot on the beaches somewhere in France the trip was more like a pleasant cruise than a landing operation. Everything is OK so far: the weather's been good, we get plenty to eat and I am very satisfied with the way the situation has developed. I'm not worrying and that's a very good reason why you should not worry about me. There are plenty of bangs but things are actually not a quarter as bad as you probably imagine them to be.

Goodness knows when this will be over but I am inclined to take an optimistic view. In a couple of months we'll be able to see the picture pretty plainly.

On 20th June, 1944, by which time there were half a million Allied soldiers ashore in France, Stanley's Troop fired their first shots in anger. Over the next two days, they advanced and dug into new positions in preparation for Operation Epsom. This was the code name for the attack whose objective was to pull the enemy reserves on to the British Second Army so that the First American Army could carry out its task more easily. But the weather had deteriorated and a great storm raged for three days destroying the US Mulberry Harbour and damaging the British one at Arromanches.

This freak June weather hampered the Allied build-up in Normandy. Fortunately Field Marshal Von Runstadt, whose forces were mainly in the Calais area, was still convinced that the FUSAG threat existed and refused to move his troops westward.

Stalin kept his promise to Churchill that once the Second Front was established the Russians would launch their summer offensive. It began on June 22nd, the third anniversary of the invasion of Russia, with over one and a half million troops and twenty-five thousand guns. The Allies were determined that Hitler should not be able to transfer troops from one theatre of operations to another. Altogether there were six fronts now on which the Axis had to fight.

At 7.30am on 26th June Operation Epsom began in which V111 Corps were to make the main attack. They had sixty thousand men, six hundred tanks and three hundred guns at their disposal plus support from other forces. Facing them were the famous German 12 and 26 SS Panzer Regiments.

Stanley's Battery Commander, Laurie Thomas, was sent forward to an OP in support of the 29th Armoured Brigade and Captain Dimbleby, Stanley's Troop Commander, to an OP in support of the 4th Armoured Brigade. They were firing on the area between Cheux and St Mauvieu. By the evening they had reached Colville on a line one mile north of Grainville-sur-Odon.

Although Cheux was now in British hands this shattered village was heaped with rubble and overturned, wrecked vehicles, slowing the advance of the 15 Scottish Division. Nevertheless the Scottish salient across the River Odon caused such acute alarm at the German HQ that their Commander, General Friedrich Dollman, died of a heart attack.

Unfortunately one of Stanley's fellow officers, Major P. T. Hollins, the 104 Battery Commander, was killed by a sniper's bullet whilst observing the fire of the Regiment. When he was first appointed to the rank of Major, Hollins was probably the youngest one in the army. The Tanks and Infantry were continually harassed by snipers who either strapped themselves in trees or hid in the ripening corn. In the letter he wrote to me the same day Stanley played down this particular hazard.

BWEF   *Monday June 26th, 1944*
(Note new address. God knows what it means)

Your letter which reached me yesterday after being re-addressed was a very pleasant surprise – partly because it is so long since I heard from you and partly because it was about the longest letter you have ever written to me.

The photo will henceforth be my most treasured possession. This means it will be quite a few weeks before I lose it. Amazingly I've still got 99% of the belongings I brought over here with me. I haven't lost much sleep, either, and all things considered we are very well fed. No fresh vegetables or eggs, everything's tinned of course, but it's very tasty and we are well supplied with chocolates and cigarettes.

I suppose you'll worry but your fears will be exaggerated. The Luftwaffe has had it and the rest won't be very difficult. I have spoken to quite a few French people and they've all been very friendly. There have been wild rumours about civilian snipers and there is, it is true a very small hostile element, but nothing of any consequence, so I am quite happy. We can take care of them.

I shall be happier still when the Mobile Laundry and Mobile Bath Units come across. To say nothing of the Mobile Bakery. Even Army bread will be a change from dog biscuits. I broke part of a tooth a couple of days ago.

The pack rations were very good apart from the lack of bread and most of the troops enjoyed them, though they began to pall eventually. Meals were enlivened by local Camembert cheeses, which appeared as gifts, and by the less welcome ack-ack shell splinters which splattered the roofs of the vehicles like rain.

The following day the 77th Medium Regiment were supporting an attack on the River Odon by 227th Brigade and 29th Brigade (with Stanley's friend, Captain Duerr, at the forward OP). The troops were so keen that even the Regimental cooks, clerks and mechanics volunteered for spells on the guns during the opening barrage. Since June 6, the Germans had suffered 43,070 casualties which included six generals, sixty-three commanders and four General Staff – equalling those of the Allies in spite.of being in prepared positions of defence. (The ratio of attackers to defenders is usually expected to be about three to one.) The Allies had also lost seven hundred and fifty armoured vehicles.

By 28th June a bridgehead had been formed at the river but the enemy counter-attacked heavily.

Meanwhile on the Cotentin Peninsular the battle for Cherbourg became very violent as the Americans reached the outskirts of the city. The battle raged for a week until 29th June when the Americans were finally in control of the whole of Cherbourg.

The invasion was beginning to take its toll. Roughly five thousand Americans, two and a half thousand British and five hundred Canadians had been killed but three quarters of a million Allied troops were now ashore. And on D-day the Allies had only lost one ship.

In England the V1 death toll had reached sixteen hundred, including twenty-four babies under one year old at a nursery in Westerham, Kent.

BWEF   **Saturday, July 1st, 1944**

Looking at my watch (General Service) I see it's July, if you get me. Incidentally I almost thought they had got me just now. There've been dozens of bangs ending up in the right direction (from me) but the odd one just came from the wrong direction (towards me).

As for sleep I still haven't missed much but the more I have the more I

*seem to want. Perhaps it's because I cover my head with the bedding to
drown out the row. But I could do with a decent book to read during quiet
spells. I was just going to say I wish you were here but that might be a little
selfish.*

*We've passed through villages which have seen very heavy fighting. In
one small town of three thousand inhabitants hardly a house was left intact.
A Tiger tank lay overturned in one of the streets. In the next village a
thirteenth century church had been practically razed to the ground. People
still live there somehow and fortunately they are pretty well nourished as
this is a fertile country district.*

Montgomery commented that the French civilians in Normandy did not
look in the least depressed: there was plenty of food, he said, plenty of
vegetables, cows, milk, cheeses, and very good crops. He often wondered
if they wanted to be liberated!

*My Foreign Equipment course came in useful the other day because some
Guardsmen wanted to know how to lay and fire a German Infantry gun they
had captured. I hope I told them correctly!*

*Now that I have finished my spell of all-night duty I shall retire to my bed
– or, rather, my slit trench. Even I wouldn't have the audacity to ask you
to share it.*

The Regiment had been in action that day and suffered one casualty. Their
objective was the control and water towers at Carpiquet aerodrome, to the
north-east of Caen. Captain Duerr was in the OP and although they
succeeded in damaging the tower it was not destroyed completely till July
3rd. The cost was two further wounded and a gun badly damaged.

There were now over one million Allied troops in France.

In England everyone was talking about the flying bombs. There was so
little warning – just the engine cutting out and then the few seconds wait
till you knew how close it had fallen. One fell quite near my home whilst
I was drinking a glass of milk, which shot out of my hand and all over the
books and papers I was working on.

Appeals to the Pope were suggested in the House of Commons and the
Sunday Times in its July 2nd editorial said: 'The killing of women and
children by this robot will not intimidate our people – it will move them
to righteous anger.'

It not only moved them to anger but also to action. On July 4th British
bombers raided the large underground flying bomb arsenal at St Leu. Two
thousand V1s were buried in the ruins.

It's 5am and I've just about smoked myself into a stupor. Unfortunately I can't eat myself into the same state. Yesterday morning I was called for duty at 3am and after three calls I eventually arrived at twenty-five to five. Disgraceful, I know, but I am just so sleepy. I spend about fifteen hours a day on duty.

Our recent offensive has gained quite a bit of ground and we all hope it will be only the preliminary to something even bigger. The Americans have done extremely well so far but their success was only possible because we contained nearly all the best German divisions on the British sector. I have made quite a few well-timed dives into the old slit trench.

But I am not likely to emulate James. Did you know he has won the MC? I had a letter from Molly — he's somewhere in Italy, still.

This must be a very quiet and gentle countryside in normal times but now every village is a tragedy. I've seen streams of refugees moving back from our front line — old men harnessed to handcarts holding all their worldly belongings, old women carrying large suit-cases. Well, we know the culprits and we are going to do something about it. But we can never restore what they have smashed.

Caen was now the main target for an all out attack by the three Services. It had been one of the initial objectives of 1 Corps. After the failure to capture it in the first rush, the artillery situation in the bridgehead, plus the shortage of ammunition supplies caused by the worsening weather, made it impossible to support a large-scale attack in June. By early July the situation had so improved that a large-scale attack with the necessary support was now possible.

From the sea the British battleship, Rodney, bombarded the city. From the air the RAF dropped two and a half thousand tons of bombs and on the land the 77th supported an attack by 1 Corps, opening fire at 2.30am on 8th July. The German artillery facing 1 Corps was attacking them ferociously as they tried to advance so the 77th switched their targets to destroy the German guns. They suffered five ORs (other ranks) wounded and lost three vehicles plus their wireless.

By the evening of July 8th, the city of Caen, save for one suburb, was in British and Canadian control. Like earlier towns liberated by the Americans, the battle had been bloody and reminiscent of the terrible First World War battles, such as Ypres.

At home, apart from the bombs, civilian life was becoming a little easier. Theatres were opening again and the thirty mile coastal ban was lifted from Cornwall to Hampshire, whilst in Germany no-one was allowed to travel anywhere without permission. July 9th was also the day on which Rommel was contacted by the conspirators, led by Count von Staffenburg, who were planning to kill Hitler.

And on July 11th, the date of Stanley's next letter, the bacon ration was increased from 4oz to 6oz. This would have pleased him as he was very fond of bacon.

BWEF   ***Tuesday, July 11th, 1944***

> *I started this letter on Sunday but then I was on my feet continuously for twenty-six hours, so I couldn't concentrate on writing a decent letter. I hope you are managing to get some rest. From what we've heard over here the flying bombs are causing quite a lot of trouble. I guess it was a pretty shaking experience to lose your glass of milk that way. Next time you feel like having a drink you'd better go to a pub.*
>
> *I think we shall have solved the flying bomb problem by the most direct method before very long — that is, by getting hold of the bases. All of us are still very confident since that marvellous Channel crossing. It was the most amazing thing I have ever seen in my life. I could hardly believe my eyes, and I am sure I will never forget those hours. And I've seen a few things since — a Bomber Command saturation raid accompanied by Godalmighty barrages and concentrations of artillery fire.*
>
> *Well, the war correspondents can all say that better than I can but nobody can say how much I am missing you. I just don't know when I will see you but I hope it's before I am 23. I'm sure we've got Hitler taped now in spite of any local resistance he may put up. Only a few weeks ago I was expecting grim years of Army life.*

The horrors perpetrated by Nazi Germany received solemn confirmation on July 11th as Churchill learnt the full details about Auschwitz, based on the reports of four escapees. The Camp huts had earlier shown up on a reconnaissance photograph but their real purpose had not been recognised. Invasion or no invasion the extermination of unwanted humans still proceeded. But we at home were unaware of the extent and bestiality of the process until the Americans liberated the first concentration camps in 1945. Total defeat was the only thing that would save the lives of those the Nazis were determined to destroy. And Stanley was perhaps a little too optimistic about an early victory.

Much of Stanley's time was spent in OPs from which gun-fire was directed and observed. The OP team typically consisted of an officer, a driver and vehicle, a radio operator/signaller and an Assistant (known as Ack). Often OPs were located in a tall building, such as a church tower, overlooking the enemy lines. On these occasions Stanley would arm himself with a bottle of brandy and a box of cigars, saying that if he was going, he would go out enjoying himself.

Once, when he was in a church tower that was hit, he and his Ack fled as the roof started to cave in above them. Half way down the steep stone stairs, the Ack went back to retrieve the still unbroken, half full bottle of brandy. As they got clear of the building the room they had been in was hit again and caught fire.

But sometimes there was no suitable high view-points and then OP tanks would be used to get as close as possible to the enemy. Fortunately Stanley was not OP Officer on the night of July 13th, '44. At 1am the enemy dropped two UXB's (unexploded bombs) on 103 Battery. Even though they failed to explode both OP tanks were damaged. One tank driver was killed and Captain Duerr was wounded and sent to Bayeux Hospital.

The Regiment continued to support the infantry, the 15th Scottish Division, as they advanced. On the 14th July their targets were three villages to the south-west of Caen – Malmot, Amaye and Feugerolles – and on the 15th July Esquay, Gavrus and Bougy. The attack was carried out by artificial moonlight produced with the aid of searchlights. By the 18th July the Regiment had moved up to support 18 Corps in the breakout, code-named Operation GOODWOOD, onto the Falaise plain, using the bridgehead north-west of Caen. Falaise was where the last successful invader of Britain, William the Conqueror, was born.

The objectives of GOODWOOD were to destroy the enemy in the area Caen-Mezidon-Falaise-Evrecy and to cut off the enemy in the area of Evrecy-Caumont. The Regiment's new gun area was centred on Gruchy where many of the dead had not been cleared. The stench of death in the moist, warm air wafted over the Batteries in sickening waves.

Captain Dimbleby, Stanley's Troop Commander, was in a tank being used as a forward OP in support of 29th Armoured Brigade. At 3pm he reported that his tank had been hit but he was trying to get back. His wireless operator was badly wounded. Nothing further was heard of or from him for two days.

In a chance strafing attack near Caen on July 17th, by a British fighter-bomber, Rommel's car was hit and Rommel himself seriously injured. He was out of the war both as an army commander and as a conspirator. Three days later the attempt on Hitler's life was made and failed.

Thursday	*July 20th, 1944*

I've begun this letter twice and both times I have been interrupted for so long that it has become out of date. Now I am hoping not very confidently that there won't be any targets coming down for the next hour or so.

I suppose by now you are looking forward to going back to Cambridge in two or three weeks. Who wouldn't be? Particularly if I could do fire-watching with you. I am so glad you passed your Inter BSc. London can't be much fun just now. I know some of my relations have been staying in Wycombe to get a few days rest from the strain of flying bombs. It's a very nasty business and it doesn't look as though there'll be any let up for a while.

At the moment we're not in a very pleasant position. We are surrounded by the corpses of cattle and German tanks. The stench is pretty horrible and we are also cursed with various forms of insect life. Every night beetles of diverse species hold a picnic in our dug-outs.

From what I can gather the BBC sends back the latest news from the war fronts as quickly as we get it here so you must know plenty by now about the current 2nd Army offensive. The weather's been much better and this has made the colossal air support possible. Admittedly it's given me dozens of blisters and bites but still with sublime self-sacrifice I am praying to God for this hot weather to continue.

Some of the villages in the coastal belt aren't too badly knocked about but when you go further inland you find absolute devastation. Our bombers and guns have razed everything to the ground. But the chase is on now and the faster we chase him the better we like it, for it all speeds up the day when all this nightmare will be over. I can wait patiently for the day when I'll see you again so long as I know we're doing a first class job of work here. And I know that.

PS The grub is much the same except that we get one slice of bread a day now. Also beer and whisky have turned up! Beer is 1/6d a pint and whisky at 8/6 a bottle (about 85fr a glass).

This was the day of the bitterest fighting for Caen but Operation Goodwood succeeded and at last the city fell. Leaving 'C' Troop behind to harass the enemy positions, the other three Troops of the 77th Regiment drove through the centre of Caen to the southern part of the town. The route was a scene of utter devastation with rubble piled high either side of the narrow track.

On 29th July in the early hours of the morning, the Regiment went into a hide area just south of Bayeux to rest up. The following evening, shortly before midnight and whilst firing their last concentration of the day, 103 Battery's Command Post was hit by a shell. Two OR's were killed – Gunners Irving and Powell – one OR, Gunner Byass, was seriously injured and Lieutenant Laverack was also seriously wounded. He had lost an arm. But by noon the following day they were back in action assisting the 29th Brigade's advance towards the River Souleuvre. They were eventually halted at St Martin-le-Besaces having advanced ten miles.

The terrain was dangerous and the 15th Scottish Division were soon exposed on their left flank, but they still drove forward. Two cars – one armoured, the other an ordinary scout car – left the main body and raced down a wooded track. To their astonishment they found themselves travelling in the dust cloud behind a German armoured vehicle which led them to the bridge carrying the Le Beny-Bocage-Vire road over the River Souleuvre.

The British quickly disposed of the sentry on the bridge and from six miles behind the enemy lines began sending messages back. V111 Corps immediately revised their plans and 29th Armoured Brigade, supported by the 77th Medium Artillery, followed the trail of the two cars. By July 31st our tanks were happily rolling over this intact bridge.

Meanwhile the Anglo-Americans had broken out from their Normandy beachhead, opening the road to central France. The Americans had also succeeded in breaking out of the Cherbourg Peninsula because the British had kept the major German forces tied up by the battle for Caen which at last was in our hands.

July ended with excellent news on the Russian and Far Eastern Fronts. The Russians were only twelve miles east of Warsaw. In the Pacific the Americans had landed on Guam and Tinian. The resulting battles cost the lives of twenty-five thousand Japanese defenders for the loss of two and a half thousand Americans.

At home a V1 fell on a Lyons Corner House killing about fifty people. Another one fell on London Zoo in Regent's Park killing two cockatoos and upsetting the inmates of the monkey house for several hours. Fortunately all the dangerous animals and reptiles had either been removed or destroyed early in the war.

CAEN – JULY 1944.

Battle honours

'there is a certain exhilaration in danger safely surmounted and comradeship..'
September 9th, 1944

With the Russians only a few miles from Warsaw the Poles in the city rose against their oppressors. They appealed to the Allies for help but, despite Churchill's attempt to involve both America and Russia in aiding them, nothing at all was done for several days. When help finally came it was too late to save the majority of the insurgents and thousands of civilians.

Help was also too late for Anne Frank and her family. This fourteen year old Jewish girl, who had kept a diary during her two years in hiding in an Amsterdam attic, was arrested on August 4th and later died in a concentration camp.

In Normandy the battle of the Falaise gap had begun. Falaise, a town some thirty miles to the south-east of Caen, was at the bottle-neck of a German push towards Mortain. Hitler was determined to take Mortain, which lay south-west of Falaise, and the German forces managed to keep a bulge some forty miles long and twenty miles wide open against strong Allied attacks for over two weeks.

But south and west of the Falaise gap the Americans were nearing the Loire and had reached the Atlantic coast. To the north Stanley's Regiment had been in continuous action since the beginning of the month. In spite of Panzer troops in the area, no further than a thousand yards away, the Batteries did not suffer any attacks from them though the Division which took over from 77th eventually was subjected to the enemy's strongest counter attack. On August 10th, after forty-six days continuous fighting, the 77th moved into a hide area near Bayeux to refit and rest. The Regiment was now under 2nd Army Command.

(address torn off)   **August 10th, 1944**

It's so long since you wrote to me − or at least since I have heard from you − that the absence of news from you doesn't hit me as hard as it used to. If I can adjust myself to the way of living out here I can also adjust myself to not hearing, though this is the harder of the two. I had hoped you would write twice a week.

You will (I hope) be pleased to know that I am absolutely OK although we've been in most of the hardest battles and have put down some very effective fire. Three times we have been congratulated by the Brigadier on the results of our shooting. Although I can't tell you our position, I personally have been over practically the whole of the British Front. The towns which have taken a bashing from our heavy bombers are in a simply shocking state; others, which the Germans evacuated quickly, are almost intact.

The countryside differs, too. So do the numbers and species of insects. The worst things in this war are the smell of dead cattle and the insects which inhabit some areas. I can take shelling and even bombing, but not stenches and beetles.

In the Command Post they say once I get into bed I fall into a coma. That's a good thing because if you lose sleep through bad nerves you'll only create a vicious circle. We're being well fed although we grumble about it – well, we have to grumble about something – so we don't go to bed hungry. And I've developed a certain fondness for the bottle but I'm not a dipsomaniac yet. Still, there's plenty of time for that. I've only been in this game for a couple of months.

At our last gun position we did feel something like a Liberation Army. The peasants couldn't do enough for us. They plied us night and day with cider, butter, milk and cream and we even managed to get some pears and red-currants. Bill Bailey and myself spent three hours talking with one of the families in their cottage. Eventually we managed to get what we wanted – a small turkey, for which we bartered soap, cigarettes, toothpaste and chocolate. They can't market their commodities at the moment and a lot of the stuff we had was surplus. Unfortunately as soon as we came back with the bird we received orders to move.

The 'move' was to a rest camp. The place reminds me of my home town in miniature and everything is laid on for us – ENSA, cinema shows and baths. Now I am clean I feel almost civilised. Life is good just now.

But it hasn't been as bad as I feared. You find a fine sense of comradeship under these tough conditions and we all feel we're doing essential war work. We even manage to take the horrors light-heartedly. It's amazing how funny shelling can be or at least people's reaction to it.

But we've also taken some knocks that are hard to bear. Poor old Bert Dimbleby – the best chap in the Battery – has gone. He was my old Troop Commander. John Laverack caught a packet, too, and he's out of this war. I've taken over his job which is at Battery HQ and slightly more elevated than Troop Leader.

The only real difference is that we receive rockets directly, instead of indirectly, from the CO and then we chew up the officers on the gun positions. We are surrounded by masses of wirelesses and telephones; the latter always seem to buzz when I am having a quiet pee outside. One thing is definite – no telephones in our house after the war.

While the regiment was resting, other Allied forces were pushing the Germans back towards their own frontier. On the 10th August the Allies were less than 140 miles from Paris. By the 12th they had occupied Mortain at the base of the Falaise gap. The following day they reached the Loire at

Nantes. Germany could no longer hold back the invasion in France. Town after town fell. On August 17th Falaise was entered, the same day as the Germans began to flee from Paris. General Eisenhower reported that after the town fell it was possible to walk through its streets treading on nothing but decaying flesh and corpses.

On the 18th August St Malo fell though a small island off-shore held out for another fortnight. It was to overcome the Germans' refusal to surrender the island that napalm was used by the Americans for the first time in Europe. Three days later, at Dunbarton Oaks just outside Washington DC, the Allied powers agreed to set up the United Nations.

In the middle of August the Allies landed in the south of France. The operation, known originally as Anvil but later called Dragoon, was aimed at tying up German Divisions to ease the pressure on the Allies advance in northern France. It was a plan conceived by the Americans many months before but it had the effect of slowing down the Allied advance in Italy, from where many of the troops that took part had come.

Churchill adhered to his promise to supply a number of Divisions for Dragoon though he was far from certain that it would achieve its objective. He thought it more likely it would merely weaken General Alexander's forces. On August 23rd he visited Italy to raise the morale of the Alexander's troops who were about to start a major offensive.

Meanwhile in England some Italian prisoners of war were helping to bring in the harvest. Their efforts sometimes extended to providing unusual meals for other farm workers. At one farm they were given a hare and produced a delicious dish made with olive oil, onions and cocoa. Rationing was still in full force but other restrictions were gradually being lifted. Parts of the beaches in southern England were cleared of mines and obstacles and the public allowed access for the first time in four years.

August 18th was also the day on which the first Russian troops reached the German border but the greatest news of all in August was the fall of Paris. French troops entered the city on the 24th and the next day General de Gaulle himself was there. On August 26 he walked once more down the Champs Elysees, home after four years absence.

BLA   *Monday, August 28th, 1944*

Yesterday I got about three days mail in one. But I was disappointed once again. I hope to God you are alright and I have asked my people to get in touch with your home to find out. I can't understand why you have to treat me like this. Surely I have meant something to you at some time or another. The postbag is empty for me unless I hear from you.

You should be fire-watching in Cambridge just about now so it's the Cambridge post-mark I'm looking for. Doesn't this soften your heart enough to put pen to paper? Please!

I'm pretty well browned-off at the moment even though material

*conditions are extremely pleasant. I must know where I stand. Anything —
however shattering — is better than the present state of affairs.*

I hastened to reassure Stanley that I was well. But I was a very poor
correspondent now that I had so many other interests and so much academic
work to do. And I did not want to encourage him to expect too much of me,
only to be disappointed later. Stanley was not the only one who suffered
from my apparent indifference. A similar appeal, which also used the phrase
'browned-off', arrived from John Pincus, couched in his inimitable style.

I replied immediately to both letters. I had given up trying to convince
them that I wasn't in love with either of them. They were both exposed to
considerable personal danger and it would have taken a harder heart than
mine to stop writing whilst the war was on. But I was not very good at
prevaricating and Stanley did not seem too pleased with what I had written.

Although Stanley was worried about the flying bomb attacks on London,
they were at last being beaten by the defensive ring around the south of
England. The day he wrote this letter only four out of ninety-seven V1 bombs
launched fell on London. The rest were destroyed by fighter planes, anti-
aircraft guns or barrage balloons. By the end of the first week in September
the V1 menace was over. But the next night the first V2s, the rockets which
the Germans had been developing at Peenemunde, landed near London.

On 2nd September a twenty-year old pilot, based on an American aircraft
carrier in the Pacific, was shot down six hundred miles from Tokyo. His name
was George Bush. He became President of the United States forty-four years
later.

On the fifth anniversary of the outbreak of World War Two, the Allies
captured Brussels and the following day Antwerp was liberated. But the
Germans still held the coastal areas to the north and to the south there was
a big bulge across the Franco-Belgian border. This was the area where the
77th Regiment had been in action.

On 1st September the Regiment, about to start a two week training
exercise, was ordered to move to Morgny but were unable to do so because
of supply difficulties. By the end of the first week it was raining so heavily
that they had to change their location to Epreville. Soon after this Stanley
replied to my letter written at the end of August.

BLA   ***September 9th, 1944***

---

*I've just had a letter from you. I don't really know quite what to say.
When I first saw your writing on the envelope I got a bigger thrill than ever
before; but now I am thinking, what if I don't get another for a month or
more? It's very difficult when I have no answer to my letters. I think
perhaps you have consigned, physically or metaphorically, what I have
written to the waste-paper basket.*

Not hearing from you has undoubtedly been my worst experience by far over here. War consists largely of dirt, stenches and death in their most unpleasant shapes. But there is a certain exhilaration in danger safely surmounted, and comradeship, and satisfaction when one hears the tangible results of what one is doing. There is happiness and pleasure in this vile way of living. But there is nothing to compensate for the one complete void.

I give you every credit for expressing your feelings so frankly and I don't suggest you are guilty of any sort of insincerity. You seem to want to remain on close terms with me and to have to break things up would be the worst decision I should ever have to take. But I can't go through again what you have put me through the last month.

It's a lovely day and not a time for unpleasant thoughts. Perhaps there'll be another letter from you tomorrow. I will re-read this in the morning but I don't think I will change a word of it.

Far from consigning his letters to the waste-paper basket I was saving them in bunches of four or five, not tied up with purple ribbon, but carefully folded in dated envelopes. Trying to be objective about our future did not extend to destroying his letters. But he never knew that I kept them and in later years I, too, forgot that I had them stored away in an old box.

Cont: Sunday

Would you like to hear something of what I have been doing? The wine and flowers — but no kisses — are flowing. Our chief medium of exchange is cigarettes pour papa. Except they are not usually for papa. The heaviest smokers in this part of the world all seem to be under fourteen. With a bar or two of soap one can get almost anything — except what you're thinking. I'm not quite sure what it takes to get that. But my French is pretty fluent which is a terrific asset.

The open-air life hasn't done me any harm and I'm feeling healthy enough, but I hate the damp and cold. Let's hope we'll be indoors before too long. At least we won't be plagued by insects then. I felt something crunch between my teeth while I was eating my tinned rice pudding just now and fished out a rather bedraggled wasp. The other day, when I put my boots on, I put in my foot and I felt something squirm beneath it. Out jumped a stupefied frog.

The hidden talent in our Battery has emerged at last. We put on a show in a village theatre and in one highly topical sketch I received three dishonourable mentions. How do I know? Well, they used the name by which I am known to my Troop, Dog Easy. It comes from the signal for the first part of my odd surname, 'de', i.e. able, baker, charlie, DOG, EASY, fox, ...etc. It's a long time since I laughed so hard.

According to Stanley's Sergeant-major, Jack Wilson, Stanley was also known as 'Dagwood', from Dagwood Bumstead, the hapless husband of Blondie in the popular cartoon strip of that name which ran from 1939 to 1950.

> *Actually I am rather pleased with the name they have chosen for me. It's accurate because I'm certainly not a disciplinarian and it's quite an affectionate term compared to what they call the other officers.*
>
> *I'm often reminded of a cartoon I saw recently in one of the pocket monthlies: a gushing hostess at a party where dozens of men and girls were gossiping, was saying to an officer,*
>
> *"I know, Major, this must be so boring for you after Normandy."*
>
> *To those of us over here this is a first class joke. For us trivialities are the breath of life. So don't abstain from writing just because you haven't anything breath-taking to say.*
>
> *PS I am so very sorry to hear about John Pincus. It must be a shattering blow to his sister and parents.*

At the beginning of September 1944 John's parents were informed that he had been shot down over the Channel and was reported missing. John had always maintained that he would never be defeated in a dog-fight but that there was virtually nothing one could do to avoid enemy flak. It was just chance if anti-aircraft fire hit you rather than the next fellow in the Squadron.

One of his friends visited the Pincus' a few days afterwards and told them he had been flying alongside John when his plane was hit. He saw him get out of the cock-pit before the Spitfire burst into flames and crashed into the sea. John's parachute opened safely and when John's friend did a return sweep over the area a few minutes later, John was being picked up, apparently uninjured, by a German fast patrol vessel.

On September 11th John's mother gave me an envelope that John had left for me should he ever be reported missing. It contained a copy, in his own handwriting, of a poem by Christina Rossetti entitled 'Remember'. I read it and remembered with pangs of remorse his Querulous Quroon which he was alive and had sent me the week before. Did he ever he get my reply? Perhaps I would never know. We all prayed as we waited for further news, hoping against hope that he was alive and had been taken prisoner.

That night RAF planes bombed Darmstadt. The firestorm which followed killed over twelve thousand people. The next day Le Havre surrendered.

BLA   **September 16th, 1944**

> *You'll see this is written on decent note-paper bought in a local shop. Yes, life still functions more or less normally in quite a lot of towns now that the*

battle has swept on. At one time I thought that every town and village we liberated would be a wilderness, but in point of fact that applied only near the beachhead. What a shambles some of those places are! As for Caen — I am glad that no town in Britain has had to undergo such a martyrdom.

We've a pretty gruelling time immediately ahead of us, but the harder we get stuck into it the sooner this Goddam war will be over. I'm convinced it can't last more than another two months — and probably a good deal less. Before the month is out I hope we will be marching triumphantly through Deutschland, taking care to dodge the brickbats, etc. which will presumably descend on us from the liberated roof-tops.

The rest period has left me with one legacy which I hope won't be permanent — that is, an unhealthy relish for cognac and sundry expensive liqueurs. I'm afraid the charms of the bottle are very potent.

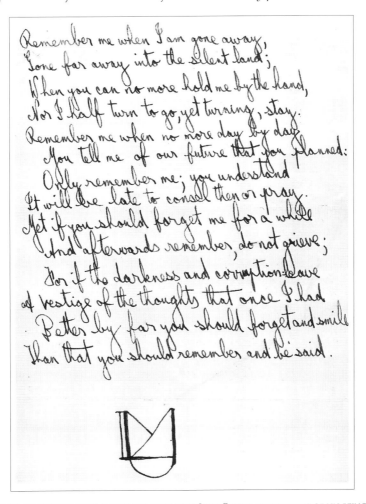

Remember me when I am gone away,
Gone far away into the silent land;
When you can no more hold me by the hand,
Nor I half turn to go, yet turning, stay.
Remember me when no more day by day
You tell me of our future that you planned:
Only remember me; you understand
It will be late to consel then or pray.
Yet if you should forget me for a while
And afterwards remember, do not grieve;
For if the darkness and corruption leave
A vestige of the thoughts that once I had
Better by far you should forget and smile
Than that you should remember and be sad.

POEM BY CHRISTINA ROSSETTI, LEFT FOR AUTHOR BY JOHN PINCUS IN THE EVENT OF HIS BEING SHOT DOWN.

Before Stanley's Regiment reached Belgium the first Allied soldier, an American, had already crossed the German border. Dunkirk, the scene of the British retreat from Europe four years earlier, was besieged. And three daring paratroop landings had taken place behind the German lines: at Nijmegen, Eindhoven and Arnhem. Their objective, a bridge over the Rhine, was not achieved and in the five-day battle over a thousand paratroopers lost their lives and many thousand more were taken prisoner.

In France, as the 77th Regiment came to the end of its training/rest period, the Regiment was ordered to move to an area South of Brussels. They were now back on operations and still had to cross the border into Belgium. Recce parties crossed the border, taking a northerly route, and went out far in advance of the Regiment to meet 8 Corps at Petit Brogel on the Belgian/Dutch border. Meanwhile the Regiment pushed through to the Bapaume-Cambrai road, south-east of Arras, in the Picardy region.

They were moving through the battlefields of the First World War, softened by cultivation but their scars still apparent. In the battle of the Somme (1st July-November 1916) between Bapaume and Albert, the Allied Front Line had pushed forward against the German Line, which was well-defended with barbed wire and deep trenches. One hundred thousand Allied troops were killed on the first day, most of them mown down by German machine guns. In the Battle of Cambrai (November 1917) prospects for eastward progress in the Ypres salient had faded with the onset of autumn because of the mud. The battle shifted to the Cambrai area where the firmer going made the attack there initially a brilliant success. But the breakthrough was squandered by lack of reserves. This was the first time tanks were used in battle on a large scale. Now, twenty-seven years later, the Bapaume-Cambrai road was congested with modern tanks, blocking the progress of the 77th Regiment who had to harbour for the night, exposed on the road.

North-east of Cambrai, in the direction of Valenciennes, lies a river called the Escaut. The canal alongside links the two towns. It was in crossing the Escaut Canal, in the middle of September 1944, that Stanley acted as forward observation officer which later led to him receiving two Belgian awards. The citation reads: At the crossing of the Escaut Canal in September 1944 Lt de Smith 'acted as forward observation officer. He travelled in a carrier, the only lightly armoured vehicle amongst a squadron of tanks, and the support provided by him was of the utmost value in enabling the tanks to advance, and was frequently directed from very exposed OPs in close proximity to the enemy.'

Once across the Escaut Canal, the Regiment moved rapidly through Belgium to their new battle area in Holland. Just after midnight on 20th September the Regiment passed through Achel and Lille St Hubert. The enemy still held Marheeze but it was clear by the following day.

Both Batteries were involved in the firing on Son and Someron that morning and just after midday they moved forward to Geldrop. Their guns were still firing at nine o'clock that evening with Captain Duerr – now recovered from his injuries – reporting the accuracy of the shots. On the morning of the 22nd September 103 Battery sent out a recce party to see if German troops still held Asten. At midday Captain Duerr reported it clear and established an OP in the church tower. When he gave the somewhat unexpected order 'target cavalry', it turned out not to be a ghostly regiment of the First World War but merely German soldiers trying to escape on farm horses.

The Regiment then moved up to support the advance of 11th Armoured Division from their bridgehead. Stanley replaced the Battery Commander at the Observation Post. Captain Duerr went forward to support 159 Brigade HQ and by the evening Stanley was delegated to support the 15/19 Hussars. In twenty-four hours 103 Battery had expended eighty-seven rounds of ammunition.

The next few days saw the fiercest fighting the Regiment had been involved in since the battle for Caen. The Germans were counter-attacking but very accurate gun-fire by the 77th pinned them down. By the 24th September 103 Battery was in Leisel. At 5pm an urgent message came from HQ RA:

'Lt de Smith to stay with 15/19 Hussars at all costs. To find their CO and arrange Direct Fire tasks and get them back to us as soon as possible.' This he did.

On the 25th the Regiment was ordered to cross the Willeim Canal. 104 Battery got across but 103 was held up till the following day. The position then reversed itself. 103 crossed the canal and occupied the positions previously held by C and D Troops (104 Battery) whilst they moved back because of enemy action to the south-east. Stanley was then located at Gemert.

That evening Captain Duerr reported that the enemy were withdrawing north-east very fast and by 5pm both Batteries had reached Deurne. Here they halted and got off the road for the night. Next morning Laurie Thomas, 103 Battery Commander, brought in a German POW.

On 27th September 103 Battery was still in action though they had lost five three-tonners, two 15cwt vehicles, one jeep and two motor-cycles. Stanley was now at 159 Brigade HQ. The next two days he was in the forward OPs and while sitting in one of these he wrote his next letter.

BLA   *September 25th, 1944*

I am writing this perched on a truck in the middle of nowhere. It's been hectic the last few days and I wish you could have seen what happened.

I was with the first regiment to enter a number of towns and villages. The people went absolutely crazy with joy. They showered apples, pears, peaches, eggs, milk and cognac on us (one thing at a time) and as for cheering, we might just have won the Cup Final. That's the only thing that could work British people up to such a pitch.

Almost everyone was wearing the national colours which had been forbidden under the German occupation. All work stopped and even the monks came out of their monasteries and were fraternising with the nuns. Of course we didn't know what lay in front of us and that restricted our pleasure somewhat but it was absolutely terrific.

I'm beginning to wonder when I shall see you — or Cambridge for that matter. The demobilisation proposals are fair enough but they don't suit me at all. I should have liked to send you some sort of souvenir from over here but there's been nothing suitable where I've been. I have got one thing, though, a sort of 'favour' with national colours on it. But we are not even allowed to allude to what country we are in.

It's rather chilly with a helluva lot of rain. War is even more unpleasant under such conditions. I'm in the grip of the first cold I've had since we landed, due to wearing wet trousers for too long.

The final split is very close at hand and I predict that the dim-out (which had replaced the black-out) will be washed out before the Michaelmas Term is over.

PS Now that the lines of communication are so extended the mail is likely to be held up so don't wait for replies to your letters — just keep writing.

It was a month before I heard from him again.

Stalemate in Holland

'Things don't look quite as bright as when I last wrote'
October 28th, 1944

B y the end of September the attempt to secure the bridge across the Rhine at Arnhem had failed but the stand made by the paratroopers helped the progress of the Second Army in Holland.

On September 26th the encircled troops at Arnhem surrendered. Altogether five Victoria Crosses were awarded, some to those who took part in the original landings and one to a pilot who tried to airlift supplies to the surrounded troops.

The fighting in Holland was made much more difficult by the watery conditions in parts of the country. Large areas were flooded deliberately by the Germans as a defensive measure. Then, on October 3rd, the RAF bombed the dykes which held back the sea from the island of Walcheren. The attacks continued for over a month before the island was taken.

Conditions were becoming difficult in Italy, too, because of bad weather. It was recognised that there was a limit to how long men could stay in action without breaking down, not only through the actual horrors of battle but also through the physical environment in which they fought. There was no such thing as 'getting used to battle' and the British combat troops in Italy were given four days rest after every twelve days fighting when this was feasible.

For the citizens of Antwerp there was no such relief. V1s fell on the city continually. My brother, Peter, was stationed there with the RAF and on his twenty-second birthday, October 13th, 1944, the first V2 fell on the city. Thirty-two people were killed.

V2s were still falling on London but in Dover there was rejoicing. Dover had been one of the worst hit areas in the South-East. It was said that children there could not remember sleeping in their beds. With the fall of Calais, from where German guns had fired directly at them, people danced in the streets. Life was slowly returning to normal.

'Blackout' had been replaced by 'dim-out'. The deep tank traps which had been dug in the South Downs were being filled in. The cheese ration went up to three ounces from two, lamb was more plentiful and often had suet left on instead of being fatless (the meat ration was then 1/2d per person per week) and every child between the ages of six months and eighteen years was promised an extra half a pound of sweets for Christmas.

In addition eighty million packets of Iraqi dates – intended for the forces but no longer required – were to be sold at 3d a packet at Christmas time. There were also minor shortages: the supply of milk was limited – two half-pints a week – golden syrup vanished from the shops and coal was very difficult to obtain.

But conditions for the German civilians were very much worse. Refugees from the advancing Soviet Army were fleeing west and from the advancing American Army around Aachen they were fleeing east. Food, coal and transport were all in short supply due to the sustained bombing attacks by the Allies.

To the north of the American Army, which had crossed the upper reaches of the River Meuse (otherwise known as the River Maas), Stanley's Regiment was everywhere in the thick of the fighting. On October 1st the 77th was ordered to clear the area of Venraij, west of the River Maas. In order to observe the east bank of the river, Captain Duerr went forward to an OP in Boxmeer Church. It was an excellent OP and thereafter each day one of the Regimental Troops occupied it. The civilians went about their normal business ignoring the gun-fire. One Sunday the OP Officer found himself locked out of the tower as there was a church service in progress!

On the 3rd, 'A' Troop were sent forward in daylight with Lt Wagner in the OP. He reported a windmill was being used as an enemy OP and one hundred rounds were fired at it. Although 103 Battery scored ten direct hits it was still standing but by 5pm the enemy had wisely left. 'A' Troop continued in action with Captain Harrisson at the OP in support of 151 Field Regiment. Then for a couple of days the Regiment was in 'silent' role, ready for action but not actually firing. The enemy were holding the line on the River Maas from Roosteren in the South through Wessem (near Roermond) and Overloon to Groeningen in the far north of Holland. They were occupying the villages of Overloon and Venraij, fighting stubbornly and carrying out active patrolling. On the 11th October Gunner O'Brien was reported missing. Although he was eventually found he was badly wounded and died the following day.

On October 12th, at Oploo, 103 Battery came under heavy mortar fire. Unfortunately at midday 'C' Troop received a direct hit on one of their guns by a mortar bomb. Two Other Ranks, Gunner Goldsmith and Lance Bombardier West, were killed and eleven wounded, plus one officer, Lt George Amman. Nevertheless all guns continued firing and they played an important role in Operation Constellation, which aimed at pushing the Germans back across the river. Two MCs and one MM were later awarded to the Regiment for this operation.

Fighting continued in difficult terrain throughout the next week. A rum issue was authorised on the 16th October. In spite of being hampered by bad weather and appalling roads, patrols reached Venraij by the 17th. Maarheeze was still held by the Germans but 103 Battery scored ten direct hits on their OP on 21st October. The Germans then began a heavy counter-bombardment which seriously wounded two ORs. But the shell fragments were collected and helped to identify the German artillery being used against them. 103 Battery was so heavily shelled that night that they moved to an alternative position.

Stanley was now Gun Position Officer, having moved up from Troop Leader, taking the place of the officer who had become Troop Commander after Bert Dimbleby's death near Caen.

On the 25th, a flying bomb passed overhead, was reported and heard to explode some miles away. 103 Battery were now firing at four targets, including Tienrag, Oostrum and Maarheeze. Meijel was subject to an enemy attack and was recaptured by the Germans. On 28th October 103 Battery received a direct hit on their OP but there were no casualties. Lt Amman, who had been wounded a fortnight before in a similar incident, returned to duty.

Captain Harrisson reported that a sketch map of the minefields at Vierlingsbeek, on the River Maas, had been given to him by a civilian. But as yet they could not get that far.

The month ended with some accurate gun-fire. On 29th the Battery Commander took on a church tower in Bergen and scored seven direct hits out of fifty. The tower was destroyed and the following day he scored nine hits on the second church tower though that remained standing.

As Stanley wrote to me after a month's silence the Regiment were withdrawn from action and offered vacancies at 8 Corps Rest Camp with tickets for Helmond Theatre.

BLA   *October 28th, 1944*

> *Don't think I have forgotten you for one hour. I stopped writing for several reasons, which all amount to the same. I just found it impossible to write as I do and feeling as I do and then to be answered by ''yours sincerely''. So I thought it better not to write at all. But when I got your letter the other day I had to change my mind. Whatever may happen and whether I shall ever see you again I really don't know. I just hope.*
>
> *Things don't look quite as bright as when I last wrote. Of course that was before the Arnhem business. Still I don't believe organised resistance will last another six months. Perhaps that's wishful thinking but I hope not because shells and autumn weather and long nights make a nasty combination.*
>
> *Our lads have had more than their share of bad luck and I've seen a few things I had hoped I would miss. We get a nightly lullaby of Moaning Minnies though I brought down a packet on them last night.*
>
> *(Moaning Minnies were multi-barrelled mortars fired in rapid succession which made a banshee-wailing noise as they came over. The noise sounded as if 'a thousand gates on rusty hinges were being opened', according to a private in the Worcestershire Regiment who was in the battle around Cheux.)*
>
> *One thing I was curious about before I came over here was my reaction to individual German soldiers. Now I've seen quite a few prisoners all I've felt is a violent revulsion with not a grain of Christian charity. Likewise whenever I've had a chance to shoot them up in the trenches. This is the*

*normal feeling out here and in other respects – e.g. being shot at – my
reaction has been the average one. There seems to be three general types as
far as physical bravery is concerned:*

the strong, (10-20%) who just have no normal fears,

the weak, (10-15%) who crack up completely,

*the medium, the majority, who have normal fears but who overcome them
(in varying degrees) in the face of danger because they know that is their duty.*

*I'm as allergic as the next bloke to high explosive but luckily I haven't
given way yet. It's absolutely hopeless for an officer to do so, anyway. I've
known officers lose every vestige of respect from their men merely on the
suspicion of weakness.*

*You will gather that I am more interested in personality and philosophy at
the moment than in society. I'm caught up with the swirling tide instead of
being just an academic spectator of events. I'm still very interested in politics
but I picked up a book yesterday called 'Marxism and Democracy' by Lucien
Laurat and quite honestly I couldn't stomach the old invective and insults
and the rehashing of the Bernstein-Kautsky-Plekhanov controversies.*

*When you next write tell me more about yourself. I was interested in the
BIPO. job (British Institute of Public Opinion). They're the Gallup people,
aren't they? And I hope you enjoyed your weekend at Brighton. It's a very
nice place in many ways.*

*It was there that I first fell in love. I was just 16 at the time. The object of
my affection was just two years younger, the same age as you were when we
met. My passion was unrequited and when I found her with a rival in a
darkened room I came to the conclusion that I had had it. Only my youthful
enthusiasm prevented my becoming a hardened cynic there and then.*

*The second affair you should know all about. There has been no third and
I don't think there can be now. How can you be so heartless as to make me
an embittered man?*

*Are your parents living in Brighton now? Or was it just a rest from the
V1s and V2s? Mine are likely to move back to Westcliff in the New Year.
Apart from its wooded slopes and you, the Wycombe area never had much
attraction for me. Maybe one day I'll write a poem entitled 'Downley
Revisited' or 'Ode to Keephill' but I'll never live there.*

*PS I've heard from James Clarke. He's well again and back with his unit
in Italy. I've also heard from Natey. He's OK but his sister's husband was
killed near Caen.*

The stray bullets which had hit Field Marshal Rommel near Caen did not
kill him and for a few months kept him out of the danger of the front line.
They also prevented him taking an active part in the unsuccessful attempt
on Hitler's life on July 20th. He was nevertheless implicated in the conspiracy
and, on October 14th, he was offered the choice of suicide or public trial.
He chose the former.

October had seen two major events in other theatres of war. In the middle of the month Athens was liberated though there was soon inter-factional fighting amongst the Greeks. In the Pacific the Americans had landed an enormous invasion force in the Philippines and three days later engaged in the Battle of Leyte Gulf, perhaps the greatest sea battle in history. Churchill congratulated Roosevelt 'on a brilliant and massive victory'.

At the beginning of November British and Canadian soldiers crossed the Scheldt, freeing the way for mine-sweepers to clear the sea route to Antwerp. By the end of the month supplies were pouring in through the port to replenish the advancing Allied Armies. But on November 5th Churchill reported there had been 'very hard fighting in Belgium and Holland', resulting in forty thousand dead or wounded.

For the next two or three months the battle area in Holland remained more or less stationary, as the British Army fought to secure crossings of the Maas and the Rhine. The 77th were in the thick of the fighting and seemed to be everywhere at once in the battle area shown in Map 2.

November began badly for the Regiment with a gun out of action. A premature detonation had occurred when firing an 80lb shell. The engineers recommended using a longer lanyard but 103 Battery were not at all keen on this solution. Nevertheless the gun was back in action the following day. But the Battery was heavily shelled by 88mm German guns and had to move to an alternative position. During the move a tractor was written off in a head-on collision.

Each man was allocated a pound of coal per day but the Battery Commander complained that he didn't have enough boots and socks for his men. The next day he ordered the issue of compound vitamin tablets – 1 per man per day – and also allowed a rum tot each. The Battery Commanders were worried both about the men's morale and about maintaining hygiene under their present conditions.

On November 4th Lieutenant Bailey was relieved by Harry Duerr.

BLA   *November 6th, 1944*

I've been to Rest Camp again, this time somewhere in Holland, (Helmond) *with – believe it or not – Bill Bailey. Possibly the BC thought we had had the toughest time recently. The whole thing was good fun but restful rather than riotous. We knocked back several whisky rations and we also went to a number of dances – there haven't been any in Holland for the last four years.*

As a dancer I was worse than ever though your expert coaching might have made a little difference. As for the Dutch girls, they're very nice types, like the men, but good looks and sex appeal are practically non-existent. You would have been far and away the most beautiful girl in the room. (This is meant to be a compliment though after re-reading the last paragraph it doesn't look much like one.)

I've done quite a bit of reading: detective novels, philosophy and straight forward novels like 'The Moon and Sixpence' (Somerset Maugham), 'Burma Days' (George Orwell) and 'Unchanging Quest' (Philip Gibbs). But as always I'd rather read your next letter which is awaited as eagerly as ever. I think I am a pretty hopeless case.

PS I hope you like the souvenirs. The stockings were rather hard to get and I trust they are not too dark.

In the United States President Roosevelt was elected for a fourth term of office – an unprecedented event. He was not, however, destined to serve much of it. Meanwhile, in Paris, Churchill and De Gaulle were preparing to honour the soldiers who fell to regain France's liberty. On the anniversary of the First World War armistice, November 11th, they drove together to the Arc de Triomphe and laid a wreath on the Tomb of the Unknown Soldier.

Ten days later P.G.Wodehouse, the English humorist and creator of Jeeves and Bertie Wooster, was imprisoned in Paris for broadcasting for the Germans to the United States. He was interned when the Germans overran Le Touquet in 1941. His broadcasts were recorded at the time with a view to prosecution 'for lending his services to the German propaganda machine' (Anthony Eden to the House of Commons, 7th July 1941).

The day after the wreath laying ceremony in Paris, Germany's only surviving battleship, the Tirpitz, was at last sunk. Still lying in a Norwegian fjord, she capsized after being attacked by more than thirty bombers from Scotland.

In India, Kohima and Imphala were once more in British hands and the River Chindwin, key to any advance south towards Singapore, had been crossed in several places. But in Holland, where the population was on the edge of starvation, little progress was made.

Recces by the Regiment were made of the area south-east of Asten and once more Major Thomas engaged a third church tower in Bergen. After several direct hits the sixty-sixth round finally brought it down. He promptly ordered another rum issue and the distribution of seven wireless sets, of which three went to 103 Battery, for entertainment.

On 10th November the Battery were firing all day at thirty minute intervals but at 3pm a Red Cross flag was raised. All firing ceased, whilst wounded were evacuated on both sides, till it was taken down at ten past five. The next day was spent in 'silent role' but an unfortunate accident occurred to one of 77ths officers. AGRA (Army Group Royal Artillery) had recently announced there would be forty-eight hour leaves in Brussels for three officers and thirty-eight ORs every fortnight.

One of the first officers to be granted leave under this scheme was Captain Harrop, who was Troop Commander of 'D' Troop in 104 Battery. He was on his way to Brussels when he was involved in an accident with an American convoy on a narrow road. Roger Harrop was sitting in the front passenger seat of a right-hand drive vehicle driving on the right-hand side of the road (the Army made no concessions to the strange habit of Continentals of driving on the right). With a wet, muddy road and ditches either side the vehicles could not avoid hitting each other although they were only travelling at a few miles per hour. Captain Harrop's leg was badly broken and he was evacuated to a field hospital and then home to England. He never rejoined the Regiment and later was sent out to SEAC.

On the 15th November 103 Battery were ordered to knock out Afferden Church Tower. The Regiment was firing every day from 13th to 19th of November. Stanley probably wrote this next letter in a quiet interval.

BLA   *November 15th, 1944*

I'm replying to your letter on some respectable Dutch notepaper which , like most things Dutch, is clean, plain and unadorned.

Am I really a mystery man to you? Basically I haven't altered though some of my opinions have. I'm rather more worldly and I am more interested in the particular now than in generalisations. There is a good deal less of the 'after you, Claude' attitude about me. Well, the Army's done that.

Also I've learnt to be rather more ingratiating towards outsiders. That sort of thing is absolutely indispensable in the Army, especially when one is commissioned, and it is largely true of other walks of life. Even a certain amount of insincerity is necessary. I may have been too reticent formerly but I was also too honest.

Perhaps the Army has made me cynical but what I said about German prisoners was absolutely true though my remarks seem to have annoyed you. This is a subject on which my views – and the views of all but a tiny majority in all countries – have changed. What would your reaction be if you came face to face with an SS man? You don't know. I didn't till it happened to me, but I felt no love or charity. Nor when I saw some of them getting into a slit trench when I was up at the OP and had guns at my disposal.

You ascribe my attitude to the fact that Germans have been killing and maiming my men and my friends but you are entirely wrong. Some weeks ago, on October 12th at Oploo, we took a terrible pasting which resulted in one of my troop's guns being hit, one man being killed outright and a number of others wounded. Two of those men died later that day and another two lost limbs. It wasn't exactly pleasant in that gun pit, particularly as shells continued to fall close by all the time. But that didn't make me hate them. It was just war.

My attitude isn't governed by sentiment but by the hard and inescapable fact that after all the horrors and atrocities and massacres, after the denial of all humane values, after the unprovoked attack on Russia, the majority of Germans are still prepared to defend Hitlerism with all their might.

I used to think that apart from a minority of fanatics the German people were rather lukewarm about Nazism, But there is almost no real anti-Nazi feeling amongst German POWs and even those who dislike the Party still venerate Hitler. It would be ridiculous to assume that the Army is not representative of the people – though admittedly it contains a higher proportion of younger men. The demand for 'unconditional surrender' has probably helped to bolster them up; but the plain fact is that the vast majority fight willingly and for the Führer.

This is no doubt unpalatable to us but it is, unfortunately, an absolutely indisputable fact. You may say, what of the German Underground, who cannot express themselves inside Germany because of the Gestapo? The number of prisoners both here and in Russia who have any constructive thoughts whatsoever is infinitesimal, and a large proportion of those are reactionary. All this is much less true of the Austrians.

What then am I to think? Obviously that the mass of the German people strongly approves both of the war and of the Nazi regime. And if they have been duped the injections were voluntary.

All these conclusions I resisted for ages because I had a deep faith in human nature. But I should be half-witted if, granted these facts – and they are hard facts – I were to think that the majority of Germans were really decent, ordinary people. As individuals they may be hospitable, jovial, sentimental, anything you like; but as social beings they are a menace. It will take decades to extirpate this horror which has entrenched itself in their minds.

This may sound like Vansittartism – but I ignore the 'historical guilt' arguments – and I don't want to impoverish Germany or slice her up into little pieces. But somehow after reading my case I don't think you can imagine that my views are based on the fact that my feet are cold and that I have to duck shells rather often. My heart does not rule my head.

In fact at the moment I am sitting in a civvy cottage with a peat fire going and a paraffin lamp burning. We're incredibly well off considering we are still in action though it's freezing tonight. I'm probably better off than you are in Cambridge – I've certainly been a damn sight more uncomfortable in my college rooms – though I'd be better off still if you were here. Or would I?

In England the severe frost was followed by a terrible and continuous gale which lasted twenty-four hours. The bad weather seriously hampered the Allied offensive which had just begun along a four hundred mile front. It was becoming increasingly obvious that the war was not going to end in 1944.

CHAPTER 16

Christmas on the River Maas

'Whenever there's a casualty the cry seems to be ''Send for Dog Easy''
Letter to Sylvia, Autumn 1944

ambridge was bitterly cold. I can remember trying to warm my
hands over the butt of a cigarette. The new digs I had moved to
had little heating – an open fire with about three lumps of coal
per day in my sitting room and no heat at all in my bedroom. There
was one cold tap in the basement kitchen/family-living room and the toilet,
originally part of a corridor, had a broken window stuffed with torn up
newspapers.

The house was tall and narrow with two rooms per floor. The old sash
windows rattled and the lino struck cold to bare feet on frosty winter
mornings. But, unlike the policeman's modern semi-detached house where
I had spent my Freshman's year, my new digs were very central, located in
a street just behind the Guildhall and opposite the Rutherford Laboratories.
The site is now a car park.

The only other student there lived on the floor above me. Our landlady,
a Mrs Niedergedasse, did all she could to make us comfortable with
enormous old-fashioned eiderdowns and frequent cups of hot cocoa. Mr
Niedergedasse was a retired glass-blower and had made the glass
instruments for Rutherford's experiments in atomic physics. I think we paid
37/6 per week each for bed and breakfast and I was still only receiving £3
per week to live on.

My fellow student, Irene, was the elder daughter of the founder of Tesco's
and was certainly not used to living in such primitive conditions. But there
were compensations – food parcels which we shared and the books and
clothes which we borrowed from each other. She was a charming and
intelligent girl to have as a co-lodger and I do not remember her ever
complaining about the contrast between home and college life.

Odd shortages continued to make civilian life difficult. The chemists'
shelves began to look bare as Dettol became unobtainable, toothbrushes
vanished, quinine was reserved for the Forces, saccharine disappeared. On
the positive side we were told that everyone would get four pounds of
oranges and one egg between mid-November and Christmas.

In Holland food shortages continued and it was decided that to try to clear
the entire country of Germans could only result in an unacceptable loss of
civilian life. Further flooding was halted and action concentrated in the south
of the country.

The Regiment continued to have more than its fair share of bad luck. On
15th November a booby trap was discovered by 103 Battery which put

everyone on edge. On the 18th, at 6.40am, there was another premature explosion in one of the Battery's guns. The gun was completely destroyed and there were two serious casualties – Sergeant Manser, who had severe body wounds and a broken arm and Gunner Bradwell, who lost a leg.

But even the horrors of war could not prevent our soldiers from expressing concern over animals. On the 22nd, 104 Battery reported that livestock at the OP they were using were not being properly fed or cared for as the owners had been evacuated. Arrangements were swiftly made for neighbouring farmers to look after the beasts.

BLA   *November 25th, 1944*

> *You'll have plenty to think about when you sit down to answer my last letter. But I wasn't going to let the intellectual challenge of your last letter pass unanswered.*
>
> *At the moment I am sitting in a chair in a Command Post, complete with a stove and an electric light. But the atmosphere in here is so thick you can hardly see across the room. I'm sleeping on a spring mattress which gives a remarkably high bounce but here there are no suitable collaborators. Never mind, my 48-hour leave will be coming up in a month or two.*
>
> *I was hoping to go to with Bill Bailey when the time comes but he has just had the most unfortunate accident. Yesterday he was shot in the groin by another officer. He was operated on today but he'll probably have to spend a few weeks in England to recuperate. Actually I feel almost as sorry for George Amman who shot him. The CO takes a pretty serious view of it.*
>
> *I'll give you a run down on the chaps you know from Southwell. Charles Harrisson is Battery Captain (second-in-command), Bill Gill is CPO (the junior subaltern's job in the Battery and actually a job which should carry three pips), I am now GPO of 'A' Troop with Arthur Edwards as my troop leader. Bill Bailey is GPO of 'B' Troop, with George Amman as his troop leader.*
>
> *My job is as varied and interesting as anything can be in the Army but it's also exacting and responsible. I don't have to get covered in mud and soaked to the skin like the Gunners when they get down to the job. But morale is amazingly high. On that shocking day I wrote about last time the chaps never faltered for a moment. They literally stuck to their guns and carried on firing to the last round.*
>
> *The Army may have withered my mental faculties but it has taught me more about human nature than ten years of civvy life could have done.*
>
> *The other evening I got rather browned off reading some of the tripe and mushy sentimentality that the men were writing on their Christmas cards so I amused myself by writing some light, satirical verse. My genius owes something to Rabelais, but a simpler, more genteel and semi-emasculated Rabelais. Don't, however, ask for a specimen as it's slightly vulgar and all implicated with GPOAs and DAQMGs so you wouldn't understand it.*
>
> *While on this topic I have just put up my first pin-up in the Command*

STANLEY'S SISTER, SYLVIA, HIGH WYCOMBE, 1944.

Post. She is semi-nude (at least I think so but there's a wall in the way) and the fellows here think I have a penchant for semi-nudes. But though I blush to mention it and wouldn't tell anybody the real reason is that she reminds me of you.

PS I wrote to Sylvia recently – hope you are keeping in touch with her.

Sylvia still has that letter of which the following is a condensed version:

'My dear Sylvia, I'm glad you are still functioning in the canteens and dance-halls of High Wycombe. I don't know how you view the prospect of going back to Westcliff. I can't say I should be wildly excited but I'd certainly be delighted to say goodbye to Wycombe, even though Borshams is a rather fine house.

My own plans are very hazy. The recent hold-up on some sectors may be disappointing but it's too early to say whether this affair is going to last through the whole winter. By the time you get this letter somebody over the other side will have taken a very severe pounding – you should have seen some of the towns we passed through with the leading troops of the Division. But, even provided I get through this lot OK and get demobbed (God knows when that would be), I shan't have any job to go to.

On the other hand there's no lack of jobs for me here. At the moment I'm doing a slightly different one again. Whenever there's a casualty the cry seems to be ''Send for Dog Easy''. I've done more jobs in this campaign than any other officer in the Regiment. In this case I expect to resume my old job when the person concerned recovers.

You've just about had this letter, I'm afraid. The top of my Brylcreem bottle has unscrewed in my greatcoat pocket – so I'd better clear up the mess. Write again soon.

The details of Bill Bailey's accident were as follows: 103 Battery had established a command post in a small farm-house. They were then warned that a local farmer, a fanatical Nazi, was roaming around with a gun. Everyone was a bit jittery and the guards were doubled. Returning to the farm-house in the early hours of the following morning after visiting the Battery Command Post, Bill Bailey opened the door and went in. The room was dark and shuttered. Suddenly he heard a movement behind him and swung round raising his .38 pistol but, before he could fire, the figure silhouetted in the doorway shot him. It was Bill's Troop Leader and friend, George Amman.

There was tragedy at home for many families. As Stanley was writing this letter a Woolworth Store in London was hit by a V2. It was lunch-time. A thirteen-year old girl described the scene:

'Bits of people were falling out of the sky: a horse's head lay in the gutter: a little baby's hand, still in its woollen sleeve lay in a twisted pram: underneath the piles of rubble and bricks people were screaming.'

One hundred and sixty people were killed and a further two hundred were seriously wounded. The V1s and the V2s had taken a heavy toll in other ways. Out of thirteen million houses in the UK four and a half million were destroyed or damaged by enemy action.

Two days later, in Burton-on-Trent another dreadful incident occurred when an RAF underground arsenal of bombs exploded. They were stored in a gypsum mine ninety feet below the surface. The noise could be heard sixty miles away and sixty-eight people, farmers and factory workers, were killed.

In Antwerp, now open to Allied shipping, V2s were causing widespread devastation. In one incident twenty-nine Allied servicemen were killed, together with over a hundred civilians, when their convoy was passing a cross-roads as the rocket fell.

Shortly afterwards the 77th Medium Regiment moved again to a new area, near Sevenum, as the enemy pulled out and withdrew towards the River Maas. They remained in action until 30th November thus completing a whole month on operational duty.

From the beginning of December the Regiment, now at Sevenum, were on operational duty though not much happened. This enabled 103 Battery to take full advantage of their quarters. They were the fortunate occupiers of a brewery. On the 1st and the 2nd they were in 'silent' role but, early on the morning of the 3rd, their guns opened up on Blerick, just west of the Maas from Venlo. Soon Blerick was in British hands. Over the next week the Battery moved quietly forward, visibility preventing any effective gun-fire from either side. They trickled through Baarlo and Kessel, villages that were now clear of the enemy.

They suffered the loss of another officer, Captain Sweetman, who was evacuated on 13th December with suspected diphtheria. Lieutenant Bailey, who had been evacuated from the Advanced Dressing Station on the 25th November to the Casualty Clearing Station, was now in Queen Elizabeth

Hospital, Birmingham.

Although it seemed that stalemate had been reached in Holland, to the south the Americans had succeeded in taking Metz after a bitter two-month battle for this ancient Alsace-Lorraine city. In Italy both sides were bogged down and in the Far East the Japanese Kamikaze pilots were beginning to take a serious toll of American warships.

But at home December began with a positive sign that victory for the Allies, though a little delayed, was inevitable. On December 3rd, in a broadcast to thank them for their services, the King told the Home Guard that they could now 'stand down', having worked together voluntarily for four years in a great cause.

There was no let up in Germany from the RAF bombing attacks. Although most raids now concentrated on fuel targets on December 4th another firestorm was started by the RAF in the city of Heilbronn. Over seven thousand German civilians were killed. When criticised on both practical and moral grounds in Parliament Sir Arthur Harris, chief of RAF Bomber Command, replied, 'I do not regard the whole of the remaining cities of Germany as worth the bones of one British grenadier.'

BLA   *December 14th, 1944*

Thanks so much for your most interesting letter — enough for two ordinary ones.

I was really astonished to hear that you voluntarily attend Winfield's lectures, though I am sure they are most interesting. I can assure you that he really is almost stone deaf; if he notices you whispering it is probably because he was already giving you an appraising glance.

I consider Professor Winfield a most charming and gifted man and one of the most eminent legal historians and interesting exponents now living. He is entirely absorbed in his work. He told me one day "I have worked at law for 40 years and I've loved every minute of it".

So Hughes Parry thinks Winfield is the most brilliant lecturer in the faculty. Have you been to a lecture by Glanville Williams on Jurisprudence or Constitutional Law? He is about 35 years younger than Winfield but his analytical capabilities are greatly superior. Incidentally as far as I know Hughes Parry and Glanville Williams marked my papers when I was awarded the George Long prize. Perhaps that's why I am well disposed towards Welshmen.

I'd like you to send me your complete law syllabus so that I can suggest the most worth-while reading to you. I have no real inclination to pick up Cheshire's Property Law or the Bills of Exchange Act now but once I had got stuck into them I found them quite absorbing. Reading history, though, is almost effortless by comparison.

As I see it the Law is a heterogeneous mass of statutes, decided cases, rules orders and regulations, lacking any shape whatsoever and conditioned only by the peculiar situations which gave rise to them. It's true that there are certain principles which underlie the administration of justice in England, as you'll see in Jenk's 'Book of English Law' but these generalities are over-stressed by the liberal idealists and the conservative pundits. The garden is less lovely than that.

I am sorry you didn't say anything more about the Germans because I am not quite sure that everything I said was right. But I think it was a fair comment on the men under the age of thirty.

It's beginning to freeze now. A dry cold spell is infinitely better than shocking mud with rain every day. It's been bloody awful out here but we're not in the Infantry, thank goodness. They're the boys who get the really rough time. Of course there are hundreds of thousands of troops here, at base areas and on lines of communication, who've never seen a German shell bursting. Conditions vary so much for different arms of the service.

This is developing into a James Agate book. But I must just say that I was intrigued by your apparent preference for my more satanic characteristics. I agree I am not the young Lord Fauntleroy which so many misguided people think me to be but I don't think I shall ever become an absolute swine. I admit the poetry I have written shows my predilection for a rather coarse type of humour, smeared with a thin veneer of literacy which is admired by the illiterate. But since you are both literate and a normally sensitive girl I haven't the slightest intention of inflicting the poems on you.

I'd give anything to be with you right now but I can't get home by the quickest route as there aren't mines around here that I can step on conveniently.

In Greece, which had only recently escaped the yoke of the Axis, civil war threatened as violent clashes occurred between the different partisan groups and the provisional government of George Papandreou, the Social Democratic premier installed by the Allies. British forces tried to separate the warring factions and keep the peace but were themselves besieged. Churchill himself flew to Greece, at great personal risk, just before Christmas to try and sort things out.

The Germans were still busy trying out new weapons. On 17th December the first jet-propelled aircraft (German) flew over RHQ at ground level, at a speed of over 400 mph, though it was not used as a bomber until Christmas Eve, 1944. The next day RHQ came under heavy fire and one of 'A' Troop's guns was damaged but there were no casualties.

The Regiment received recognition for its part in the campaign to date in the form of the award of two Military Crosses – to Captain Charles Harrisson and Lieutenant Bill Bailey, both 103 Battery – and of the Military Medal to Lance Bombardier Galbraith, a regimental medical orderly. The citations each refer to the bravery of the men on October 12th, 1944 when one of the four guns ('c' sub gun), in 'A' Troop, received a direct hit.

Forty miles to the south of Stanley's Regiment the Germans launched a last desperate counter-attack, which became known as the Battle of the Bulge aimed at pushing the Allied line back to Antwerp and the River Schelte. To cause confusion they infiltrated thirty-three English speaking commandos behind the American lines. As this became known even American Generals were liable to be stopped and challenged by suspicious GIs though most of the infiltrators were caught within twenty-four hours. General Bradley was asked to name Betty Grable's latest husband and failed to do so. However, his challenger was so pleased at having caught him out that he let him pass.

In ten days, more than nineteen thousand American troops were killed for the loss of forty thousand Germans. Dreadful massacres of prisoners took place on both sides. The Allied air forces were unable to help the ground forces because of dense, low-lying fog which covered most of Europe. The Germans succeeded in penetrating over thirty miles into Belgium and Luxembourg before they were halted but as the fog cleared on 23rd December the Allied counter-attack began. There were also heavy losses in Antwerp where nearly six hundred people were killed when a V2 struck a cinema. About half of them were servicemen.

Because of the enemy breakthrough in the American sector, defences were re-organised around the Regiment's area on 22nd December. There were warnings of heavy frost on the night of the 23rd but the expected crossing of the River Maas on Christmas Eve by the Germans on the eastern bank did not take place. Civilians reported that the enemy spent the night in a state of drunken orgy. His only fear, apparently, was that the Regiment might attack!

At home Christmas was being celebrated in traditional manner. On 17th December a carol concert was organised in the Albert Hall, conducted by Sir Malcolm Sargent. The choir numbered four hundred and the audience some five thousand. Some traditional things, though, were nonexistent, like crackers, oranges and currants, and Christmas cards were a wicked price. But people were determined to enjoy the first Christmas since war had begun that presaged victory.

I went to a wonderful party on 21st December. It was held at the Pincus' and they had invited all John's Air Force friends that could get leave, plus many of Margaret's fellow students from Art College and Bobby's school chums. It was the day of John's twenty-first birthday and, although we had had no news of him since he was reported missing in September, it was as if he was there in spirit. For me the evening was made all the more poignant as we danced to the radio music of Glen Miller's band in Paris. Major Glen Miller's plane had been reported missing a few days earlier on his flight to the French capital.

On Christmas Eve the Germans launched a final attempt to cow London's population with a heavy V1 attack. But in the States a more deadly weapon was another step nearer to becoming operational. On Christmas Day the first irradiated uranium slugs were produced and the first atomic bomb was less than six months away from completion.

The Germans still had one more secret weapon up their sleeves which was to cause the Allies great anxiety in 1945. It was the 'schnorkel', a revolutionary breathing device which enabled the improved U-boats, then under manufacture in Kiel, Hamburg and Danzig, to stay under the surface for long periods.

On New Year's Day, 1945, the cold spell ended, lemons appeared in the shops and the last rusty wire guarding some of Britain's beaches was removed by soldiers.

BLA   *January 2nd 1945*

Now for a crawling apology. I've committed the horrible offence of forgetting your birthday. The excitement of Christmas must have been too much for me. Perhaps Freud would be able to prove that I had really wanted to because I couldn't bear to think about you reaching the mature age of nineteen.

I saw the New Year in with whisky and champagne. Auld Lang Syne was ten minutes late because we broke two cork-screws trying to get the cork out of the champagne bottle. It was the first time I had tasted it since 1939. Perhaps I'll get some more when I get my forty-eight hours leave in Brussels which is coming up on 9th January. As for my seven day leave in England, I should know more in a few weeks time as the rosters are being prepared now. I wish I could hire a suit of armour till then.

James Clarke is hoping for some leave soon, too. He is still functioning in Italy according to the letter I had from Molly. I also had another letter from Marjorie, who is working very hard but having a fine time in Alexandria.

I've hardly mentioned politics recently but the shocking affair in Greece has shaken me considerably. I don't believe the last word has been said in Belgium, either. The Central and Eastern European countries are, I think, too remote for anyone to have much say except Russia. There may be a good deal of trouble in Albania and possibly also in Spain and Austria. But I'm not very often in the picture about political possibilities these days.

When I get to England I shall certainly try and see my academic friends in Cambridge to get some advice about the remote future. I must know which way the wind is blowing but of course it may always blow me out to SEAC.

The champagne must have still been affecting him when he wrote this letter because he did not forget my birthday. In fact he sent me a Christmas card with a birthday card slipped inside. He also sent me a carved ivory paper-knife which I used until it broke quite recently.

Waiting for the final assault

'I lick my lips feverishly when I see the old sign saying Achtung Minen'
February 24th, 1945

On 9th January Stanley went on leave to Brussels and the same day the Regiment moved to new positions about ten miles south of Maasbree. The site was waterlogged and the tracks gave way under the weight of the guns. When the mud turned to ice and snow these problems were replaced by others. Fires had to be lit under the recoil systems of the guns to keep them ready for action at all times. Most of their artillery battles were aimed at pushing the enemy artillery further and further back whilst remaining stationary themselves.

One of the gun troops' more enjoyable roles was being chosen to go out with a roving gun (sometimes called a pistol gun) to harass the enemy by shooting up specific targets. As soon as they were spotted they moved on, sometimes leaving a dummy gun behind to confuse the enemy as to their whereabouts.

BLA   ***January 10th, 1945***

> *I am writing this in a luxurious hotel in Brussels, having spent about thirty of my forty-eight hours leave. It's a very intriguing city and one had to maintain a terrific tempo to do half of what one wants. There are plenty of things which are just unobtainable in Holland.*
>
> *I've just had my first real bath since 'D-day and you can't imagine how clean I feel. I'd like to come here with you some day. It is certainly the place for a 'good time'; there seems to be an abundance of alcohol and anything else you need. Too much of this flashy brilliance could be a bad thing, though.*
>
> *PS I'm hoping to be home in the latter part of February.*

By the time Stanley returned from Brussels the amenities around 77th's position had improved a little but the battle had stagnated. He was, he realised, unlikely to see the war end before his twenty-third birthday.

Like his predictions about the end of the war and demobilisation, Stanley's proposed home leave dates gradually became more remote, though he did manage to get back to England once before V-E day. And we did visit Brussels together – but not till the Bruxelles Exhibition in the summer of 1958. We went by boat-train, a service which had not run for five years until

January 15th, 1945, when the London to Paris service was re-introduced. Transport generally was getting easier in England and petrol could now be bought at any garage.

Newspapers were still delivered in some areas but most people had to collect them each day. They made grim reading on January 16th, 1945. The numbers of service people killed so far in the War were announced: approximately 138,000 Americans, 200,000 British, 28,000 Canadian, 18,000 Australians, 17,000 Indians, 9,000 New Zealanders and 6,000 South Africans, a total approaching half a million of Allied dead. But it was reckoned that the use of the Mulberry Harbours in Normandy had saved between 100,000 and 150,000 British and American casualties by facilitating the swift unloading of troops and supplies.

A couple of days later it was reported that Hitler had returned to Berlin, in order, one of his staff is claimed to have said, 'that he could take the street-car from the Eastern to the Western Front!' Both Warsaw and Budapest had been freed.

The Hague, Copenhagen, Oslo and Prague were still in enemy hands.

BLA   ***January 19th, 1945***

The hideous mauve hue of this notepaper indicates some un-English and slightly indecent origin; yes, it does come from Brussels.

Since my leave I've received the familiar letter in green ink. Sorry about the birthday-card confusion. I told you the Army had numbed my wits.

You're assuming you'll be in Cambridge during my leave, which is not at all certain. I feel pretty sure it will be the latter part of February or early March. Do you realise I haven't seen you since early April '44? The most pleasurable experience I can possibly imagine is to be with you (preferably alone). I'm quite sure my personal efficiency would jump about 100% if I could have you on my knee while I was controlling a target or taking an ammunition return.

In the Far East the Burma Road had been re-opened. And in East Prussia the road to Berlin was cut as the Red Army reached the coast, trapping half a million Germans.

BLA   ***January 25th, 1945***

I had a bad cold two days ago but I've cured it in the Spartan way by exposure to the elements. I don't think the thermometers we use in England would be much good just now – they aren't usually graded below 0 degrees Fahrenheit.

I'm on a job tonight and under conditions which require a certain amount of stimulation. I've got plenty of whisky, rum and tea and an assistant who's a member of a temperance society. With alternate swigs at the flask and dissertations on the evils of alcoholism, time passes quickly enough. Yes: it's a very queer life.

The leave allocation has been altered again. I shan't be coming home in February but I'm fairly certain it will be some time in March. I feel very strongly about the whole business of leave and I imagine that the matter will be brought up in Parliament.

The news from the Eastern Front is first-class, isn't it? I cannot believe the Germans will be able to last much longer but at the same time I'm not expecting the final crack-up for some time.

That night there was a severe frost warning – 0°F but the following day the 77th's guns were in action, firing at Belfield water tower and a suspected enemy OP in Belfield church spire. They remained standing though badly damaged. The Regiment then received orders to move to Oostrum in the Venraij area.

At home the cold was intense and fuel short. Soldiers in East London who were home on leave pushed their old coster-mongers' barrows around full of logs for sale. Two eggs and a packet of mixed fruit from Australia was swopped for a pile of logs by one desperate woman. People took empty sacks to the coal yards at the railway sidings and trundled them home full in old prams. But somehow everyone managed by helping each other out, sharing the evening fire with neighbours, wearing unlikely collections of layers of clothing and looking after the elderly who lived alone. No such neighbourly comfort was available for the millions freezing in death camps.

Dreadful scenes were greeting the Russian forces as they pushed further into Nazi Germany. On 27th January, 1945 they entered Auschwitz. The guards had gone, after a final murderous bout of killing, leaving behind over six hundred corpses and more than seven thousand skeletal survivors. The pattern of deliberate death, though on a smaller scale, was echoed in the Japanese POW and internee camps that were gradually being freed by the advancing Americans.

By the end of January the Russians were only fifty miles from Berlin.

BLA   *January 31st, 1945*

I haven't got much to write about but I want to release the pressure valve or else I'll be talking to myself before long. I am still functioning, sometimes in decreasing circles, and managing to find enough amusement in a small way to make things bearable.

The most pleasant thing I could talk about is the Russian offensive which has been wonderfully successful. But there's a very wide river still to be crossed and I don't think we are facing the last fight yet.

The weather is pretty bad but we've been supplied with enough kit to keep us warm and dry under most conditions. The men have got things like cards, darts, draughts and magazines and a wireless set to relieve the monotony.

All the same it's difficult not to feel browned off now and again and little difficulties become magnified. My blood pressure is mounting steadily and my outbursts of frantic rage are more frequent. Yes; I'm definitely one of the objectionable military types these days. 1942 seems a long way off to a disillusioned and bitter man.

Even my mother wrote that she is feeling old but I wrote and told her that when I come on leave people will think I am her brother. In any awkward situation I could easily pass as your uncle.

Actually the occasion for this outburst is 1) damp socks and 2) reduced leave allocation. I'm afraid the official dope about leave ending in March with all the BLA fixed up is absolute tripe. Present indications are that the roster will take twice as long to complete.

I gather your family are living in Brighton now though I take it they will return to London once the debris stops falling. My mother has offered to have you down at Wycombe for a few days during my leave. I really am delighted that you have managed to get her to come round. Nothing upset me more than the long period when she disapproved of our relationship – not that it made any difference, but I'd rather things were OK between you for obvious reasons.

I heard from James Clarke the other day. He's got a bar to his MC and he's now OC of a well-known divisional battle school in Italy. He's done incredibly well. I also had a letter from Bill Bailey who is on sick leave in Ireland. He's much better but he tells me he has a horror of entering a dark room.

James' citation for the Bar to his Military Cross reads;

ITALY, Faenza   27th November, 1944

'On the evening of October 7th, Major Clarke, MC, and his 'D' Company were given the task of capturing Point 382 on the Condranco Ridge. This position was held by a Company of Germans sixty strong. Major Clarke led the assault at dusk and after two hours succeeded in taking the church and other buildings at the bottom of Point 382.

In the meantime the Company was too close to the objective for further artillery support, surprise had been lost and the enemy was putting up a fierce fight. However, the attack was renewed and for several hours a bomb and small arms fight continued around the foot of the hill and in the houses beside it. Owing to a very steep slope and the mud, 'D' Company were unable to get a foothold and the Germans were able to roll a steady stream of grenades down.

'D' Company finally consolidated around the church with the enemy in position 200 yards ahead. The whole of the next day Major Clarke directed artillery, mortar and machine gun fire on Point 382, in spite of being practically on top of the place himself and getting all the 'shorts'. When day came, of course, his Company were completely pinned down.

Major Clarke attacked again at dusk and the assault was successful. Two prisoners were taken and twenty three dead were found, the remainder of the garrison having fled. 'D' Company's success in capturing this important feature was entirely due to Major Clarke's skilful planning and leadership which has been characteristic of his conduct in all the previous operations he has taken part in. During this action he was suffering throughout from acute fever.'

signed H. R. Alexander, Field Marshal

In Germany, on February 4th, the Americans breached the outer defences of the Siegfried Line and on the 8th the Canadians pushed south from Nijmegen to clear the area between the Maas and the Rhine. Cracks were beginning to appear in Hitler's impregnable German Front.

The 77th Regiment were now in support of 6 Airborne Division, who daringly crossed the Maas at night to capture German prisoners or to set booby traps. On 11th February shells were fired across the river by 103 Battery to discourage some Germans who were yelling abuse in broken English about the previous night's raid. One Other Rank was wounded that day.

As the war progressed inexorably towards the final battle both the Americans and the British were getting more worried about the role Russia would play in post-war Europe. The Yalta Conference held that month extracted promises from Stalin, which later proved worthless, that Poland would have free elections. The Western Allies promised in return to step up the bombing of German cities to prevent German troops being transferred to the Eastern Front.

On February 13th the British sent eight hundred bombers in two waves to destroy Dresden's marshalling yards. This was followed by a raid by American bombers. Over six hundred and fifty thousand fire bombs were dropped on the city which was to burn for seven days.

In Peenemunde, Allied artillery fire could now be heard and on 17th July the rocket scientists pulled out of their base there. But rockets continued to fall on London. On the other side of the world the Americans were just liberating the first capital held by the Japanese – Manila, in the Philippines – as Stanley wrote his next letter.

BLA   **February 17th, 1945**

At last we're on the offensive once more, so things look a bit brighter. The quicker things move the better I like it. And I've just had a stroke of luck. I've been put in for a course on mines in Belgium. Admittedly it's about the world's most dangerous course but it is a course and it's in Belgium. You can't have everything.

As Stanley was preparing to go on the mines course the 77th Regiment were sending out recce parties towards Oostrum and Oorloo in the Venraij area.

Two important events took place on February 19th. The Americans landed on Iwo Jima and the bloody battle for this tiny, eight-mile long, island was to last for six weeks. And in Germany, behind Hitler's back, Himmler talked to Count Bernadotte, the Swedish Red Cross Official, about possible peace negotiations.

On 23rd February Turkey declared war on Germany but when Egypt did the same the following day their premier was assassinated.

RE Training School, BLA   February 24th, 1945

You will see I have changed two things, my notepaper and my address. I hope the former meets with your approval, the latter I don't approve much of myself but it's only for the duration of this mines course. I'm once more in the lap of luxury but I still lick my lips feverishly when I see the old sign 'Achtung Minen' surmounted with a skull and crossbones.

The Army is pampering me for some reason. The Battery sent me here with my own driver and batman. Moreover I'm staying in Brussels overnight both coming and going. I arrived a day early and tonight saw 'Hold Back the Dawn' with Charles Boyer, Boyer murmuring with restrained tenderness and Paulette Goddard as the bad girl. I had a balcony seat, classified 'club' and it only cost me 10d.

I'm glad you like the scent I sent you though I wish it had been called something other than Obsession. I'm just about obsessed at the moment with the thought that inside six weeks I shall be seeing you again. This knock-about life with the many casual acquaintances it brings has only emphasised what you mean to me.

Is Peter on leave at the moment? If so he's extremely lucky for only about 40% of our 'D' + 9 boys have drawn lucky numbers in the Jan-Feb allocations and nobody who arrived here later than July 1st will go home on leave much earlier than that date in 1945.

No Allied soldier had yet crossed the Rhine although on the Eastern Front the River Oder had been breached in several places. Nevertheless the German Eastern Front still held the Russians from their prize of Berlin. The night Stanley wrote his letter about leave the prospect was brought slightly nearer by the worst raid Berlin had yet suffered. More than half a million incendiaries fell on the city.

Whilst he had been on his Mines course the Regiment had moved up to the Ventraij area and then sent out several recce parties to find a suitable rest place near Sevenum where they could refit and re-calibrate their guns prior to the battles for the crossing of the Rhine. On 27th February they were firing at Kevelaer with temporary OPs at Wansumm and Geijsteren. The weather had improved and it was now showers/fair/rain rather than the frost/ice/fog they had suffered during their long sojourn in Holland.

BLA   *March 4th, 1945*

I'm back with the boys again, this time in a dug-out and as usual it's raining. I had a very pleasant week – worth the fear and you never know when that knowledge might come in handy – though we had to work very hard. A most attractive country, is Belgium – entirely different from Holland, except in the border regions. Some of the seaside resorts are unhealthy these days because of the innumerable mines and booby traps left behind by the Germans, and they're all disfigured by the fortifications of the Atlantic Wall.

Now I know just about enough to make myself really dangerous. The BC, of course, is already talking about mines classes within the Battery. The best policy in the Army is undoubtedly to know as little as possible. Did I tell you that the BC has just been awarded the MC? I'm still waiting to see the citation and so are all the gunners.

Sorry I didn't mention your puppy. You seem almost as possessive as if you had acquired a baby. I suppose he attends lectures and Union meetings. If he is the right breed I could possible train him to detect mines.

The puppy had been given to me by John's parents. He was a delightful little black retriever. I named him Jake after John's Spitfire 'J for Jake', and when he was very small I did sometimes smuggle him into lectures.

On 5th March the Regiment moved into comfortable quarters in Sevenum where the mornings were spent in maintenance and the afternoons in sport. They were even able to visit Brussels in the evenings occasionally. The weather was excellent and the Regiment enjoyed its first period out of action since the winter battles had begun.

As the Regiment was not under such pressure from the enemy the CO decided it was time the men knew a little more about mines. The enemy were scattering 'schuh' mines behind them as they retreated and it was part of Stanley's job to deal with these. He welcomed the chance to impart his recently acquired knowledge and recruit some more volunteers to help clear the gun sites.

The enemy had been pushed back to the east of the Rhine along most of its length and only the German bridgehead at Wesel remained to be taken in their area. The fact that we had not yet officially crossed the Rhine did not deter Churchill. On 5th March he visited the Front and briefly set foot the other side. He was the first British statesman since Chamberlain to set foot in Germany.

Encouraged by his visit people in England began to turn their minds to peace. MPs found that housing was the matter of greatest concern to the overwhelming majority of their constituents. Shortages of all sorts, of course , continued to feature in their lists – lack of fuel, lack of domestic help, lack of accommodation – and queues formed for fish, fats and fowls.

BLA   **March 7th, 1945**

It won't be too comfy when the main assault does go in but at the moment we are pretty well off. I understand Germany is decorated mainly with white flags and booby traps. As Mines Officer I am not particulary enthusiastic about the latter.

I can't imagine organised resistance will last more than another six months but my father is the world's greatest optimist. Every time there is an air-aid over Germany he proclaims the great crack-up is imminent.

PS My love to the little dog. Is he a lady or gentleman – or can't you tell the difference?

On 7th March Remagen, just south of Bonn, was reached by the Americans and on 9th they entered Bonn. By 10th March the Allies were across the Rhine for a distance thirty miles south of Remagen most of the way north to Nijmegen.

At home, on March 8th, a V2 fell on Smithfield killing over one hundred people.

BLA   **March 10th, 1945**

I have been most terribly busy the last week or so chasing over North West Europe on a variety of minor missions.

Germany is in a pretty bad state. Material damage is at least as bad as in Holland and we see the same streams of refugees, most of them carrying their belongings in hand-carts, that we saw in Normandy, but without feeling the same emotional reaction. In one town I have passed through, the damage is as bad as in Caen although the place was captured without a fight. The RAF have made a shocking mess.

The only laughing faces I have seen up to now belong to the Poles and Russians – slave labourers. But then they have a future. All Nazi signs have been obliterated except one, Sieg oder Sibirrien (Victory or Siberia).

Let's talk about something more pleasant – leave. I'm hoping to get home about midnight on April 2nd and have asked my parents to invite you to stay on either 4th or 5th. Till then I am keeping my head well down.

PS This watch-dog racket leaves me slightly uneasy. Jake will be relegated to a position of total insignificance in my household.

Although Stanley was being kept busy on special missions in Germany his Regiment was not yet across the Rhine. They were ordered to recce Menzelen, a village immediately opposite Wesel, the last remaining German bridgehead on the Rhine. A smoke screen protected them as they moved into position. Gunpits were dug at night and camouflaged before dawn.

Menzelen had suffered severely and its farmhouses were in ruins. Burnt out barns contained the charred remains of horses and cattle. Those animals that survived were pressed into service, either to move equipment or to provide food. Even hens played their part. A coop was improvised in a slit trench covered by wire netting. Apparently unaffected by the gunfire they obligingly layed eggs for a different sort of battery from the ones their descendants would become used to.

Allied bombing continued without let-up. In the Far East on 9th March two thousand tons of incendiaries were dropped on Tokyo causing the biggest firestorm to date. On 14th March the marshalling yards at Dulmen were heavily hit. They had already been badly damaged by 103's guns at the end of February. The Remagen bridgehead had been extended, cutting the Cologne/Frankfurt autobahn and the Regiment was standing by, ready now to support the crossing of the Rhine at Wesel.

But for once my thoughts that week were not with the Allied advance in Europe, not with the Regiment whose officers I had come to know through Stanley's letters, not even with Stanley.

I will never forget March 17th, 1945. Myrtle Pincus rang me – I was staying with my parents in Brighton for the weekend – and invited me to visit them the next day on my way back to Cambridge. Rather to my surprise when I arrived she was alone in the house. She handed me a letter from the Air Ministry saying:

'It is with regret that we have to inform you of the death of your son, John David Pincus, in action on 19th July, 1944.'

I left their house shortly afterwards and wandered over Hampstead Heath where John and I had walked so often. I loved that family as if it were my own and I did not know how to contain the pain at the news.

The poem I had received the previous August – A Querulous Quroon – arrived several weeks after his death. How could that have happened? Who posted it and from where? Why didn't the Ministry of Defence inform the family earlier that he was missing? But I now knew the answer to one question – he could not have received the letter I wrote to him in reply.

The following day I received a letter in Cambridge from his mother:

London   18.3.'45

My dear Joan,
I do hope I wasn't too hard this afternoon. I've been steeling myself to tell you ever since we knew and came to the conclusion it was better to be as calm and simple as possible. At the least unbending I am liable to become completely unstuck and that upsets the family very much indeed. Believe me

it is very difficult for me. I can't allow Marg and Bob to feel ever that my feeling for them isn't at all times equal to what I have for John.

I must thank you for the truly great joy your friendship was to our boy. Cling to the happy memories! Remember only the forgotten are truly dead. John is eternal!!

With much love, Myrtle Pincus.

My only comfort was Jake, the little black puppy I had named after John's plane. It was the first time that I had had to face the death of someone I truly loved as a friend. The dreadful wastage of war was no longer an abstract statistic.

I did not write to Stanley about John Pincus. I knew he was in the thick of the battle for the Rhine. There was no hurry. Time enough when he was home on leave in April to break the news.

Into Germany

'The Herenvolk regard us with blank and apathetic stares'
April 23rd, 1945

The war in Europe was almost over. For Stanley's Regiment there was one last battle to fight and his one fear seemed to be that he would not survive long enough to enjoy his leave. It was now over a year since I had seen him and I knew nothing at the time of this secret dread of his. His letters certainly didn't give any indication.

BLA   ***March 22nd, '45***

While I am writing these lines I am having to pick up the microphone to control gunfire. We've undoubtedly reached the climax now, and it may be that this is the last great battle. But what a battle!

The weather is absolutely first class and I'm feeling fine. It won't be long before I'll be with you again and perhaps we can make amends for the last twelve months.

The crossing of the Rhine at Wesel on 22nd/23rd March by 1 Commando Brigade was later described as a perfect operation. Path-finders dropped flares around the town, sticks of high explosives followed, the guns of 77th Regiment opened up in support and soon after the 6th Airborne Division, together with the 17th American Division dropped into the area on the far side of the Rhine.

By 25th March the link-up with the airborne divisions was established. Churchill, determined not to miss the fun, went for a short cruise up the river and later flew in a small plane for a hundred and forty miles along the Rhine, east of the Maas.

On the evening of 26th March the guns of 103 and 104 Batteries rolled across the bridge over the Rhine. Stanley was in Germany at last, just a few hours before his twenty-third birthday. The wish expressed in his letter of July 11th, 1944, was almost, but not quite, fulfilled. On his birthday the Regiment came under the command of 6th Guards Brigade with the task of capturing Munster. With them they had some members of an American Parachute battalion, who hitched rides on their tanks. Those who could not find room commandeered German vehicles and some even seized motorized bath chairs to keep up with the advance.

His birthday was marked by another event. The last V2 of the War fell on England. It landed in Orpington, Kent.

You realise that the Front is in a somewhat fluid state at the moment and I am enormously pushed for time. Unfortunately we are not exactly moving in the direction of the embarkation port, but there's always some traffic moving in the reverse direction. I shan't be able to tell you if I can't get away but if there is a general postponement of leave it will be in the papers.

Resistance was gradually stiffening and Stanley must have written the last letter under very difficult conditions. On 28th March the Regiment's tanks were sniped at from woods and houses and were shot up by German Panzer troops concealed in the ditches and hedges. Even the enemy ack-ack guns were turned on the Regiment. By the evening they were just east of Dorsten.

The next day the Americans captured Frankfurt. The 77th advanced fifteen miles to Dulmen but on the way had a tractor blown up with a direct hit. The gun was damaged, the driver killed but the rear-most Battery soon silenced the enemy gun. Progress slowed and on 30th March – Good Friday – the Regiment only advanced five miles.

But by 31st March they were targeting 104 Battery's guns on the Dortmund/Ems Canal, in the area of Munster, as planned. Prisoners came in in ever increasing numbers and the Burgomeister of Munster tried to negotiate a surrender for the following day, Easter Sunday. But the negotiations broke down and by the evening of Easter Monday Munster was captured.

On Easter Sunday in the Far East the Americans invaded Okinawa. Again the Japanese defended the island to the death and that spring and summer a quarter million human beings died in and around Okinawa.

The 77th Regiment's objective having been achieved it was a fine time for Stanley to take his well earned leave. He arrived back in England on 3rd April and a day later I joined him in Wycombe. He looked fit and confident. Not older, but then he had never looked particularly young to me. I, of course, was more self-confident and physically more mature so that I was less in awe of him than previously. And perhaps this made our relationship easier. I don't know quite what I had expected but I remember being overwhelmed by my emotions and wondering why on earth I had been so aloof and careful in my letters. But mainly I remember how happy we were that leave apart from the sadness of a visit we paid in London.

I had decided to wait till Stanley was home on leave to break the news about John's death. They had never met although they knew all about each other's existence. I was therefore very surprised at how badly Stanley took it. Several of his own friends had been killed or injured yet John's death really shook him. He insisted on coming with me to meet John's parents and to express his sympathy personally. They, in their usual open-hearted way, made us very welcome.

They put on a splendid meal for us which must have used up much of their rations. As the war drew to a close it was still very difficult to find certain commodities in some locations because of uneven distribution. Myrtle told us that she had recently swopped lard for washing soap, dripping for sugar and custard powder for seed potatoes. But these were such small inconveniences compared to the great news from the Western Front.

By April 7th British troops were only twenty miles from Hanover, Russian troops were on the outskirts of Vienna and the Americans were only one hundred and thirty miles from Berlin. On 11th April they entered Buchenwald a few hours after the administrators had fled. A sickening scene greeted them – emaciated corpses and starving survivors. One of Buchenwald's inmates later wrote of the Americans: 'You were our liberators but we, the diseased, emaciated, barely human survivors are your teachers. We taught you to understand the Kingdom of the Night.'

For America's President news of the final victory was to be denied him. On 12th April, 1945, he died quite suddenly. American soldiers wept for him and Churchill was dismayed and shocked. 'I have lost a dear and cherished friendship forged in the fire of war'.

We went to the theatre once whilst Stanley was on leave to see John Gielgud's production of 'Love for Love'. It seemed no time at all before his leave was over and he was on his way back to Germany.

BLA   *April 13th, 1945*

Here I am back again with the Unit. The return journey was very swift but rather uncomfortable and less exciting than the previous cross-channel journey to Normandy. Was it really only ten months ago? I didn't manage to get very much sleep though it wasn't at all rough.

I'm afraid I can't even tell you where we are or what we are doing at the moment. Don't worry about me. I'm not where I thought I might be.

I shan't write much tonight because I'm tired but I want to tell you once more that I love you very much and had a really delightful few days with you. John's death has brought home to me how transient our lives are and it made every moment with you that much more precious. Always yours.

Stanley's cryptic letter concerning his whereabouts became clear when I knew what the 77th Regiment had been up to whilst he was on leave. During the time they had been battling for Munster, other Units had made considerable progress. Osnabruck had fallen and on April 5th the 77th Medium Regiment took over the town, moving into the scarcely damaged barracks, Caprivi Kaserne. Their guns were left in action outside the town, ready to deal with any emergency, as there was still unrest.

Military Government had been established and it was the Regiment's task to restore law and order. Two days later Stanley wrote again.

My Darling,

I am missing you as much as ever but the return here hasn't made me as depressed as I thought it might. Things in our present location are working smoothly enough but it is a strange and difficult job that we are doing. Nevertheless my temper is fairly well under control and I've only had one violent outburst today which caused me to use unparliamentary language.

The weather here is far warmer even than it was in Wycombe, at least 10° higher. A German summer is supposed to be very hot and I can well believe it if it is like this in spring. My personal temperature has been reduced by about 100°, though. How about yours?

I've just finished Trollope's book ('Barchester Towers') which unfortunately became frightfully moral and Victorian, with the usual impeccable heroine and a dear, good old clergyman as hero, but it was still very much worth while reading.

I'm miles from where I expected to be and we've had some more bad luck in our Battery. Just before I came back off leave my driver, Barker, was accidentally killed by an American sub-machine gun discharged by another chap in the Troop. Barker hadn't been married long and he was very devoted to his wife.

The fellow who shot him is the best man in the Troop in action – he's absolutely fearless – but this business shook his nerves as no enemy shell or bomb has ever done.

On the day Stanley wrote this letter, 15th April, 1945, British tanks entered Belsen. Three of the soldiers riding those tanks were Jews. But, although they wanted to stay to help their desperately sick and tortured brethren, the tanks had to move on. For the next forty-eight hours, until more tanks arrived, the Hungarian guards were still in charge. In that interval they shot a further eighty-three people.

Other prison camps were being overrun by the Allies. One of them was Colditz where Wing Commander Bader, the legless air ace captured in 1941, had been held.

Every day brought fresh news of towns and cities captured. On April 15th Arnhem was finally seized by the Canadians, seven months after the abortive Allied paratroop attack. By 17th April the Americans had reached the outskirts of Nuremburg and the Red Army offensive on Berlin had begun.

Churchill, who was worried about the Russians advancing too far in northern Germany, ordered Montgomery to reach the Baltic port of Lubeck before the Russians.

I've had a letter from you yesterday. Wonderful. At the moment letters take about four days but this may be reduced somewhat when things get organised again. Still, it's obviously quite hopeless to wait for replies before writing again.

Another man dropped dead of heart failure yesterday. I had to arrange the burial. With the body in the truck I was unfortunately directed to the wrong cemetery many miles from base. This rather pained the padre – already very unhappy at being expected to conduct a service in a Roman Catholic churchyard – and I was left standing for an hour with an unwanted corpse on my hands. I was so annoyed that I almost threw a fit myself and in fact I stamped around the cemetery swearing for fifteen minutes without a break. An ugly sight!

The trouble was that the poor man had 'Atheist' inscribed on his identity disc. Army procedure dictates that, except in action, a man must only be buried in an appropriate cemetery with a padre of his own faith present.

If he had had nothing on his disc it would have been simple – we could have made him honorary C of E and taken him to the nearby Protestant church. But they wouldn't have anything to do with him. And we couldn't find an atheist padre.

Eventually we found somewhere to bury him – in the grounds of an abandoned private chapel – and the padre finished by discoursing for an hour on the unhappy lot of Army padres. Yes: it's a weird life.

OSNABRUCK.

163

Meanwhile rioting and lawlessness broke out in Osnabruck. 103 Battery were trying to guard fifteen points round the town – including a metal factory, wine store, ammunition dump, displaced persons barracks, margarine dump and goods yard – an almost impossible task as bands of different nationalities roamed the streets looting and taking revenge on their erstwhile persecutors. It was difficult to blame them.

City after city continued to fall before the swiftly advancing Allied troops. On 19th April the Americans entered Nuremburg and the following day it fell. It was Hitler's fifty-sixth birthday and he marked the occasion by awarding the War Merit Cross to Lt Waldheim, the same Lt Waldheim who had previously received an award for his efficiency in helping to deport Jews, and who is now President of Austria. On the 21st April French Forces entered Stuttgart. The early capitulation of Germany was certain.

The 77th Medium Regiment began to fear they would not be in at the death, so enmeshed had they become in the affairs of Osnabruck. However, on 22nd April they heard they were going to be relieved by another artillery regiment. Recce parties were sent off to the north of Luneburg to look for suitable gun sites. They were to support the 15 Scottish Division in the crossing of the Elbe.

BLA   *April 23rd, 1945*

As far as we are concerned the Army Postal Service has ceased to function and so I haven't heard from you or anyone else for nearly a week. It's twelve days since I left you, darling, and it seems much longer than that. I'm certainly not too happy at the prospect of not seeing you for several months.

It's a good thing in a way that we have never spent very long together. I can appreciate that it must be very hard indeed for a married man to come back here after seven days at home. But my bed here is too uncomfortable for me to imagine you sharing it with me; and you've never shared one with me yet, anyway. Actually I believe you are fundamentally too conventional to do so except under the recognised conditions of connubial bliss. How delicately I put things!

So I have to content myself with work. It's very interesting on the whole, and sometimes exciting, as we have to go out practically every day to round up SS men or civilians who have murdered Russians. But military government isn't exactly a hair-raising job. The Herenvolk regard us with blank and apathetic stares, but they haven't very much to be cheerful about.

I'm extremely glad that I studied German and I wish I knew something of Russian for it is almost impossible to make myself understood to a crowd of excitable comrades, particularly if there are any German malefactors around. I can well understand the Germans preferring our relatively mild form of government to the Russian. However, I have every sympathy for the Slav prisoners and workers. They have been treated like pigs.

April 24th – While I was writing I was called out to arrest a German policeman for looting and as soon as I returned I had to go off on a round

trip of three hundred and seventy miles. But there were no letters from my
favourite correspondent when I got back.

In Italy the River Po had been crossed and the Italians rose up against the Germans still occupying the north of their country. Milan was liberated by the Italians on 25th April.

Shortly after midday an historic meeting occurred on the west bank of the Elbe, south of where Stanley's troop were dug in. An American Lieutenant met a Russian soldier. The Allied forces had cut Germany in two from east to west. By the evening the Russians had also surrounded Berlin and three-quarters of the city was in their hands by 27th.

The next day Stanley's Regiment were in action though they did not start firing till 2am on 29th April. Stanley was in one of the two OPs with 44 Brigade but they had an uneventful battle and found no targets.

In Italy Mussolini and his mistress, who had been captured and shot the previous day, were hung upside down from railings in Milan. The German forces in Italy had surrendered unconditionally.

On the last day of April the Americans entered Munich. In Berlin the Red Flag flew from the Reichstag building. Hitler killed himself though, according to Eisenhower, Himmler had told Count Bernadotte on April 24th that Hitler had had a brain haemorrhage and was only expected to live a couple of days. After the announcement of Hitler's death De Valera, the Irish Premier, called on the German Minister in Dublin to convey his condolences.

On May 1st Goebbels and his family committed suicide. Goering, whom Hitler had stripped of all his offices and placed under arrest on April 23rd, was captured by the Americans. May Day came and went and the war still rumbled on. Berlin surrendered on May 2nd. In Holland the starving Dutch population behind the German lines received six thousand tons of food dropped by British bombers. As for the 77th, they were now across the Elbe and were supporting 15 Scottish Division who were pushing towards Hamburg. They only fired their guns once and on 3rd May were ordered to cease fire whilst German emissaries came through the lines and surrendered.

BLA   *May 3rd, 1945*

It's about a week since I last wrote to you. Blame this bloody war which
was supposed to be 'all over'. After our spell of military government in a
large German town a certain formation, which I very much admire, decided
they couldn't get any further without the 77th Medium Regiment, and, in
particular, without de Smith at the OP. It's proved to be an extremely tiring
job.

But, as you will have read, resistance is almost negligible now and the
general collapse is nearing completion. So I am afraid I wasn't as much use

to them as I had hoped to be. All the same it also means that we haven't had very much stuff flung back at us.

The last few days I have been spasmodically tormented by the thought of catching a dose of lead poisoning just before the Armistice – as they do in all the stories about the last war. But I think that possibility can almost be ruled out now.

I wasn't feeling too well yesterday – I had a stomach chill – but the news of the Fuhrer's death (which I heard from a German who seemed pleased about it) did more than anything to cure me. The circumstances of his death aren't very clear but I think it will be found that it was suicide. Well, thank Christ this affair is nearly over at last. It hardly seems possible, dear, but I feel that the British role will be completed in a very few days. When I was home I said victory would take four to six weeks so it looks as if at last I may be right.

Re: our future – I can talk about it now – I have no certain prospects and no real idea of where I might be sent next. I realise our parents' attitude would be very unfavourable if we were to get married whilst you are still at college but against that is the fact that I want you so much and being separated from you, and not being able to sleep with you when I am with you, is hellish.

There's not much chance at all of my getting leave again till after the summer unless, of course, I am switched out east. So I am not in any position to say what I want to at present. But I'm thinking it just the same.

In England the Civil Defence was stood down, the air raid warning was discontinued, street lights went on at night and preparations for Victory celebrations got under way.

On 4th May the Regiment moved to north of Hamburg and maintained their guns ready for whatever operations came their way. That evening news of the capitulation of all German armies on the British Front was received at RHQ 103 and 104 Batteries discharged their Very lights and as the flares lit up the countryside they were joined by neighbouring Units far and near.

The war in Europe ended officially on May 8th, 1945 – VE Day – but the war was virtually over by the 5th and Stanley's next letter, dated May 6th, begins 'Now that the war is over......'

Peace in Europe

'Today I had what was perhaps the most interesting conversation of my life'
May 29th, 1945

The war in Europe was now virtually over and although pockets of resistance remained it was time to count the cost.

On May 4th it was announced that the War Damage (Private Property) Fund would hand over £30 million to local authorities so that they could compensate owners and rebuild houses damaged by enemy raids. There was a similar industrial and commercial fund. A few days later in the House of Commons the Chancellor of the Exchequer said that German air attacks on Britain had done over £1,000 million worth of damage.

In London people whose homes had been so badly damaged that they had slept in tube shelters, even when there were no air raid warnings, had to look elsewhere. On May 6th the seventy-nine underground passenger tube stations on the London Transport system were closed for use as shelters for the first time since 1940.

The damage caused by Allied raids on Germany was immeasurably greater and problems of accommodation, not only for the German civilian population but also for hundreds of thousands of displaced persons and German POWs (of whom there were seven and a half million), almost overwhelmed the Army of Occupation.

BLA   ***May 6th, 1945***

Now that the war is over I have time to sit down and write a letter. It's Sunday afternoon and the fact that I know it's Sunday shows that things are beginning to return to normal.

I'm waiting for ''Combat Diary'' at 15.30, for the 77th are at last to be publicly boosted. This may be the last occasion on which I feel a glow of regimental pride. When I came back from leave I applied for a staff post dealing with Military Government affairs, and yesterday the CO told us that the officers who have made such applications (in 103 Battery, Harry Duerr, Bill Gill and myself) will probably be posted for those duties within a few days.

The Unit meanwhile is preparing to take a slice of Deutschland to govern as the Army of Occupation. We shall be responsible for the entire civil administration and all the innumerable problems raised by the presence of Allied and German prisoners and foreign slave-workers. My new job (if I get it) may be similar or it may be better or worse: I just don't know. The primary consideration is to get a settled job in this theatre. One thing it will do and that is rake in an extra five bob a day.

At the same time I've had my disengaged fingers put into another sort of pie. I've been recommended as Unit Education Officer. God knows what sort of education that will be but if I stay with the Unit and if the recommendation is accepted by higher authority, I shall get at least one course (possibly in England) and also a third pip. But knowing the Army as I do they will probably shove me into something quite different and for which I am totally unsuitable.

I feel particularly mournful at this moment but whether that is because I am deprived of your caresses or whether it's because of the effects of the victory celebrations the night before last, I don't know. I quail at the thought of another night like that. You would have strongly disapproved of the drunkenness and smell of alcohol. I was with the Sergeants and it was a really filthy party: the Alphabet song and other similar. Actually I behaved pretty well and came through unscathed except for a large bump on the back of the head administered by the beak of a stuffed bird.

The 21st Army Group should have had one leave by the end of June and, if privilege leave on a peace-time basis is accelerated, the second round should start within a few weeks. There is bound to be much more shipping available soon, though things like the repatriation of POWs and 'displaced persons' and food shipments to the allied countries and also, of course, the Far Eastern racket, will limit availability.

This seems a very factual and business-like letter but I've just got to be objective until my immediate fate is decided. My only bright prospect is my next leave with you. There is no harm done by keeping your eyes open for a comfortable and non-squeaking double bed, even if you won't let me use it. The twin-bed idea is probably more suited for the time when we value sleep more highly than pleasure.

PS My people will be moving back to Westcliff at the end of this month.

Stanley was taking rather a lot for granted, both in this letter and the next. It was true that marriage had been discussed between us – theoretically – when he was home on leave in April. We had been very close and our discussions had covered a wide range of topics. It was wonderful to be with him again and there was no doubt about the warmth of our feelings for each other.

But he had not proposed formally. Knowing his cautious nature this did not surprise me and gave me a little more time to reflect. I had certainly not committed myself in any way. I was still far from sure that I wanted a domestic role in life though if I did I knew it would be with him. And the war was not yet over. There were still twenty-one hours to go as I slept peacefully that night in my double bed in Cambridge.

In the early hours of May 7th General Jodl signed the unconditional surrender of all German forces, to come into effect at one minute past 11pm on May 8th.

The 49th Armoured Brigade entered Utrecht in Holland on May 7th to a tumultuous welcome. Queen Wilhelmina was already back in her capital and celebrations were widespread throughout the country. The same day, in the North sea, a German U-boat sank two merchant ships, killing seven Norwegians and two British seamen, the last sea casualties of the war in Europe.

In Prague the fighting went on till 5am, six hours after the official cease-fire. In the Channel Islands the Dame of Sark raised the Union Jack even though the island was still occupied by over two hundred German soldiers with not a British uniform in sight. But over the Channel a plane carrying British POWs home crashed, killing twenty-nine soldiers. Still, of the ninety thousand British and Commonwealth POWs, some fifty-three thousand were already back in the UK.

May 8th was a beautiful day and for the first time since the war began the weather report censorship was lifted. But the censorship had never been 100% effective. It was a well known fact that there was always a very high probability of the weather off Valentia, in Southern Ireland, reaching London and the South-East twenty-four hours later. Much to the chagrin of RAF pilots Dublin continued broadcasting weather reports from Valentia throughout the war in spite of British Government requests to discontinue them.

BLA   *May 9th, 1945*

By the time this reaches you, darling, you'll have heard about my spell of inglorious isolation in support of the 15th (Scottish Division).

Since my last letter we've been on the move again — this time on what we hope will be our last journey. We are now the pukka Army of Occupation or at any rate will be tomorrow. We are even better off here than we were during our previous spell of Military Government in Osnabruck. Myself, I'm established in a single room in a pretty good hotel, with decent furniture, central heating, hot and cold water and electric light — the last two are very rare luxuries in present-day Germany.

We are surrounded by vast herds of the sheep-like Wehrmarcht. Their military discipline is still remarkably good and, either through a fundamental stupidity or a lifetime's education in blind obedience, they execute our orders in as docile a manner as the civilians. We come across the odd danger-man, like the SS Colonel from Dachau concentration camp — a blackguardly-looking type who at first refused to carry his own luggage to the truck which was taking him away, or even to shut the door of the car himself. He will no doubt be tried as a war criminal, anyhow.

Today I came across another revolting case: two little Polish boys on an outlying farm who had been so neglected and maltreated that they couldn't walk till they'd had their legs and feet bandaged by our MO. The farmer cleared out of his home when he grasped our attitude but I'm going to run the swine in tomorrow.

Maltreatment of Poles and Russians is very widespread. In fact to my certain knowledge at least twelve Russians were murdered by German gangs around Osnabruck after the Occupation. We detained thirty men in respect of these crimes. There's always a chance that somebody in one of these cases may try to shoot his way out but it hasn't happened yet, thank goodness. Having survived the war I am pretty confident of my ability to survive the peace.

I haven't told you much about VE day or days but that's because we've been in a state of mobility all the time. I managed to hear Churchill's short speech yesterday, though. These last few days I've been steadily sampling cellars and doing pretty well but I've had enough sense not to try and maintain the furious fun of the glorious Fifth of May.

At the moment I am no wiser than I was before as to my future movements. I'm afraid it is going to be rather a long time before we are together again. Use the time to concentrate as hard as you can on your work but if you care to include some domestic science you'll be killing two birds with one stone. Admittedly no cooking could be worse than some of the stuff I've had today but I am rather fond of my stomach and I doubt whether I'll ever be able to satisfy it with my own efforts. But I promise to collaborate in the cuisine department if you keep me on a tight rein.

Both May 8th and May 9th were declared public holidays in the UK. On May 8th there was an estimated hundred thousand people outside Buckingham Palace and the Royal Family made five appearances. In Whitehall fifty thousand gathered to cheer Churchill, who stood giving the V-sign on the balcony of the Ministry of Health. Public buildings, including St Paul's, were floodlit and there were fireworks, bonfires, flags and dancing in many public places.

In Cambridge the town went wild. Dancing round huge bonfires went on throughout the night. One of these gatherings was on Parker's Piece, a large area of common ground on the outskirts of the city, and there my friends and I celebrated victory with linked arms, singing popular romantic songs round the fire.

In New York more than a million people crowded the streets. Broadway, Wall Street and Manhattan were knee-deep in ticker-tape paper. Moscow celebrated May 9th as Victory Day, with parades and speeches.

In Europe several more enemy notables surrendered: Quisling in Norway, Goering (head of the Luftwaffe) in Germany and Kesselring in Austria. Fighting ceased on the 9th in Austria and Czechoslovakia but continued on Germany's Eastern Front. Pockets of resistance fought on in East Prussia, Latvia and Yugoslavia. Nor was the sight Stanley described in his letter of May 13th uncommon.

I am writing this by the window of my hotel apartment. It's at the main cross-roads of this little town but the generally attractive view is marred by the presence of two uniformed SS men walking down the road. This really is the most fantastic situation and no-one is at all happy about it. When I woke up this morning armed columns of the Wehrmacht were marching through the streets singing military songs. Admittedly they were marching to the demobilisation area but even so it's enough to provoke me beyond endurance.

It's an absolute scorcher today and I rather imagine that you are in the vicinity of Grantchester where it should be cooler. As we are on a large artificial waterway there is a chance of swimming and boating. I haven't summoned up the courage yet to overcome my prejudice against cold water but I'll soon be finding out whether I remember how to swim.

This is a mighty strange life. In barracks it was always pretty bad but there was always the thought that it was going to lead to something worth-while — as indeed it did. Now there stretches forth a dreary vista of existence in a land of untouchables. It isn't so bad for officers, who live reasonably comfortably most of the time but it's going to be frightfully hard for the men.

You know that I put in for Staff Officer about a month ago? Well the BFs in the Regimental Office sent the application to the wrong people, so I think you can rule out the possibility of my leaving the Unit for some weeks. I believe that on my new application I'm being recommended for GS03 (Intelligence) which would make me a Captain. With no recommendations for promotion the next logical move will be to receive a posting to the Far East as a Lieutenant.

But perhaps I belittle the Army.

PS My mother said that some of those snaps taken at Wycombe were pretty good, so I'll send you a copy when I get one.

At home the Government was faced with the problem of returning a country, which for five and a half years had been on a war footing, to a normal democratic society. Many of us did not realise the full extent to which our lives had been controlled. In the second week in May no less than eighty-four of the Defence Regulations were swept away.

For example, it was no longer illegal to communicate with persons living in enemy territory, except Japan, or to keep or liberate racing or homing pigeons without a police permit. Looters of bombed property could no longer be sentenced to death. Of the three million acres set aside for D-Day training by the Americans, only fifty thousand acres were to remain in their control.

And it would soon be possible for some of those requisitioned sites to be used again for pleasure by the public. On May 16th a White Paper proposing the formation of National Parks was tabled. A drive out into the country on Sunday – for most of us only a pre-war memory – was about to become a reality again. From the beginning of June a basic petrol ration for non-essential use was to be introduced. Cars of 9 horse-power or less would get four gallons a month rising to seven gallons a month for cars of more then 20 horse power. The allowance was sufficient for 120 miles per month.

It was not surprising petrol had been in such short supply for civilian use. Two extraordinary and successful methods of distributing and using it were revealed in May. The first one was PLUTO – Pipe Line Under The Ocean – which provided a continuous pipe, from England under the Channel to France and beyond, through which petrol was pumped to supply Allied troops as they pushed the front line forward through France, Belgium, Holland and Germany.

The second one, which solved the problem of pilots landing in foggy conditions, was FIDO – Fog, Intensive, Disposal Of – which fed fuel alongside airstrips to smokeless, petrol-fired flame burners. (I had a cousin who was one of the scientists working on that project.)

BLA *May 15th, 1945*

I've just received your VE day letter. From all accounts I read, VE day must have been a clean break with the preceding five and a half years. I wasn't quite sure whether Cambridge would go haywire or remain aloof but as I should have guessed it went haywire.

For us things were very different. Unfortunately we were stranded somewhere in Schleswig-Holstein having moved up with 15th (Scottish) Division after the assault crossing of the Elbe. We were so far forward that we couldn't even get any beer for the men and they had a really wretched time. On VE day I went out as interpreter on the recce of our Army of Occupation area, so there was none of that feeling of being at one with a happy crowd that you describe. Of course our real celebration was when the German armies opposite 21 Army Group capitulated.

How old were you, darling, when war broke out? Thirteen, weren't you? It makes me feel a real cradle-snatcher. I remember at that time I was young and ambitious and I wanted to know everything. Well, I'm still ambitious but I have a bigger and better ambition now – you.

I'm still entirely in the dark regarding my future. Today I missed an ideal job in connection with the Army Education scheme because I happen to be under twenty-five. But I'm still hoping for a stroke of luck. The capture of the 'Bremen' and the 'Europa' may possibly facilitate the leave scheme.

Today I had a letter from home which included the snapshot taken of us together. Do you realise that's the first of us as a pair – but not I hope the last. The sight of the photos made me feel rather miserable as well as happy. Roll on that leave!

Nothing definite about it yet but 1) it will now last eleven days; 2) our Unit intends to carry on with the second round in about four weeks time when the first leave list is completed.

Censorship of mail at the Unit end finishes today though it's still subject to censorship at Base but I don't think I'll be giving away any vital information when I say we are in Rendsburg about 20 miles west of Kiel on the famous Canal. It's quite a pleasant place but on account of the non-fraternisation order the general atmosphere is strained. A rotten state of affairs but one which I always expected. We are actually very lucky that there is no active resistance. The whole nation seems to acknowledge defeat.

You know my application for a staff job was wrongly sent to Civil Affairs? Well, apparently AGRA (the next higher formation) HQ said they thought I was very young for such an appointment and that I should apply for a staff post (which I had originally done) getting some preliminary experience on a temporary attachment to their HQ.

The application was duly sent in from the Regiment but the Brigadier then stepped in, having looked at my language qualifications and said that at the present stage of operations I was most useful to my Regiment (which is unfortunately true as I'm used as everyone's interpreter) and I therefore had to stay where I was.

So we are back to square one. The Army is an unpredictable animal.

PS How about starting a softening up process on your parents preparatory to any announcement we might have to make?

If the Army was an unpredictable animal so was the electorate. On May 18th the Conservative Party issued a twelve point manifesto, which was to be the basis of their election campaign. It was confident of victory and decided to end the Coalition Government which had run the country ever since May 10, 1940. Parliament was to be dissolved on June 15th and a General Election held. Although the current Parliament had been in existence for over nine years it was not the longest in history: four others having lasted longer.

On May 23rd Churchill tendered the resignation of the Coalition Government and formed a new government. A week before he had announced that the Women's Land Army, a conscripted and uniformed force which could be directed to any part of the country, was not eligible for post-war gratuities. A small but increasingly active part of the eligible voters was thus alienated. The Armed forces, too, were beginning to be disillusioned by the slowness of leave and demobilisation.

Governing Germany was proving very difficult for the Allies, though disagreements between the four victors were on the whole resolved by reference to the Potsdam Conference decisions. The main problem was finding non-Nazis with any experience whatsoever of administration, even at the lowest level.

At the top level many of the leading Nazis were captured in May and a number committed suicide. One of the most notorious, Heinrich Himmler

(Reichsfuhrer, Chief of German Police and Minister of the Interior) was arrested by troops of the British 2nd Army on May 21st. The following day he was taken into Field Security custody at a villa near Luneberg, the Intelligence branch to which Stanley was later transferred.

When arrested he was travelling in the name of Hizinger, having shaved off his moustache and put a patch over one eye. Nothing had been known of his movements since his negotiations with Count Bernadotte in April. On May 23rd he asked for an interview with the Camp Commander and announced his true identity. A counter-intelligence officer confirmed this and Himmler was immediately confined under special guard. He was stripped and searched to find any hidden poison but, when the medical officer attempted to examine his mouth, Himmler crunched and swallowed a glass phial containing cyanide.

Within fifteen minutes he was dead. He was buried in an unmarked grave in unconsecrated ground and the British troops who buried him were sworn to secrecy. A few days later eleven sacks, sealed with Himmler's stamp and containing £2 million in twenty-two different currencies, were found on the floor of a barn.

BLA   *May 22nd, 1945*

I'm still visiting guards, interpreting and making surveys of our area. Today I had the job of moving a hundred and sixty Italians in six vehicles from one Camp in the town to another. It took forty-five minutes to load them in and the Italian officer in charge took one and a half hours to get them out at the other end. I thought I was going to burst a blood vessel. I'm afraid they will never win wars until they submit to some discipline and organisation – things which I dislike intensely but which are unfortunately very necessary if anything practical is to be done.

I'm afraid your remarks about cookery and housework sent cold shivers down my spine. Any co-operation I attempt to give you in these spheres will be quite valueless. I am inordinately fond of my stomach and if my appetite isn't satisfied I am apt to become really brutal. You have been warned!

At the moment though my chief pleasure is careering around Schleswig-Holstein in various types of automobiles. Funny, I haven't managed to write one off yet.

I envied Stanley because I had always loved cars and was very keen to learn to drive. Since there had been no petrol for civilian use for many years this had not been possible. Now, with a petrol ration about to be introduced in England, I hoped to persuade my father to teach me. Other rations were being decreased. On May 27th cooking fats were reduced from 2oz to 1oz, bacon from 4oz to 3oz and soap was cut by one-eighth.

We were aware that there was still a war to be finished in the Far East, a war to which Stanley might easily find himself transferred. As if to remind us a massive air raid, by five hundred US bombers, took place on Tokyo on May 26th. Military targets in the city suffered severe damage.

BLA   *May 27th, 1945*

We have been here eighteen days now but it seems more like eighteen weeks. I knew all along that the Army of Occupation would be like this but reality is even more unpleasant than I expected. I suppose it's better than the Far East but I'm not at all sure that it's better than our dash from the Rhine. The chief trouble is the virtually complete absence of any society outside our own small circle and the absence of any immediate goal that we are aiming at, as there was during the campaign. On the whole I agree with the policy of non-fraternisation but it's mighty hard in practice.

As you will realise the question of frat, in its various forms, is very prominent in our minds at the moment. But we're well in just now with the local Rumanians — a very hospitable crowd — with the odd Pole and Dutchman thrown in. They have an extraordinary good international dance band with a fleapit of a dance-hall which is also their sleeping quarters. Nothing is too good for the British officers. Unfortunately though German girls (who have lost all their Wehrmacht boy-friends) have been infiltrating into the dances and I'm afraid even this outlet will have to be closed.

I was delighted to hear of the receptive attitude of your parents and that I am no longer persona non grata. But I have no intention of living with a woman who keeps a pack of dogs. One is enough, God knows. I fancy this wretched creature will have to be put in his place before too long. I'm not sharing your affection with a hound. And I am convinced that men who own dogs grow to look like them so take pity on me before it is too late.

PS I love you in case you are still not sure about it.

Stanley expressed some sympathy with the bereaved German girls and certainly German manhood losses were enormous compared to Britain's. Nevertheless the figures for the total UK casualties, issued on May 29th for the period September, 1939, to February, 1945, showed the level of disruption to the lives of a whole generation of British youth. There were 1,128,000 injured, including 300,000 deaths (this was about one third of the First World War figures) and in addition 61,000 civilians killed plus nearly a quarter of a million injured.

BLA   *29th May, 1945*

Today I had what was perhaps the most interesting conversation of my life. It was with one William Joyce (Lord Haw-Haw to you). He was captured at Schleswig last night and was shot through the bottom in the process. This morning he was taken to Rendsburg Military Hospital where I was placed in charge of the guard that was mounted over him.

I discussed a number of political questions with him as he lay on his bed in the ward, particularly in relation to the present situation of Germany. The recent SHAEF edict against publication of interviews with prisoners and also the British rules of evidence precludes me from making public his remarks but I shall disclose them after his trial.

He is personally more agreeable than I had expected and he didn't appear in any way perturbed at the prospect of what he must know is his inevitable doom. I do not think he will raise any serious defence once he is put on trial. Charles Harrisson has carted him off to 2nd Army Headquarters now and I don't expect to see Mr Joyce again, except in the 'News of the World' and 'Madame Tussaud's'.

Among the things Stanley later told me about his conversation with Joyce was Joyce's comment that he could smell a Jew a mile off. Since one of his guards, with whom Joyce was on quite amicable terms was Jewish, Stanley thought this comment particularly obnoxious. However he made sure his prisoner was never left alone with that particular man just in case the soldier decided to exact immediate revenge. Stanley was determined to see Joyce got his just desserts at the hands of the British authorities.

William Joyce was captured only a few hours before being brought to Luneberg Hospital. The son of an Irish-born naturalised American, Joyce was born in the States in 1906. He had last broadcast on April 30th from Hamburg and was on his way to Denmark when challenged at the border near Flensburg. He was carrying a passport in the name of Hansen, but the sneer in his voice, known so well from the opening words of his propaganda broadcasts to England – 'Jairmany calling, Jairmany calling' – gave him away. The border guards thought he was about to draw a gun and shot him in the buttock, though he was not seriously injured.

The case of William Joyce was an interesting exercise in the interpretation of international law. Could he or could he not be hanged as a traitor? He claimed at his Old Bailey trial that he could not since he was an American who had become a German citizen in 1940 – before America was at war with Germany. But in 1933 he had obtained a British passport in order to go to the Nuremberg Rally. On his application he falsely gave his place of birth as Galway, to which the family had returned when he was three. That was the lie which was eventually to hang him for treason as a British subject. But the legality of that decision was still being questioned in the House of Lords and the columns of the Times newspaper in 1991.

Military Government

'I'd be happier fighting in some other theatre of war'
June 15th, 1945

Most foodstuffs were still heavily subsidised and on June 1st, 1945, the Ministry of Food published the following list to show how little change there had been in prices during the war.

PRICE per lb

Oatmeal	3½d
Potatoes	1d
Sugar	4d
Cheese	1/1
Bacon	1/10
Meat	1/0¾
Eggs	2/– per dozen
Milk	9d per quart
Bread	9d per 4lb
Flour	⅓ per 6lb

I was beginning to take an interest in food prices as it seemed likely that I would have to start catering for myself, if not for two people, before very long. LSE were already making plans for returning to London and I did not want to lose the independence I had gained by living once more in the family home. Rented accommodation in England was, however, likely to be very difficult to find. I toyed with the idea that I might emigrate to Australia or New Zealand after finishing college.

BLA   **June 2nd, 1945**

Today for some reason I am feeling rather feeble and lonely and that makes me want you more than ever. I think it is a serious case of Joan-starvation. I'm beginning to dream about how, when and where we are going to live together. I just hope you still love me enough to make it come true. Anyway, you'll be leaving Cambridge for good soon. I hope you are having a damn good last week of term.

At the moment I am in charge of an Anglo-German guard over a combined fertiliser factory and naval warehouse. Amongst the exhibits is the damaged floating dock from Kiel. The factory is populated by millions of flies who are making a very good meal of the masses of decaying bones and vegetables which are eventually to be used on the good German earth. The smell resembles Normandy's least pleasant places.

In private Stanley told me that he was almost certain the bones were human. Many years after the war he took his two sons to Rendsburg to revisit the factory. It had vanished from the face of the earth and he could not even identify the street. The local population must have been equally keen to obliterate all evidence of their country's gruesome past, for no-one could – or would – answer his questions on the subject.

By contrast where we are living is quite decent except that I have to fight my way into my room of a night past the insect population. I am also living among the men which is an opportunity I don't have normally except in action.

We had a Regimental Dance on Wednesday with foreign workers as partners. Most of them speak German and our chaps have already learnt the essential phrases. But sooner or later they'll all be moving homewards or else electing to remain in Germany and be treated like any German, so I am afraid this peculiar state of affairs won't last very long.

I'm still trying to get out of regimental soldiering but the lists held by 21 Army Group are very long. Of course Intelligence is the branch which has always interested me most and the one in which I could probably serve best. But the Army is quite unlike Civvy Street and nothing is more unusual than to put a man in a job he can do.

The weather here stays lovely. I shall be rummaging for that bathing costume soon and if I can't find it I shall have to manage like most of the men with a fig leaf.

PS Please note last month's Mess Bill: Bar account £2/10/6.

I had mentioned to him that I was rather worried about how much he seemed to drink when under pressure, and that now the danger was over perhaps he might moderate his daily alcohol intake. Hence his PS. I had also told him about my own lack of domestic training – I had never even boiled an egg for myself, let alone studied domestic science or cooked a meal.

BLA *(undated)*

I've just got your letter dated 30th so it seems mail takes about four days to get here.

Your attitude towards domestic work is most lamentable and if you are not prepared to minister to the tired warrior in every necessary respect I shan't consider our union fully consummated. Actually I know what all this is leading up to. You want me to provide, out of my negligible financial resources, someone to do the dirty work for you. A bad business but if I am to lay my hands on your salary I suppose I shall eventually have to give way. Seriously I do feel domesticity is a worthwhile career and I shan't want any wife of mine working for long, or at any rate not once there are children.

That is not to say you shouldn't get yourself a useful job for a few months — preferably a well-paid one.

There, I have answered one of your comments. The reason I don't always reply to points you have raised is generally because I have lost the letter. However I have started to number them w.e.f. this one. You also wanted to know about my attitude towards Law. Well here goes.

I am still interested and as it is the only subject on which I can speak with any show of authority I shall expect to continue to use it in some way. I used to think it in many ways uninteresting but after two years of Army administration it seems positively fascinating.

As for living in England: I am an Englishman, I am extremely fond of England and one of the things I have tried to fight for in a small way has been the preservation of England. So I have no desire at all to live elsewhere and I doubt whether I ever will until the country gets too hot for me.

It was still uncertain whether Stanley would stay in Germany. Unknown to all of us decisions were being taken at the end of May and beginning of June, which affected not only British troops being sent to SEAC but also countless American servicemen's lives. The atomic bomb had become a reality. Should it be used and if so where? And if it were not used what were the likely Allied casualties that would result from invading the Japanese mainland?

At the Pentagon on May 31 Oppenheimer described the probable effects of dropping such a bomb on different types of targets. Four possible cities were considered as targets – Kyoto, Yokohama, Hiroshima and Nagasaki. Tokyo was ruled out as it was already mostly flattened by conventional bombing. Hiroshima, being surrounded by hills which would focus the effect, was favoured. It was also believed erroneously that there were no POW camps there. The alternative – to invade Kyushu, the southermost, large Japanese island by sea and airborne forces – might cost one million American lives.

BLA   ***June 6th, 1945***

At the moment I am not frightfully optimistic about my prospects of remaining in this theatre. But I am trying to remain long enough for at least one leave during your holiday time. I suppose you are going to live at home now. There would obviously be a great deal of friction if you didn't.

Today is the anniversary of D-Day and has been proclaimed as a public holiday for the Army of Occupation. This means in practice that about 25% of our regiment had half the day off. I had to sort out some minor contretemps between the Russians and the Germans whose relations are somewhat strained. But we haven't had the murders here that we had in Osnabruck.

I'm afraid I am not at all impressed by the discipline and the general behaviour of the Russians but they have lots of enthusiasm. Of course we nearly always support them against the Germans but it's a very tricky business at times.

Incidentally the Battery has just had some news: the BC is being posted away to become second in command of a Heavy Regiment.

This posting, which resulted in several officers in the 77th Regiment being promoted, proved only temporary.

BLA   ***June 10th, 1945***

My Darling, Your letters are arriving very well these days and now I have two to answer. First politics:

I believe that democratic habits have a very real value in this topsy-turvy civilisation and that social democracy should therefore be supported. The attainment of socialism may be possible by democratic methods in a particular society. Recent shifts in party politics (which have all been strongly influenced by Keynes' new economic theories) lead me to believe – which I did not before the War – that social democracy may prove workable in England as it has done in Scandinavia.

Broad differences in national temperament are enormously significant in shaping the course of events (vide Germany, Italy, France, during this war, for example) and it is quite possible that the governing classes in Britain will react differently to the threat of expropriation, from their continental counterparts, as they did to the threat of military defeat. I may be wrong of course but I have come to place such a high value on the liberal political freedoms that I shall not easily be persuaded to cross the fence. Are you prepared to debate with me dialectics or the materialist interpretation of history?

The Army hasn't altered my outlook very much except that it has made me less ready to make vague generalisations on subjects I know nothing about. These may seem queer after the diatribe above but I am gradually getting to know something about the real subject matter of politics. I consider the result of the Election far from obvious: in fact I expect Labour to win by a small majority, probably with the help of Liberal and Commonwealth support.

Re: Lord Haw-Haw: he won't be shot, he'll be hanged. A military government couldn't settle his fate and it has no jurisdiction to try him. Haw-Haw announced himself on the radio as William Joyce and has given his life's story. He has also written a book, called 'Twilight over England' and subtitled 'The Autobiography of a Traitor' when in Germany. Also there is the evidence of his colleagues and he has shown absolutely no desire to whitewash himself.

Admittedly it might be difficult to prove that any one particular broadcast was by him but there is so much against him already. If he really is a German he has, as far as I can see, committed no offence at all. But I am certain that no British court will uphold his claim to German nationality (if he makes one) and in fact I believe it will be held that his purported naturalisation was itself an act of treason (cf. R. v. Christian 1902 or thereabouts). I've had part of the interview published in a broadsheet within the Regiment.

I agree with almost all you say about non-fraternisation except the situation is even worse than you imagine. I quite seriously consider that the best move would be to introduce licensed brothels for those who want it so badly that they can't do without it. Griggs' statement in the Commons the other day was another blow to the chaps out here — no increase in leave, no wives over here. However as long as the status of Displaced Persons remains we're pretty well off in Rendsburg.

Sport is beginning to get organised again and I've decided to run a Troop magazine which I hope to publish in a week or so. One has to maintain interest somehow.

Today I had rather more fun: I ran in two fellows for stealing. One of them was our own interpreter who had been taking stuff from the Guard. But so many forms have to be filled up and so many statements prepared that it is more of a punishment for us than for the chap who's arrested.

This was not the case for one particular German, known as Herr Riese, who was arrested on June 14th. He turned out to be Von Ribbentrop, the Third Reich's Foreign Minister and former ambassador to England. He was staying in a private boarding house in Hamburg under that assumed name when he was seized by the same field security forces who had arrested Himmler. At Luneburg, where he was taken, he was identified by his sister, who had been arrested the previous evening, and by a Hamburg wine merchant. Like other Nazi leaders Ribbentrop was found to have poison on him though he did not attempt to use it. He also carried letters addressed to Churchill, Eden and Montgomery.

According to later reports from 21st Army Group HQ, he had arrived in Hamburg on April 30th and unsuccessfully sought refuge with the wine merchant whom he had known for twenty-five years. Ribbentrop was the last of the leading Nazis to be rounded up. At the Nuremberg trials, which found him guilty him in October 1946, he was amongst the twelve German war-time leaders sentenced to death. Goering escaped the hangman by committing suicide. The others were hanged on October 16th and their bodies taken to Dachau to be disposed of in the crematorium ovens.

I rather doubt whether this Regiment will survive as a Unit until Christmas. Frankly I am beginning to feel unless I get some sort of Intelligence job pretty quickly I'd be happier fighting in some other theatre of war. That's probably exactly what the War Office wants me to feel. But don't worry — I am not volunteering yet. I can't honestly pretend that I prefer Siam and Singapore to Schleswig.

It was on this day at this time a year ago that we set foot on the beaches of Normandy. It was the most wonderful and memorable and strange sight of my life, and I don't think I shall ever lose the feeling as I stood, a puny spectator of the war above and around me, that night on board the landing craft. The Commander was chivvying our fellows over the loud-speakers for not off-loading fast enough: and all the time there were air attacks and the most stupendous ack-ack fire from hundreds of guns, mostly on ships.

Normandy itself was a fertile and pleasant land and with all the stench and dust and ruin it still retained a peculiar delicacy of its own. There was something exotic and attractive about the buildings even in the most ruined village. There was also so much in those weeks which now appears even more revolting in retrospect than it did at the time that I am unwilling to think back.

The country is polluted with horrors which only generations of time can efface. I do not believe that any other large area of Europe is so scarred by battle. In our Battery we lost four killed and twelve wounded in that first campaign and we might have lost three times as many if we hadn't dug such deep slit trenches. Most of us hardly knew fear then and it wasn't until October 12th last year, at Oploo in Holland, that we saw what happened to a dozen chaps who were unlucky.

The campaign was a tremendous experience altogether. The most significant feature from the human angle was the all-pervading spirit of optimism which proved quite justified. The trip across the Rhine, after the colossal barrages and the airborne landings, was right up my street. So was the Elbe crossing though I couldn't find anything to shoot at.

But now I am down to my lowest ebb. Unless I am driving for a clear objective I simply go to pieces. I am sitting tight for the moment and trying to keep my bar account down.

PS Charles Harrisson is now our Battery Commander and he has been promoted Major. Excellent.

The election campaign in England was well under way with all the normal 'dirty tricks' and, on 20th May, Harold Laski had issued writs against certain newspapers. They had claimed that the Labour Party would, if necessary, resort to violence to attain its political objectives.

News came through the following day that the Americans had at last captured Okinawa though they had not taken many prisoners. Emperor Hirohito urged his Prime Minister to make all possible efforts to end the war by diplomatic means. In Britain the final German POW count was given as seven and a half million, but they were a nation not given to the unpleasant tradition of fighting to the death or committing hara-kiri like their Far Eastern allies.

BLA   **June 21st, 1945**

This evening I played my first football match for four months in a temperature of 80°. That was four hours ago and I am still red in the face. I came into dinner late on account of the match and I had my jacket off. The CO informed me that if I wanted any dinner I had to go and put my jacket on. That's the Army for you.

The Election campaign is now more or less a slanging match which tends to obscure the fact that there is not an enormous gulf between the parties. Poor old Harold Laski is the shuttlecock at the moment. Beaverbrook or Laski would appear to be the elector's choice: the all-powerful newspaper magnate or the sinister foreign head of the Transport House Gestapo.

It would all be a huge joke if it didn't mean that it may lose a lot of votes for Labour. But if the recent Gallup Poll is accurate Labour can afford to lose plenty. It's really a farce. First the Zinoviev letter, then the PO Savings scare, then Baldwin's 'collective security' swindle and now the Laski menace.

I've been writing this in the Adjutant's office. The CO2 is writing a report and keeps asking me how to spell different words so I am sorry if this is disjointed. I think I'll go and write to Sylvia from whom I have just had a twelve-page letter. She says our parents will soon be well settled back in the old house at Westcliff but that she can't join them there. The Ministry of Labour's decided that she's got to stay at her war job in Wycombe so, pending her appeal against them, she is staying with a friend.

PS Don't tantalise me by writing your telephone number on the top of your letters. The line from Kiel to London isn't through yet.

On June 24th the notorious bridge over the River Kwai, carrying the railway which had caused so many Allied POWs' deaths in its construction, was destroyed by British bombers.

BLA   **June 26th, 1945**

I'm glad you are enjoying your walking holiday with Margaret. The only time I've been to Scarborough was on a flying visit at the head of thirty-two guns and tractors on the way to a twenty-six hour exercise on the moors to the north-west of the town. There is an Artillery range there. It was our

Brigadier's idea of fun. But I've been bestirring myself too. I've played two sets of tennis in the last three days and tomorrow I'm playing cricket. I've been out in a motor-boat on the Eider a few times but I'm not risking a yacht until my swimming has improved.

By the time this reaches you I may be on a course for Regimental Instructors under the Army Education Scheme. We have nothing at all in our Unit and it seems unlikely that we will until we reduce our guard commitments. While the good weather lasts there is also no demand for it. It doesn't look like being a frightfully useful course. My previous two courses on German Guns and Mines were almost valueless to anybody but myself so that will be nothing new.

We've had an ENSA party staying at our hotel. However there's always a small clique of Captains and Majors who make a concerted dive for any presentable women so we poor Lieutenants don't get a look in. Talking of majors, the news has come through that our BC who was posted as second in command of another Regiment is coming back because his posting was a mistake. This means that Charles Harrisson must come down to Captain again and Bill Gill to Lieutenant and, I suspect, two hundred faces in the Battery will go two shades gloomier.

Since I wrote those lines the Battery Commander has ambled into the Mess with the old familiar grin on his face. Well, I've no doubt he'll do his best to make life pleasant for us especially after the send-off we gave him.

I shall go and amuse myself writing an editorial for the magazine. The contributions we have had so far have been of an unprecedented vulgarity. I'll send you a copy when it is printed just to show you the depths to which a soldier's mind can sink. Two of the less reputable contributions are mine.

June 26th was a memorable date for the World Powers. It was the day that the United Nations Charter was signed in San Francisco by fifty nations after nine weeks of discussion. It was agreed that the maintenance of world peace was to be the responsibility of the Security Council, on which Britain, the Soviet Union, The United States, China and France would each have a veto.

BLA   *June 29th, 1945*

I note with trepidation that you are determined to show me all the beautiful places on the Yorkshire moors some day. I take it you intend to reveal these beauty spots in easy stages – just a twenty-five mile walk every day. My dear girl, I have seen more charming villages in Yorkshire than you are ever likely to. It's amazing how unpleasant the most innocent little hamlet becomes when viewed from an armoured OP or a motor-cycle on a wet and windy winter's day, with the Brigadier grinning fiendishly by a thatched cottage. No thank you.

We are now having a spell of bad weather, just like it was last June in

Normandy. It reduced the stench and dust and the insects a little but it almost completely eliminated air support. I hope it improves for I want to start a little running soon.

I'm afraid the Regiment wasn't allocated a vacancy on the Army Education course in Brussels so that's that. I still have vague hopes of Intelligence but the shadow of Singapore is looming larger. I am particularly anxious to have my leave before Nemesis overtakes me. You may be able to guess at my dark designs.

Exams over, Margaret and I had gone up to the Yorkshire Dales for another holiday together, the first since we had been told about John's death. We stayed as usual in Youth Hostels, sometimes spending two nights in one place so that we could devote the intervening day to walking unencumbered by back-packs. I think I came to know her better in those two weeks than in all the years we had spent together at school. She was now more tolerant and understanding of my failings as a correspondent. She told me that since John's death she had no wish to remain in England. She had changed her sense of values and wanted to start afresh. As soon as possible she intended to return to Australia where, as she put it, 'no-one knows all the stupid mistakes and errors I have made'. I repeated Stanley's admonition to me – that she was too young to revise her values – and that I for one would feel a terrible sense of loss if she were to go but I couldn't dissuade her. I even told her that I had thought about emigrating myself and that I might go with her.

BLA   *July 3rd, 1945*

It's almost as great a tonic to hear from you these days as it was in action though I hear from you much more frequently now. I am sorry I upset you by calling you 'my dear child'. At least half the things I say have to be given their reverse meaning and it takes a good deal more than five years intermittent experience to understand my rather distorted sense of humour.

Since I last wrote we've had a Brigadier's inspection. Almost incredibly it's been enormously successful. I think we dazzled him in the first five minutes with new paint, scrubbed floors and the general spit and polish. As the only officer present in 'A' Troop I had rather a nerve-racking job, particularly in the preparatory work, and I was with him for nearly two hours but the result justified the trouble. All this nonsense is most repellent to myself and most of the chaps but it's one of the penalties I always knew would be incurred by occupation troops, for the simple reason that we have little else to do.

On Sunday afternoon I saw a Polish variety show put on for the troops. Some of the folk songs and dances were excellent. Afterwards I met a Polish officer who was actually in favour of the new regime. He told me that the majority of the local DPs are too ill-informed to come to any real opinion about the present conditions, but he thought most would go home when the word came. This attitude was quite different from that of most of the Poles in Britain who seem very largely anti-Russian.

Although the war in Europe was over the mass movement of displaced persons and of refugees had only just begun. Thousands of people were about to be sent to live under regimes they did not like or trust. Germans from Russian controlled territory were moved west whilst Russians who had served in the German Army were repatriated.

The political pattern of Europe for the next forty-odd years was beginning to take shape. On July 4th the British 7th Armoured Brigade and other battalions, including the Royal West Kent Regiment, took over occupation of the British zone of Berlin. The occupation zones for all the enemy territory that had been fought over were finally adopted in July 1945.

The End of the War in the Far East
'Either we abolish war or we perish'
August 7th, 1945

June had been a month of intense electioneering. Churchill had undertaken strenuous tours of all the major British cities with enthusiastic crowds cheering him wherever he went. But he was tired and glad when polling day, July 5th, finally came round. The population duly voted but the ballot boxes were sealed for three weeks pending the arrival of all the servicemen's votes. Churchill took his first proper holiday for five years though he admitted later he could not entirely shut out the mystery of the ballot box contents.

BLA   **July 7th, 1945**

I'm not quite as browned off as I was. I'm frightfully busy these days. Dammit! They're even making me work in the afternoons! I'm Gaol Governor, Sports King and Magazine Editor.

It has been most interesting producing the Battery magazine. I have also been playing tennis, football and basket-ball. I've had some pleasant evenings with DPs (don't get me wrong). I've had more responsibility through acting as Troop Commander. And I'm due to go on this Education Instructors course in Brussels at the end of next week – my chief worry will be to keep my expenditure within reasonable limits. But, above all, leave is drawing closer.

Yesterday morning we lost our CO, Colonel Wintle, posted to SEAC (South East Asia Command). He was a very good chap on the whole – though very fussy and extremely temperamental. His personal abuse of people when he was feeling liverish was quite unprintable but he usually apologised afterwards. He was a man of unusual intelligence for a Regular soldier and I consider he certainly deserves to become a Brigadier. Although we are sorry to lose him it has at least one advantage – our BC goes to RHQ as second-in-command for the time being.

At the moment I am feeling very sleepy after last night's send-off party for the CO. We had fish, chicken, strawberries and ice-cream for dinner, with Sauterne, champagne, port and cigars.

On July 9th a British scientist, named Dr Alan Nunn May, who was working on the atom bomb in Canada, handed several micrograms of

Uranium 233 to the Russians. They already knew about the bomb from Klaus Fuchs but at that time had no way of obtaining the essential element. And, had we been living in the Middle Ages, it might have appeared as if Nunn May's action had been noted on high. A celestial omen occurred that day in both America and Russia, in the guise of a total eclipse of the sun. In Britain the eclipse was only partial.

BLA   *July 12th, 1945*

This is my first duty free and party free evening for some time so this historic correspondence can continue.

The first issue of the magazine went down amazingly well with the chaps and, if it seems rather crude and vulgar to you, remember it's written primarily for ordinary working-class fellows in a condition of sexual maladjustment. The emotions of the authors should be pretty obvious. Have you managed to earmark my foul contributions yet?

The non-frat rule is going to be drastically modified. This will undoubtedly make us look fools after all our professions but of course we have been fools. I have no doubt that the relaxation order will be qualified by some unenforceable restrictions but these at any rate will provide us with some material for our magazine.

We've had some good films here at last: 'The Way Ahead' and 'Hail the Conquering Hero'. The first was a fine film and magnificent propaganda. My only real criticism is that of the infantry section, in question at least 80% would have been half paralysed with fear. A distasteful fact and one which wouldn't fit into a propaganda picture. The other film was first rate satire and very well directed.

PS We weren't allotted a vacancy on the education course, after all.

'The Way Ahead' – which described the adventures of a platoon of raw recruits – was made in 1944 and intended originally as a training film. It was written by Eric Ambler and Peter Ustinov (who also played in it) and directed by Carol Reed. The other stars were David Niven and Stanley Holloway.

'Hail the Conquering Hero' is about an army reject who is accidentally thought a hero when he returns to his small-town home. None of the stars were household names but the director, Preston Sturges, is now recognised as one of the giants of the cinema.

BLA   *July 15th, 1945*

We're not doing any Artillery Training but they're beginning to train us in Infantry tactics – to deal with the Werewolves. I have to do things like supervising the Burgomasters, taking surveys of the area, sorting out the

Guards, and administering the Troop in general. I'm beginning to feel that if I am to be called away to see more of our far-flung Empire I shall be rather sorry after all.

The Werewolves were a band of German youths – Nazi fanatics – who tried to prevent collaboration between Germany and her so-called invaders by committing acts of sabotage. They probably took their name from Hitler's headquarters in 1942 – the days when Hitler thought the conquest of Russia was a matter of weeks away. (He had moved his headquarters from Rastenburg to a new site at Vinnitsa, known as 'Werewolf'.) Mostly the acts committed by the Werewolves were of small importance but on March 25th, 1946, they admitted assassinating the newly appointed, American-backed, Mayor of Aachen. Though the Werewolves were only children the Allies said that they would try any Werewolf youths they caught as if they were adults.

Now that non-frat has been lifted I don't notice a very great deal of difference except that the more meretricious types are giving us the eye more openly and when one sees a chap with a civilian woman one naturally assumes that she's a German instead of just suspecting it. But, don't worry, I'm only fraternising in the true sense of the word – that is, I treat every woman as if she were my sister.

I'm thinking about you a hell of a lot and the more I think the more I realise what a lucky man I am.

Later, Sunday evening

I am sitting in the Adjutant's office: it's a beautiful, still night and the wireless is playing 'The Warsaw Concerto'. The Poles don't like it and I'm beginning to dislike it, too. But I wish so much that you were here listening with me.

PS Herewith a copy of 'Kaserne'.

'Kaserne' (German for Barracks), which Stanley edited for about six months until he left the Unit, was cyclostyled in small print on eight A4 pages. The first edition contained a number of anonymous entries which were by him. I guessed a couple of them; the first was a poem on the official non-fraternisation policy and in the second, entitled 'Frustration Section' he imagines how one of his contributors might feel.

Documents of a different sort were in the news at home. On July 16th, a copy of Magna Carta, 1225 (third re-issue by Henry 111) and known as the Laycock Abbey copy, was presented to the British Museum. It is one of the only two originals of the Magna Carta in this country. Other precious documents, which included the Domesday Book, Wellington's Dispatches from Waterloo, the Log of HMS Victory and the only known seal in existence of Thomas à Becket, were returned to the Museum from their war-time hide-out. They had been stored in the disused women's wing of Shepton Mallet Gaol during the war.

On July 17th the first female Prison Governor in Britain was appointed as Governor of Holloway Women's Prison. She was Dr M.D. Taylor and at the time of her appointment was only thirty years old. Stanley's prisoners that July were in a different category from those of Dr Taylor.

BLA   *July 20th, 1945*

At the moment I'm handling the SS and high-ranking Nazi types who are deposited in our gaol from time to time. I've got about thirty-seven now and there are some really horrible types among them including an SS Sergeant-Major from a Concentration Camp.

The other day I made a survey of all schools as it was believed that German schools would recommence next month. In one school there were seven hundred refugees from Kiel and Hamburg, and in five others there were military hospitals. After I had finished the job somebody discovered that it was all a mistake. Just another of those little errors. I also went to Lübeck on Monday buying wines for the Officers Mess. It's an old Hanseatic port and rather fascinating. I had lunch at a hotel there: oxtail soup, very good Hamburger steak and saute potatoes, ice-cream, tea and a pint of beer. Price: one shilling.

I'm pleasantly surprised that you really liked our magazine though you didn't guess all my contributions. It's amazing really to find how many chaps can produce the right sort of stuff and I think the next number is going to be better than the one I sent you.

This week I've seen 'Double Indemnity' and 'A Guy Named Joe' – both good even though the latter had all sorts of ghosts and Lionel Barrymore as God Almighty's Deputy Chief-of-Staff. On Sunday I am going to a Polish wedding at the DP Camp. They really are first-class people, these Poles.

The two films he mentions are interesting because both had unusual aspects. Billy Wilder's 'Double Indemnity', which starred Fred McMurray, Barbara Stanwyck and Edward G. Robinson, was one of the first films to feature the hero/villain. The novel on which it was based (by James Cain) was rewritten by Raymond Chandler. 'A Guy Named Joe', which featured Spencer Tracey and Irene Dunne as well as Lionel Barrymore, was intended as propaganda to blunt death's sting as ordinary people suffer it.

On 21st July, during a short break in the Potsdam Conference which had begun four days earlier, Churchill took the salute of the British Sector Forces in Berlin. Whilst still in Potsdam, Churchill and Truman, together with

Chinese delegates, sent a final ultimatum to Japan. Russia was not included as she had not yet declared war on Japan. Truman then told Stalin about the extraordinary power of a bomb they had just tested. Truman did not tell him the bomb was already on its way to Tinian Island in the Pacific.

The American cruiser, the Indianapolis, carrying the bomb arrived on July 26th. Awaiting its arrival was the 'Enola Gay' and her crew, the plane which had been chosen to drop the bomb. Three days later the Indianapolis was sunk with tremendous loss of life. Of her twelve hundred crew nearly nine hundred died, either in the attack, eaten by sharks, or by drowning. But the cargo she had just delivered was shortly to kill tens of thousands.

Churchill had asked Attlee to attend the Potsdam Conference with him, not knowing then the outcome of the General Election but aware that if he were not re-elected it was essential that Attlee be a party to agreements reached between the occupying powers. It was a wise precaution. On July 26th the result of the ballot was announced – an overwhelming majority for Labour.

BLA   *July 26th, 1945*

The great news today has been the election result. It's certainly the biggest day the Labour movement has ever had in this country. My early prediction for a Labour victory tended to recede as the campaign went on but like most other people I forgot the Services vote, which was almost certainly 80% Labour. As the leader of a small subversive faction in the Mess I had a very pleasant afternoon smirking at my colleagues who had assumed the Conservatives would romp home.

Your typewritten envelopes take some getting used to and so does the threepenny ha'penny stamp. You know that letters to the BLA only cost a penny ha'penny? We're not writing as often as we should these days but this letter is very well worth writing because I can tell you when I am coming home on leave. Date of arrival is September 1st.

Today I went to an Army Education Conference at Neumunster. The Director is a sincere chap but he has a thankless job, always the Cinderella. Lunch afterwards was served up by Polish girls who had only been brought in as waitresses that morning. It was rather like a Marx brothers comedy and the meal took twice as long as usual.

Moving somewhat faster than the Polish waitresses, Gundar Haag broke the world record for the mile in the third week of July. He ran it in the amazing speed of 4 minutes 1.3 seconds. It was still some years before Roger Bannister broke the 4 minute mile. He set up a new world and British championship record at Oxford on May 6th, 1954, with a time of 3 minutes 59.4 seconds. Stanley's interest in running continued when he was demobbed and each evening for some years he got me to time him on an

880 yards circuit round our neighbourhood. His fastest time was also his last lap for this specific run. He was chased the whole way round by a particularly vicious dog.

BLA   *July 28th, 1945*

This is a vitally important letter because an enormous draft for SEAC had just been published. I am almost certain to be included because of my high demob group – in fact, practically every eligible man is on it. This means I shall come home on leave at some uncertain date prior to September 1st. If I am to unite myself with you before I go a long way away we've got to move pretty fast. But it will be up to you to find out (as surreptitiously as possible) how long it will take to arrange matters and go through the appropriate ceremonies.

De Smith is definitely on the war-path this time and it's going to take something more than the War Office or sentiment to shake him off it.

On July 27th the Japanese Government announced that it would ignore the ultimatum from Potsdam to surrender. 'Japan, unlike Germany, is not on her knees'. It looked as if Stanley would be sent out to SEAC and hoped we would be married before then. He had still not proposed marriage to me formally and I still had not said yes. Nevertheless I began making discreet enquiries as he had suggested.

I resorted to my usual tactic when I did not know what to write to him. I simply wrote nothing.

BLA   *July 30th, 1945*

I haven't heard from you for two weeks and I leave the Unit on Monday morning, August 6th. We are losing three captains and five subalterns altogether – no exceptions. We shall probably arrive at Bruges on the 7th or 8th and then to England. I shall certainly get fourteen days and it may even be twenty-eight.

Later.

We've just been given our 'farewell' dinner. The inverted commas mean one hell of a lot because as soon as I arrived downstairs I received the quite staggering news that all the chaps who, like myself gave their names in as German-speaking persons are to be frozen and NOT posted outside this theatre without 21 Army Group authority.

So I sat at the bottom of the table instead of at the head. The 100-1 chance has come off (I was born lucky) and it seems that I definitely shan't be on the August 6th drop. So my leave date is changed again.

Before I received the letter above and after much heart-searching, I wrote another 'holding' letter. In it I discussed every conceivable topic I could think of that Stanley was interested in, in the vain hope that he might not notice the one glaring omission. I gave him the factual information that he had asked for but did not comment on his assumption that we would be married on his next leave.

BLA   *July 31st, 1945*

Your enormous and very delightful letter arrived this afternoon for me. But you should write two medium-sized letters instead of one huge one spread over about four days. I've definitely been taken off this draft and I think I'll stay with the Unit for the time being. They can't spare me now with all these postings. You've brought so many things into your letter that I'd be writing all night if I were to answer it fully. But I'll answer your question about the Poles.

My contacts have naturally been with the more intelligent types (because of language problems) who are mainly from the middle and upper classes. They are the best crowd of people I have ever met bar none. Politically they are rather unfriendly towards Russia – they disliked the 1939 episode and the territorial resettlement and they ask when is the Red Army going away. Living conditions in Poland are extremely bad just now and they tend to blame the Russians. But there are wide differences of opinion. I have even met officers who support Mikolaiczyk.

The Polish question is a very great tragedy. If you think of Eire you will find some similarities in the attitudes of mind involved. And just as they are beginning to realise in Ireland that it is a political necessity to retain good relations with Britain, so more Poles are coming to understand that enmity with Russia is a political impossibility. But I am afraid that hundreds of thousands will never go back home.

I can't tell you anything more about the German schools except that they are supposed to re-open in the coming month. God knows where the teachers are to come from. I am afraid that many of the Nazi teachers may be used. That would be our supreme folly.

The adjutant now says my leave is likely to be August 28th.

It seemed clear that for the time being I had been let off the hook since the urgency for us to marry had now disappeared. But my problem had been nothing compared to those facing thousands of British girls waiting for ships to take them to the United States. They were going to marry American servicemen who had proposed to them whilst stationed in England. Many of the girls had spent less time together then Stanley and I, and knew their prospective husbands less well. What was more, they were going to live in a strange new country. The total GI brides, including some twenty thousand who had already tied the knot in England, numbered some eighty thousand.

The American Red Cross ran schools for overseas brides. No such facilities existed in England to help the many war-time brides who had promised to marry, or had already married, servicemen they hardly knew. Maybe I was unduly cautious – it is difficult looking back over forty years to remember just what prompted my reservations.

At the beginning of August a letter arrived from Stanley, apologising for trying to force my hand and asking if I would marry him, if not immediately, then after a suitable period of engagement. Regrettably, like some earlier letters of his which did not survive, this one was carried around in my pocket, to be read and re-read, till it fell to pieces. I replied immediately this time, promising to marry him. I no longer had any doubts and our years of separation made me keen that we should be married as soon as possible. His next letter must have been written before he received my acceptance.

BLA   ***August 4th, 1945***

I have seen the authority cancelling my posting. It's a 21 Army Group General Routine Order saying that all German speaking officers will either be accepted for Intelligence Duties or as interpreters or become available for draft. There's also another delicious possibility. Three thousand Arts students are getting priority 'Class B' release for October but having already completed three years I don't think I stand much chance this time.

The men off on this SEAC drop held a farewell binge with all their pals from the Battery last night. Most of them still thought I was going with them and as soon as I got in the door they gave me 'For He's a Jolly Good Fellow' and three cheers followed by a short speech and a repeat ovation. I was pretty well staggered: no other officer in the Unit got such a reception and a more sentimental bloke than myself might have been visibly moved.

I haven't heard from you since my rather frantic correspondence earlier this week. If you thought I was swinging a fast one on you, you were quite entitled to, for I felt I had to act on the spur of the moment.

For now, au revoir till that vacillating date somewhere at the end of the month. I shan't let you out of my sight. I warn you – I'll just about devour you once I get my hands on you!

August 6th, 1945, is a date engraved forever in the history of civilisation. At 7.45am the first atomic bomb was dropped, on Hiroshima. There was an enormous blinding flash and eighty thousand people died instantly. In addition one half that number were badly injured and several thousand more died in the next few weeks. Two thirds of all the buildings in the city were destroyed. In 1986 the final figure of those who had died as a result of the bomb – and who had been identified – was given as one hundred and thirty-nine thousand.

What do you think of the atomic bomb? A lot of people were most excited about it here. My immediate reaction was one of horror and dismay, and I'm afraid I have no reason to feel otherwise up to now. It means almost certainly that if there is another war material civilisation as we know it will be literally obliterated and ground to dust. The secret cannot remain a closed one for many years. Either we abolish war or we perish.

Leave is still as uncertain as ever. The SEAC draft leaves on Thursday. Unfortunately it includes my best two friends in the Unit which is now a shadow of its old self. Most of the fellows are doing Infantry Training. Now the ultimate horror has occurred: I'm in an 'Officers Demonstration Section'. Up to now I've managed to avoid any of this nonsense as I'm employed almost every day on dealings with the Master Race. Talking about the Unit our old BC is going to be our CO when our present one (recently promoted) goes on a Staff Course.

Well, I've left the best thing till last. I can't express in words how delighted I was to know how you had received my proposal of marriage. If you had temporised or even rejected the idea out of hand I couldn't have blamed you. I shall never forget that letter, darling.

On August 8th Russia finally declared war on Japan and proceeded to attack the Japanese forces in Manchuria with more than a million Red Army soldiers. In spite of Hiroshima, Japan had still not surrendered.

The following day the Americans dropped the second atomic bomb – they only had made two at that time. It had been intended to give the Japanese five days in which to agree to the unconditional surrender laid down in the Potsdam Declaration. Bad weather brought the date forward by two days, cutting the time between the two bombs to three days. The intended target for the second bomb was the city of Kohura but, as the plane carrying its load of destruction passed over Kohura, nothing could be seen because of industrial haze.

The next target on the list was Nagasaki and as instructed the pilot flew on and dropped his bomb there. The sight of the destruction totally changed the life of one observer, Leonard Cheshire, who decided to devote his remaining years to helping physically handicapped people. In Nagasaki the eventual death toll was almost fifty thousand.

The Emporer Hirohito decided that his country 'must bear the unbearable' and admit defeat. The following day he formally accepted the Potsdam Declaration and surrendered but not quite 'unconditionally'. A proviso required that the Potsdam Declaration 'does not comprise any demand which prejudices the prerogatives of His Majesty as a sovereign ruler'. In reply the Allies devised an acceptable formula which stated 'the authority of the Emperor ...... shall be subject to the Supreme Commander of the Allied Powers'.

BLA   *August 11th, 1945*

Glad to hear that Peter isn't going out East. The shortening of the war is about the only good thing that is likely to result for some time from the release of the new destructive energy. It is the most horrifying thing that has happened in my lifetime.

Frankly my wits are just a wee bit befuddled, thanks to gin and martini, a Havana cigar, the atom bomb, the imminent end of the Japanese War and the still more staggering fact that I've just won the Open Half-Mile in the Rendsburg Garrison Sports. The Sports were open to over 2000 troops and my only training consisted in the pursuit of 'unclean living', wine, women and cigars.

Re: the demob situation: pay not the slightest attention to the recent newspaper forecasts! Nobody treats these disgraceful publicity stunts seriously over here. Within two days I've read that:

1) Far East Groups up to Group 36 will be coming home in the immediate future

2) Group 32 will be demobbed by Christmas

3) Group 30 will be trying on their civvy suits on June 1st next

4) Virtually all BLA will be demobbed by Christmas '46

2) is arrant nonsense. 1) or 3) or 4) could be correct but then the other two must be wrong. So believe nothing except that we'll reach Group 23 by Christmas.

There's just a slight chance of my getting a Class 'B' (priority) demob under the terms of the new ruling about Arts students. I wrote to Glanville Williams and to Steers (my college tutor) about this saying I was keen to resume my studies. On Sunday I got a reply saying the College was going to do what it could for me but because I already had my first degree they weren't very hopeful. Say I have one chance in four – it's not very likely but what a possibility!

Since June 1944 I've had a very great deal of experience – of hardship and comradeship, of courage and fear, of jubilation and frustration and latterly of a rather strenuous social life. All this hasn't changed my attitude towards you in the least. I love you, physically and in all other respects: I want no-one but you: we are ideally suited – or at least, you suit me ideally in spite of our differences in interests and temperaments.

I am quite certain that our marriage can be absolutely successful provided we are tolerant of each others foibles and don't lose our tempers with each other.

I didn't quite share Stanley's optimism. Though I felt I knew him quite well I suspected he had put me on a pedestal that I did not deserve and that I might not be able to live up to. I was not worried about the physical side of our relationship – we were tremendously attracted towards each other and I wanted his children. (I remember thinking at the time that seven children seemed the ideal number to have, if possible.) Intellectually, though, he still frightened me and I was also far from confident about my domestic abilities. But I was determined to give our marriage everything I could to make it a great success. Nothing now seemed in the way of our marrying once the war was over.

The Red Army was still continuing its fight against the Japanese in Manchuria and on August 14th American bombers, using conventional weapons, struck at several military installations on the island of Honshu. But Hirohito had already decided he had no option but to accept Potsdam and just after midnight – for the first time ever – the Japanese Emperor's voice was heard on the radio.

The Second World War was over.

BLA   ***August 16th, 1945***

It's now late in the evening of VJ+1. This morning I went round to the Cook-house with Harry Duerr and Bill Gill and at 7.30 we took tea round to all the men in bed. I'm serving my time till I go on leave in ten days.

Re: the ring, as far as I am concerned we can dispense with it if you don't want one. But would your family not expect it? I would love to get married on my next leave. Admittedly it would be rather cold at that time of the year but I am told one doesn't notice that sort of thing. It would be very amusing for you to hear the enormous amount of well-meaning advice I've had from friends whom I've told about my intentions. But I can assure you that nothing will deflect me from my essential purpose which is to marry you in the next few months.

PS This photo was taken by Major Watson of me winning the half-mile. Unfortunately the horse which appears to be jumping over my head was superimposed from the next frame.

August 15th was designated VJ Day, though the celebrations, similar to those for VE Day, carried on to the 16th. Many people, who had not heard the early morning news of Japan's complete surrender, went to work only to be sent home again for two days holiday. The weather was wet and the King and Queen were soaked on their state drive, in an open carriage, to the opening of Parliament. It was the first such state occasion since the outbreak of war and the Queen refused to have the cover of the coach raised.

Amidst the joy there was a warning note. In the House of Commons on August 16th Churchill, now leader of the Opposition, used that fateful phrase which was to dominate European politics for the next forty years – an 'iron curtain' has descended on Europe. Also in the House of Commons that day it was announced that the petrol ration was to be increased by 25% together with a reduction in cost per gallon from 2/11½d to 1/1½d.

On 17th August an increase in the rate of demobilisation was promised – a million men and a hundred thousand women would be released by 31st December 1945.

BLA *August 20th, 1945*

I've just got your VJ Day letter. I am amazed at how you write such long and interesting letters these days. Since we've been out of action my letters have all been short and uninteresting. The sound of falling shells used to make one write more freely as well as run more quickly.

Half the officers in the Regiment have been with us for less than three months and most will be demobbed within another three. On Friday 'A' Troop is holding a party before we disintegrate completely (I am making the arrangements for that) and on the following night the Sergeants Mess are throwing another party, which promises to be a real bender.

PS Your spelling is going haywire again. 'Exercise' and 'gaiety' are the versions I learnt at school.

During the next few days the Labour Government began to outline its plans to make Britain a country 'fit for heroes'. Among the proposals was one to nationalise the Bank of England. They pledged to renovate the seven hundred thousand houses in London and seventy thousand houses in Bomb Alley which still needed repairing. Britain was also to have the first normal winter hours (GMT) since 1939. During the war we had had 'Summer-time' in winter and 'Double Summer-time' in summer. Double Summer-time had already ended on July 15th, 1945.

Field Marshal Montgomery declared that the British Liberation Army was henceforth to be known as the British Army On the Rhine, (BAOR), but Stanley was unaware of this as he travelled home on leave at last.

Folkestone *30th August, 1945*

TELEGRAM – OVERSEAS LEAVE DELIVER URGENTLY ARRIVING VICTORIA ABOUT TEN TONIGHT LOVE = STANLEY

Transfer to Intelligence

'Today is an evil day.'
Saturday, November 3rd, 1945

I didn't get Stanley's telegram of August 30th in time to meet him as I was at a Promenade concert at the Albert Hall that evening, with Margaret.

August 30th was the day that General McArthur arrived in mainland Japan. The first American soldiers had set foot on the mainland two days earlier and had met no opposition. In the intervening 'twilight' period between the dropping of the atom bombs and the arrival of the Americans, the Japanese opened the Allied POW camps and some of the occupants wandered over Japan with the happy zeal of tourists. A few even visited Hiroshima. There was little to see, apart from the scarred and burnt people and though some of the soldiers picked up objects, unaware of the dangers of radiation sickness, nobody took home any souvenirs. In the words of an Australian POW who was there, 'One does not rob a tomb'.

On September 2nd, 1945, at 10.30am in Tokyo (2.30am BST), World War Two officially ended. On one of the Allied warships in Tokyo Bay that day was a young First Lieutenant whose job it was to find the POWs and bring them back to the UK. His name was Prince Philip of Greece. The warship was the Missouri, still on active service off Kuwait in the Gulf War of 1991. In Britain, German POWs were helping to bring British farms, including Churchill's farm at Westerham, back into peace-time production.

At last, with the shadow of a posting to SEAC finally removed, Stanley and I were able to discuss our future. We had not seen each other since he had landed in Normandy in June 1944, apart from his brief leave the following April, when the war in Europe was in its final stages. It was a joyous reunion and at last I felt quite sure that I wanted to marry him as much as he wanted to marry me. But there were still a few obstacles to be overcome.

Now he was no longer in physical danger I wanted to tell him face to face the reason for my coolness to him in 1944. I had met and fallen briefly in love with someone else at University. Although the affair was over it was important to me that he heard it from my own lips and not from some mutual friend at Cambridge, but Stanley brushed it aside and said it made not the slightest difference to his feelings for me.

Obstacle number two was my father. Stanley formally asked his permission to marry me. Incredible as it may seem now it was not possible to marry under the age of twenty-one without parental permission. We had no personal financial resources, though our families were quite comfortably off, nor any job prospects but that did not seem to worry my father unduly.

He merely said he thought I was too young – I was nineteen – and I still had another year to Finals. He reminded me that I had persuaded him against his will to let me go to University. Now I could choose between marriage and college.

Stanley replied that we'd waited long enough and to expect us to wait almost another year was unreasonable. Torn between the two of them, a 'lover's tiff' developed and our so-called engagement party, which Stanley had asked his parents to arrange for his last night on leave, ended with me in tears. Our proposed union was not looked upon with much more favour by Stanley's parents who considered us both too immature and irresponsible – Stanley because he couldn't support me and myself for having the temerity to go out with someone else whilst their son was away fighting.

The hero's home-coming was not turning out to be the story-book version.

BAOR   *September 12th, 1945*

I was very glad to get back among my friends again after the gloomy journey which took forty-eight hours. Two of my friends (designated SEAC officers) have returned to the Unit so things won't be too bad here. There have been a few promotions within the Regiment: our CO is now a Lt Col, Charles Harrisson and Bill Gill are once more Major and Captain respectively and I'm about to become Chief Education Instructor within the Regiment.

It's very good to get amongst the gunners again; they're a damn good crowd of chaps. In a couple of weeks we are staging a Gymkhana cum Sports Meeting so I'll have to get down to training soon. But I think I'll do just a little bit of drinking first. There'll be entrants from all over Germany, a Totalisator in the athletics as well as in the mounted events and a big dinner in the evening.

I'm feeling apprehensive about the attitude your parents are adopting. I do hope your father hasn't decided to take you away from college. If he has you must try to get him to rescind his decision and I may write to him myself. I haven't thanked your parents properly for entertaining me as they did, under difficult circumstances, whilst I was on leave. I would be extremely distressed if you had to leave college on my account apart from the tragedy of breaking up your career. But remember that whatever happens my love for you is unshaken.

PS I still consider myself engaged to you, whether formally or informally, whatever he says.

BAOR   *September 14th, 1945*

I am entered for the 880yds and 440yds which are open to several thousand troops. I start training tomorrow – it's always tomorrow – and I plan to keep fit for a fortnight. Today I should have played for the Battery

Football Team (who haven't lost a match this season) but at the last moment I was whipped off into one of those shocking officers' infantry demonstration sections.

Our CO, with typically fiendish ingenuity, set us a scheme which necessitated our standing thigh-deep in water for a half-an-hour. We had 'to prepare for battle' — stuff our packs with the local flora and fauna and black our hands and faces with burnt cork. I was No. 1 on the Bren gun and had to lie, half submerged, in a stinking, rush-edged pool by the side of a lane.

After some time a stout German Frau came down the lane with her husband. Well, the sight of me, concealed, prepared for battle and at the business end of a Bren Gun was too much for her. She almost passed out, then she galloped off down the road moaning 'Herr Gott! Herr Gott! Ach! Herr Gott!' We get a laugh even out of infantry training sometimes.

On September 22nd a new road system was proposed for London to relieve the traffic congestion. It was called the Abercrombie Plan and included tunnels under Hyde Park and under the Thames. The London County Council, forerunner of the Greater London Council, estimated that the ten-year reconstruction plan would cost them £15 million for new roads and a further £30 million for improved roads. The plans consisted of five concentric rings and included a version of the M25, known as E ring, which did not link up under the Thames. At the time it was practical to build the inner rings because of the large stretches of bombed houses but they were soon rebuilt and the scheme was never implemented.

BAOR   **September 24th, 1945**

Tonight I saw 'Henry V' at the Garrison Cinema. It was a very good show though the typical Elizabethan soliloquies and harangues would be better handled in the modern theatre. It was certainly the best historical film produced in this country and on a par with 'Alexander Nevsky'.

The film script of 'Henry V' was written by the young Laurence Olivier, who also starred in it. It begins as if staged in Shakespeare's Globe Theatre and gradually becomes more realistic. The critics of the time raved about it. In comparing it with Eisenstein's splendid historical pageant, 'Alexander Nevsky' Stanley was giving 'Henry Vth' the highest praise possible.

BAOR   **September 27th, 1945**

My form in training hasn't been too bad but I don't expect to win either the 880 or the 440 yards on Saturday. However, one never knows and the

prizes are very good. Even the third prize is 100 cigarettes. I expect to do
about 2'14" in the 880 and 59" in the 440. Wish me luck.

PS My cousin, Margery, sent us a congratulations cable from Alexandria
– extremely nice of her, I think.

Stanley had written to Margery that we were engaged and getting married at Christmas. This now seemed a forlorn hope though my parents attitude was beginning to soften. Meanwhile I had persuaded my father to let me continue at college. Grammar school and University fees were expensive and, though there were some scholarships and grants available, higher education was still out of reach for the majority of the population. The school-leaving age was fourteen and on September 28th, 1945, the Minister of Education stated that it could not be raised to fifteen until at least April 1947.

Education was not yet state-controlled and the railways were not nationalised. On September 30th, an LMS (London, Midland and Scottish) passenger train crashed in Hertfordshire at 9am. Forty-four people were killed and eighty-eight injured – the worst train crash since the First World War.

BAOR   *September 30th, 1945*

I am writing this with a rather peculiar Danish pen, with a glass nib,
which I got for coming second in the 440 yards yesterday. I also won the 100
cigarettes for coming third in the 880. The opposition in the quarter mile
was much stiffer than before and I was just pipped at the post by a
Dutchman.

Today I played in the Regimental football team down at Neumunster where
we drew 4-4 with 53 Heavy Regiment after an extremely exciting game.

BAOR   *October 3rd, 1945*

This breaks a long interval of silence. I think it is three whole days since I
last wrote.

Last night three of our newer officers, all Regular Warrant Officers, had
their demob party. It developed into a terrific rough house and two chaps
had their shirts torn to shreds, someone got a black eye, and broken crockery
and glasses were strewn all over the place. But it was all in good part and I
went to bed fully clothed and with the light still on.

The German classes are going fine though it would be easier for me to
make a series of gramophone records. I'm very over-worked – Orderly
Officer, judging Infantry schemes and worst of all being embarrassed by the
wives of my SS detainees. It's not at all easy to explain to an emotional
woman why I think her husband is a pretty bad type.

I had a letter from my father today but I find it very difficult to assess the strength of their opposition to my marrying so I've asked Sylvia to give me her view of how best to handle them. It's unfortunate really that I didn't emphasise more our estrangement in 1944. At first I was confident that I could change your attitude — we were so happy at Southwell — and until about July or thereabouts I didn't treat your stance very seriously. After that I made it clear to them that things weren't as I wished between us but I was never very specific. I never have discussed our relationship very much at home and I only made occasional references to it after that time.

Nothing could be worse from my point of view than strife with my parents — except losing you. As far as the two of us are concerned — I love you, beyond any shadow of doubt and I have absolutely no interest in anyone else. But it's very difficult to convince them of that by writing. I'm determined to get it sorted out on my next leave.

Another man whose family had disapproved of his marriage was in the news. On October 5th the Duke of Windsor visited Britain after six years of absence. It was a private visit to his mother, Queen Mary, and he did not meet King George and Queen Elizabeth.

Also arriving in Britain that week were the first POWs from the Far East. Many of them were in a pitiable state, comparable to that of the inmates of Hitler's concentration camps. They, too, had been subjected to experiments, torture and starvation. Stanley was about to become involved in tracing some of the perpetrators of similar dreadful crimes committed in Europe.

BAOR   **Saturday, October 6th, 1945**

I went off to BAOR HQ at Herford on Thursday morning for this Intelligence interview which took place today. We travelled in a comfortable Staff car and spent the night in a rather pleasant transit camp — good food and central heating.

I stand quite a good chance of being accepted for Field Security work or Political Intelligence: they're getting so short of Intelligence officers they'll take pretty well anyone these days. I'll get 2/6d a day extra with good chances of promotion. I'm due for an extra 2/3d a day anyway on November 3rd for three years service and that would bring me up to 19/9d a day. If worse comes to worst I could then manage to support you while you finish college, though goodness knows where we'd live.

Between returning to Germany from leave in mid-September and the end of December Stanley wrote fifty-two letters to me. They were all at least four pages long, in tiny handwriting, and over two hundred words to the page

– approaching a total of some fifty thousand words. Much of the content was of a personal nature and concerned our plans for the future. He had always been a prolific writer but for this period particularly it is difficult to give more than a flavour of a few of the letters.

BAOR *Sunday, October 7th, 1945*

I had a letter from my cousin, Harry Brown, congratulating us on our engagement and regretting his inability to attend the 'blessed event'. My father's family has always been rather sentimental. I take after my mother more, except in regard to my absent-mindedness. I'm delighted she's invited to meet you in town or have you down to 'Jasper', our Westcliff home.

I'm still giving my six German classes a week. We're getting to the stage now where the more gormless pupils – about 70% – get completely baffled by the grammar, because they've never been taught any English grammar. But they are getting somewhere and it's useful practice for me apart from keeping me off Infantry training.

BAOR *October 10th, 1945*
If everyone was always blunt and frank, civilised social life would be impossible. Even between us, 100% frankness would be undesirable. It is understood that some things are better left unsaid.

I'm reading quite a lot nowadays. At the moment it's 'Goodbye to Berlin' by Christopher Isherwood and I've just finished 'The English People' by Brogan: a most penetrating study.
Still no news from the Intelligence Board.

I wonder now what I could possibly have written to give rise to his comments in his first paragraph of the letter above. Whatever it was, the war had certainly made him far more cynical than the young, passionately straightforward, student I remembered.

On October 18th, as Stanley was preparing to appear at a trial in his legal capacity, the Home Secretary, Mr Chuter Ede, announced that a total of sixteen spies had been tried and executed in England during the war. Four of them were British.

BAOR *Thursday, October 18th, 1945*

On Monday I am going to defend Gunner X on his latest court-martial. In my opinion he'll be very lucky to get off with less than two years this time – absent without leave for twenty-eight days and stealing a watch: and this was while he was serving detention at the time. Possibly a superb forensic exhibition will reduce the sentence to eighteen months. I'm taking the line that he cannot be deterred by punishment. A risky line to take but it is the only one that can do any good. He is pleading guilty, anyway.

On October 24th Quisling, a Norwegian officer whose name had become synonymous with cooperating with the enemy, was shot by a Norwegian firing squad in Oslo. The same day the United Nations Organisation was inaugurated.

At home the Minister of Labour announced that a Women's Resettlement Committee would be set up to advise Ministers on the problems of resettling women in domestic life.

BAOR   **Saturday, October 27th, 1945**

I've had an absolutely first-class three days in Denmark – a magnificent country with very fine people and very fine food. The country itself is largely agricultural, very green and undulating and rather pretty. The farm buildings are extraordinarily up to date and there are large numbers of well-built modern houses.

Copenhagen itself is a pleasant, well planned city – the Paris of the North. There was an abundance of everything: all kinds of food, clothing, furniture, most of it unobtainable in England. Every morning for breakfast we got two eggs and a glass of milk. Mushrooms, cheeses, smoked eel, smoked salmon, all kinds of meat, fish and poultry are unrationed. My stomach is like a football. And the ices! Served with an equal quantity of whipped cream. I wish you could have been with me.

(Denmark was the first foreign country we visited after we were married.)

The first night in Copenhagen we were stopped by a crowd of drunks in evening dress. They took us to their flat which belonged to a leading industrialist. They were mostly the big shots of the Resistance Movement. One, named Lt Tretow Loof, was the leader of the Copenhagen sabotage group. He was condemned to death on April 1st, 1945, after he had been flogged and tortured three times by the Gestapo. He admitted having disclosed all the secrets as a result of the tortures. But the Group took five German officers as hostages and the Germans released him. His execution was originally fixed for May 11th. Another of the Group that night had helped hundreds of Jewish children escape to Sweden.

There's an inordinate admiration everywhere for things English and a very good knowledge of British politics, life and literature. Believe it or not, one of their favourite authors is Kipling and a popular song is 'Road to Mandalay'. At the Danish Parliament I sat in the Premier's seat and also noticed that Christmas Muller, the Foreign Secretary, had a biography of Churchill on his desk in the Chamber.

I've finished Virginia Woolf's 'Orlando' and I'm now reading Graham Greene's 'The Power and the Glory' and Huxley and Deane's 'Future of the Colonies'.

The future of the British Colonies was a topic which absorbed much of Stanley's time in the years following the war, when he acted as constitutional adviser both to the British Government and to the governing bodies of many of the emergent nations. The British Government had already announced the proposal to make India independent (September 19th) and that it was time for India to settle their internal differences. It certainly looked as if the Labour Government would remain in office for many years and carry out its policy of allowing self-determination to the Colonies. The Labour Party was remarkably successful in the first local elections since the war began, held on 1st November, when Labour had a majority in twenty-two of the twenty-eight London boroughs.

November 1st was the day which had been designated for the invasion of mainland Japan if the nuclear bombs were not used first. Attlee told Parliament that a research and experimental station was to be set up at Harwell and a few days later the USSR said it would start building its own atomic bomb.

BAOR   **Saturday, November 3rd, 1945**

Today is an evil day. It is the third anniversary of my entry into the Army. But it has its compensations for I get an increment of 2/3d which gives me 15/3d plus my 2/– Field Allowance – a comical survival from the campaign now we're living in a centrally heated hotel instead of a slit trench. Net income of your future husband, with tax deducted:– 14/6d a day.

Tonight I spent some of it and went to see 'Frenchmen's Creek' – pretty awful with everything in half-light and sumptuously artificial. Joan Fontaine, though, reminded me just a little bit of you.

There had been a Supplementary Budget on October 13th which reduced the wartime standard rate of tax from April 1st, 1946. Personal allowances for single people were to go up from £80 to £110. On the first £50 of annual taxable income the rate in the pound would be 3/–, on the next £75 it would be 6/– and on the remainder the standard rate would go down from 10/– to 9/–. For the whole of the war the British people had been contributing almost half their earnings to the country.

On bonfire night the Minister of Education, perhaps mindful of earlier attacks on Parliament by discontented citizens, said that every child in Wales would henceforth have the opportunity of learning in both the English and Welsh languages.

BAOR   **Tuesday, 6th November**

I heard a rather amusing story today from the Brigade Education Officer.

He applied for his present job in May. In September he happened to be at 21 Army Group HQ and asked about his application. They looked it up and told him he had been posted to this job three months previously. The posting order had never arrived.

In the Air Force some events moved rather more rapidly. On November 7th Group Captain Wilson set the World Air Speed Record at 606mph, flying in an RAF Gloster Meteor over Herne Bay.

BAOR   ***November 9th, 1945***

Today I went to Neumunster to collect pay for the Regiment (£1600) and we were held up at a level crossing for a few minutes. Going to the front of the column I saw there had been a smash. The returning leave train had hit a truck and trailer, carrying three British soldiers, on the unbarred crossing. Parts of the vehicles and their occupants were strewn all over the countryside. It happened ten minutes before we got to the crossing. War is not the only danger here.

In Britain on November 11th, 1945, there was a resumption, for the first time since 1938, of the two minutes silence – this time for the dead of both World Wars. But as a day of commemoration it was thought to be inappropriate and likely to be changed as it had no connection with the Second World War. I do not know whether the silence was observed in Rendsburg but the day was marked in another fashion.

BAOR   ***November 11th, 1945***

We chose today to play our first soccer match against the Germans, the Rendsburg Football Club. It's a rotten day – rainy, windy and cold. All the same we got a good crowd and had the pleasure of beating them 9-0. That'll learn 'em.

BAOR   ***Tuesday 13th, November, 1945***

My course has come through! I'm off to Paderborn in a fortnight (November 25th) and the course (Intelligence and Field Security) lasts till December 9th. Whatever happens I hope to be sent back to 8 Corps District in Schleswig-Holstein or Hamburg. Well, the Army can move quickly after all. It's only seven weeks since my interview and five and a half months since we were asked to submit our names. My new address will be: Military Intelligence Wing, School of Military Intelligence, BAOR Training Centre.

The set-up in the Regiment at the moment is that Thomas is CO, Charles Harrisson is BC of 104 Battery and Peter Lloyd (ex-Adjutant) is BC of 103 Battery. Harry Duerr is Battery Captain with John Wagner and Bill Gill as Troop Commanders. George Amman has gone to England and I suspect will get Class 'B' release before he is sent out to SEAC.

To answer your question about my views on Palestine: it's just about insoluble. (At the beginning of November anti-Jewish rioting had broken out in Arab territories and on 13th November Bevin announced that the UK and USA would devise a plan to settle the Palestine question.)

I find it difficult to know what policy to support. Any solution will have to be enforced by arms. I regard Zionism as a creditable view for a Jew to hold and pursue but a Jewish state in the Middle East would be surrounded by hostile Arab neighbours. To survive it would have to depend on outside bayonets. This would mean the perpetuation of imperialism in the Middle East – or the withdrawal of support by the West followed by war with the Arabs. They (the Arabs) appear to be a very backward and unreasonable race of people. Anyway, Palestine couldn't absorb more than three or four million Jews and what about the other seven or eight million? An independent Jewish state might possibly reduce persecution in the short run but I fear it will not last.

The United Nations meanwhile were busy setting up various international bodies. On November 15th, in London, UNESCO (United Nations Educational, Scientific and Cultural Organisation) came into being. In Germany the Allies were busy with the Nuremberg Trials which began on November 20th. Goering, von Ribbentrop, Keitel, Doenitz and von Papen were among the Nazi War criminals standing trial. Hess, who tried to claim amnesia, was declared fit and joined them ten days later.

77th Medium Regiment   **Friday, November 23rd, 1945**

I'm off to Paderborn tomorrow morning. It's about half-way between Hanover and the Ruhr.

Your information about Sylvia's intentions shook me somewhat. She's never lived away from home so it's natural for her to want to try the experiment. But I don't agree she'll give it up after three months because she wouldn't admit that she's made a mistake even if she realises that she has very quickly. Her new job in the West End sounds a good one and well paid, too. Anyway, I'll give her some brotherly advice when I am next on leave.

Military Intelligence School   **Sunday, 25th November, 1945**

Just discovered the School isn't at Paderborn any more: it shifted about a month ago to Bad Driberg, a little spa about fifteen miles east of the town. Of course, nobody thought to tell me. The Commandant is an old Cat's man (St Catherine's College, Cambridge) and asked if I'd like to do a staff job. Well, I've no objection to another three bob a day.

My leave date is now December 13th and should finish about Christmas Eve so I may get an extension as they won't have people returning on Christmas Day.

In England topics which had received little attention during the war were now back on the agenda. On November 27th the Government announced that it had set up a committee to advise on the establishment of a British Institute of Management. Reforestation plans were also announced and a sum of £20 million was allocated to the Forestry Commission to spend on planting trees between 1946 and 1950.

Military Intelligence School   **Friday, November 30th, 1945**

The course is a very interesting one but it involves a great deal of work. We have six hours of lectures a day and they're very meaty. Then we have various tests and quite a few fail as temperamentally unsuitable. But I am afraid I can't tell you what we are learning; I've signed too many declarations under the Official Secrets Act. As far as getting something into one's skull is concerned, I recommend the occasional sniff of Benzedrine when you're sleepy. I've just had some sent to me so that I can continue my nightly dissipations in this smoke-laden, centrally heated atmosphere. You can't beat it.

Military Intelligence School   **Tuesday, December 4th, 1945**

I've written to my mother and asked her to contact you about the allocation of my person during the leave period. I'm delighted she's asked you down to stay for part of the time but it's a nuisance that your term finishes so late. It feels like the end of term here. We've just done our third written exam followed by an amusing exercise. The instructor said I did pretty well and this afternoon we are going to be told what, if any, our next job will be in Intelligence. I leave this joint on Sunday morning, make my way back to Rendsburg and depart on leave next Tuesday.

Military Intelligence School   **Saturday, December 8th, 1945**

It's very cold today with a temperature well below freezing and it's

snowing at the moment. The course is over and I've been told my report is
'definitely above average' and I have been recommended for a Staff Officer's
post. I had asked for something on the political or quasi-legal side. But after
waiting three years to get into Intelligence I could hardly expect the Army to
use me where I'd be most useful so I'm going to the case-work branch.

BAOR, 11th December
LEAVE UNAVOIDABLY POSTPONED TILL TWENTY-EIGHTH
LETTER FOLLOWS LOVE STANLEY

Awards for services to humanity were made in Oslo on December
12th, 1945. Amongst the men honoured were Sir Alexander Fleming
and two of his colleagues for their work in discovering penicillin.

77th Medium Regiment   Wednesday, December 12th, 1945

I should have been on my way homeward: instead I have to write this
letter. A regulation has just been introduced to the effect that no-one is to
proceed on leave less than 120 days after his previous leave so cancel all
arrangements, it's now the 28th.
    Everything is fixed for my posting to Corps. I was interviewed today
(which I would have missed if I had been on leave) and I'm moving across to
Plön on Friday morning. It's about forty miles from Rendsburg and fifteen
miles south-east of Kiel. A beautiful little town in the lake district of
Holstein but over-populated by troops. The Colonel said it is an excellent job
for anyone who wants to enter the public service.

Stanley had been recommended for an Intelligence Staff Officer's post at
last and was to join Ib, the counter Intelligence branch. It was then under
the command of Lieutenant Colonel Neill McDermot who was later to
become a QC, a Labour Government Minister and Secretary General of the
International Commission of Jurists. His fifteen or so subordinate Ib officers
were lodged and fed in E Mess which occupied a couple of houses on the
outskirts of the town.
    By December 1945 the stage of arresting war criminals had largely ended
and Ib began to assume the task of vetting applicants for public office, such
as that of mayor, and for posts in the political parties, which in the New Year,
would once again be allowed.

GSI Branch, Plön   Friday, December 14th, 1945

I left the Unit with mixed feelings and my first impressions here are
equally varied. I was shown round by the chap I'm working under and by
six o'clock I was so bewildered that I lost my way back to my billet. I don't

think I'm even quite sure what job I'm supposed to be doing. It's one of those fairly simple jobs which can't be explained verbally but should become crystal clear after a week's practice.

GSI Branch   **Monday 17th December, 1945**

The Brigadier was round today and the Intelligence Colonel described our branch as the 'bottle-neck department'. I didn't see the Brigadier come in, by the way, and the Colonel had to bat me over the head with a document file twice before I awoke to his presence. I'm beginning dimly to discern the nature of my functions now: they consist mainly of moving sheaves of documents from my in-tray to my out-tray with the result that sundry persons occasionally get moved from one part of the country to another.

Yesterday I discovered for the first time the existence of five pigeon-holes which were unfortunately crammed full with documents awaiting my attention. Whenever a new bundle of files comes in I just shove them into the pigeon holes with the others. After all, I'm only here for another seven days.

The Labour Party's attitude to private enterprise was illustrated by two statements in December. On the 17th the Location of Businesses Order, which had been in force throughout the war was rescinded, thus permitting anyone who wanted to open a shop (excluding a food shop) to do so without a licence. The Ministry of Information was to be wound up.

The following day the Government declared that the Gas Industry would shortly be nationalised. And money was to be raised to build a Shakespeare Memorial Theatre on the South Bank.

For a member of Churchill's war-time Coalition Government, L. S. Amery, the dawn of December 19th must have been the saddest in his life. Leo Amery had been the Tory MP who, quoting Oliver Cromwell's words on leadership, was mainly responsible for toppling Chamberlain in May 1940. He was proud of one of his sons, Julian, who later became an MP. During the war Julian had been parachuted behind enemy lines to disrupt communications. But at dawn on that grey November day his other son, John Amery, aged 33, was hanged for high treason at Wandsworth Jail. John Amery had tried to persuade British POWs to join the Free Corps and fight for Germany.

GSI Branch   **Wednesday, December 19th, 1945**

My leave's been put off again. It's rather like 'this year, next year, sometime ....' It may be next year because the leave date is now 31st December. I shall be absolutely furious if I have to sing 'Auld Lang Syne on the platform of Rotterdam station. The Adjutant was under the unfortunate delusion that there were only thirty days in December but I've sorted that one out.

GSI Branch   **Friday, December 21st, 1945**

Today the Colonel GSI had a chat with me. He's a very decent chap for a regular high-ranking officer. Unfortunately he thought I was rather young for the political side but said I might go to a Field Security Section later. I don't know what gave my mother the idea that I may have to 'step down' for a time. I certainly can't step down much further without losing my foothold altogether. Anyway, at the moment I'm a rather superior type of Lieutenant or will be when the Royal Army Pay Corps get round to crediting me with my extra two bob.

I'm still looking forward desperately to that elusive D-Day but like the other D-Day it will no doubt arrive before the leaves of autumn fall again.

GSI Branch   **December 23rd, 1945**

Here's a card to wish you many happy returns of your birthday. I forgot to mention my greetings in my last letter. You may rest assured it won't be the last time I forget that sort of thing.

Roses decorated the romantic birthday card he sent me. But roses were not the flower featured in the most popular song of 1945 which was 'We'll Gather Lilacs in the Spring, Again'. This sentimental tune looked forward to the resumption of a normal life, free from the heart-breaking separations caused by war. I used to hum it all the time.

The Last Hurdle

'It'll be just another headache for Monty or his successor'
February 14th, 1946

Stanley arrived back in England on leave on the last day of December 1945. Whether it was the prevailing season of good will or whether they had decided to bow to the inevitable, both sets of parents had recently changed tack.

There was a hiccup over the wedding arrangements. Both Stanley and I wanted to get married quickly and quietly but this was not to be. Our respective parents had other ideas and elaborate plans were put in motion for a grand spring wedding. The proposed date was actually very inconvenient coming as it did just before my Finals, but we both felt it wiser not to demur.

There was another slight hiccup over the engagement ring. Stanley's mother, Jennie, and I met in town just before Christmas. Stanley had asked his mother to choose an engagement ring for me as he could not be sure of finding something suitable in Germany. She kindly suggested we might look at some together to give her an idea of what I liked. After a day spent in and out of jewellers' shops, where I resisted the traditional solitaire diamond, I finally spotted an old ring that I immediately fell in love with. It was very plain with a single emerald-cut diamond supported by two triangular shaped sapphires. It was also outrageously expensive so I firmly said I did not need a ring at all.

The story of our fruitless search was recounted at the New Year's Eve engagement party held at Stanley's home in Westcliff. Whereupon their next door neighbour said, 'That ring is mine. It belonged to my grandmother and is on sale or return in Bond Street. I'll get it back and you can have it'. And he did and I still have it. How I came to choose that one ring out of the millions on display in London beggars belief.

New Year's Eve was celebrated in a different way in one part of London. Wembley Ice Rink, where I learnt to skate as a child before the war, was re-opened and thousands flocked there for the first New Year's Eve of peace for six years. As the old year ran out, a game of musical chairs was played on the ice. It was pandemonium as the last few chairs were fought over but, as Big Ben chimed the hour, concentric circles of the unseated skaters formed. They sang Auld Lang Syne and skated hand in hand towards and away from the remaining chairs in the centre of the ice rink. From a distance, high in the stands surrounding the rink, it was like some gigantic, brightly coloured flower opening and closing its petals.

On January 1st test flights started from a new major international airport to be known as Heathrow. It was intended to start a regular passenger and freight service to South America. On what was then the finest runway in the world a jet airliner, the Lancastrian, took off on a proving flight to Montevideo. It had to use conventional propellers to get off the ground but, once in the air, the jet engines took over.

Soon after, on January 9th, Churchill left for a holiday in the States. He was given a hero's welcome and not even the pouring rain could dampen the enthusiasm of the New York crowds as he drove through the city. Later, at a dinner in his honour, he stated that, in spite of the Iron Curtain, he did not think the Soviet Union wanted war. Elsewhere in the States at a Hollywood Awards ceremony, Bob Hope was honoured for the first time. He received an Oscar. It was one inch high, but he said he expected it to grow.

In London on January 4th Aneurin Bevan, then Minister of Health, declared the top targets for the new NHS were to be TB (now virtually eradicated in the UK) and VD (with us still and, more frightening, its successor, AIDS).

GSI   ***Tuesday, January 15th, 1946***

It's a bit early to begin to appreciate what a terrific leave I had, but it was certainly very much the best yet. Of course, it was the first on which I'd been with you all the time. But I can't keep on saying 'I love you': women have no idea how embarrassing the constant reiteration of those three words becomes for the average man.

I was very moved by the Pincus' reaction to the news of our forthcoming marriage. They really are a remarkable family and you are very fortunate in having such friends.

Paul Pincus had told Stanley when we visited them at the beginning of January that he had always hoped that one day I would be his daughter-in-law. But since John had been killed and that was no longer possible, he could not wish for a better partner for me. He added that we would always have a home with them if we needed it. Years later we visited them in Australia and their welcome was as warm as ever.

It is so difficult to express my feelings for you without sounding sentimental. But I think I must be the luckiest man alive. You have no idea of the pain I carried throughout the Normandy battle, not caused by fear of being killed but by the dreadful apprehension that I was going to lose you to someone else. And whatever may happen in the future I shall always have the memory of these last two weeks. No-one can take that away and no-one could ever take your place.

On the 20th January Charles de Gaulle resigned. Riots had broken out in Paris earlier in the month over bread shortages. De Gaulle, a brilliant soldier and inspired war leader, had always been found difficult by his colleagues. In war-time this was tolerated but now he refused to align himself with any party and found himself isolated. It was 1958 before he became President of his beloved republic, brought back to power by the Algerian troubles.

GSI *Tuesday, January 22nd, 1946*

Last night I went over to 77 as I had just heard the Regiment was being broken up. Don Campbell told me that things are very much on the move in Rendsburg. One of the Batteries is going to an outlying village in a new area but I don't know where. Incidentally he told me that the coloured cover for Kaserne's Christmas issue cost over 700 marks. Inasmuch as we never got more than 200 marks from sales it seems that my last deed in 77 was to bankrupt 103 Battery.

It seems to me now that the comradeship developed by fighting together in the same ranks is something very much bigger than any other more or less casual acquaintanceship. I felt sorry I hadn't stayed with the chaps but I think if I had I would have definitely gone to SEAC. Tomorrow I'll be going to the Officers and Sergeants Farewell Party.

Although Stanley clearly missed his war-time companions, in his new job he met an amazing assortment of talented people. One of those whose company Stanley found particularly interesting was Hugh Carless, who later became a diplomat. Writing to me recently about those days, Hugh commented:

'E Mess had a galaxy of talent and compared with other officers messes in the Rhine Army, often seemed more of a cabaret with a colourful and gifted cast. Half a dozen of its members were Intelligence Corps officers – experts on the Nazi hierarchy, linguists, interrogators. To this core had been added others from the RAF, Parachute Corps and 15 Scottish Infantry Division which was being disbanded. Stanley, with his analytical mind, his mild appearance and gentle sense of humour, was soon welcomed as the egg-head in residence.'

GSI *Friday, January 25th, 1946*

Things are moving in Plön but the lakes aren't moving. They're frozen over. Like the lakes I expect 8 Corps will dissolve in a couple of months time and my little department will be taken over by Rhine Army so I'll have to look for another job.

Talking of jobs, I've had a letter from Glanville Williams – typically generous. He said he would always take a keen interest in my career and advised me to apply to one of the provincial universities for a lectureship. But one of my reasons for not wanting to take up an academic career is that I don't want to spend my life absorbed in concentrated study. You don't realise what I'd be like. I'd become extremely unworldly and absent-minded and generally irritating. It was very nice of you to be so amenable regarding my career — I hope you'll always be so easy to please.

Stanley's description of himself as a potential academic was very accurate but it was also quite obvious to all that knew him that he would be an outstanding success in that capacity. He had no business experience or interest in the commercial side of life, and he was too lacking in self-confidence to become a diplomat though I am sure that, with his political acumen, intellectually he would have been suited to it. But in the academic field he had already made an impression on his tutors and I encouraged him to pursue Glanville's suggestion.

As for my career, if any, it was clearly going to have to take second place. The problems of preparing for the wedding plus the disturbance caused by LSE's return to London, began to interfere seriously with the time that I could devote to study. Living at home, though far more comfortable than my digs, was also far more distracting. I discussed the difficulties with my tutor, Professor Rhodes, who was Head of the Statistics Department. He pointed out that I had gone up to university a year early and could therefore afford to take an extra year if I so wished. We agreed that, apart from two subsidiary papers, I should postpone taking Finals till 1947.

With the wedding only a few months away, I set about looking for a flat in London, searching columns of local newspapers for a second hand cooker. No new gas or electric stoves had been manufactured during the war and fridges, freezers and washing machines were rare luxuries, not always found even in well-to-do households. The problem of furnishing a kitchen with cooking utensils, though, was one I did not need to worry about. Myrtle Pincus kindly organised a 'kitchen shower party' for me. 'Shower parties' were at that time virtually unheard of in England though quite common in Australia and America. As a result I was given everything I needed, from saucepans to wooden spoons. All that remained was to learn how to use them.

On 28th January the first bananas to be imported commercially since 1939 arrived at Bristol docks. There were five million of them, destined for distribution to children under the age of eighteen who lived in south-west England.On the dockside were a committee of testers — children who had never tasted a banana. The bananas met with universal approval. But the following month a three-year old child died after eating four bananas which had been given to her as a treat.

GSI   ***January 29th, 1946***

> *I had a rather unpleasant shock today when I learnt that the RA branch at BAOR HQ had refused to sanction my posting to Intelligence. This means that I may have to return to Artillery. However, GSI have objected most strongly and now that the battle is joined it should take them some time to sort out.*

Meanwhile Stanley continued to work in Intelligence. Hugh Carless describes the section's activities: 'After the war ended, the work of Ib had been to help secure and de-nazify the British occupation zone. This was accomplished by the arrest and interrogation of leading members of the Nazi Party, Gestapo and SS and the internment for subsequent trial of the most infamous. Among these was Carl Petersen, the head of the Gestapo in Oslo, and Field Marshals von Mannstein and von Brauchitsch.' (The latter's engraved Walther pistol is still in the possession of one of the officers and von Brauchitsch's baton was inscribed and presented by E mess to the 8 Corps commander, General Sir Evelyn Barker.)

'Stanley was assigned to the casework section of Ib under Major Russell Ross. This section kept files on all those in the automatic arrest categories who were either wanted for arrest, due to be interrogated, or kept in internment locally or required for transfer from the 8 Corps area to, for example, the American occupation zone or Denmark.'

GSI   ***February 5th, 1946***

> *Yesterday I went down to the big Internment Camp at Neumünster and a sergeant took me round one of the blocks. The place is seriously overcrowded and rather insanitary and opportunities for exercise are limited; but it is very far removed from anything resembling a Concentration Camp. In fact the food ration is almost 10% higher than that of the civilian population. Internees are also allowed to receive parcels.*
>
> *The internal discipline and administration is largely managed by the internees themselves. There are a fair number of books available and there are lectures daily. Any hardships which the internees have to bear must be mental and emotional rather than physical. There are no bullying camp guards or anything of that sort. The Commandant, an English Lt Col, is a decent sort of chap who is most suitable for the job.*
>
> *Anyway, I'm not prepared to waste much sympathy on these people because the overwhelming majority are either thoroughly unpleasant types or people who've achieved high positions through their loyalty to the Nazi regime.*

Supporting the staff work as "troops on the ground" were six or seven Field Security Sections covering the Corps area and stationed in the major towns such as Flensburg, Kiel, Lübeck and Pinneberg. Each section comprised one officer, Sergeant Major or Staff Sergeant, two or three sergeants and the rest corporals making a total of thirteen. Virtually all of these would be fluent German speakers and the section would be in close contact with the local population.

GSI   *Saturday, February 9th, 1946*

By Stakhanovite efforts we have just completed the appropriately named 'Operation Bedlam' i.e. the closing down of this department. Today a comic message arrived saying that I had to go forthwith to GSI, so I gather GSI have triumphed over RA for the custody of my body. I've never been of the opinion that they'd get me as far as SEAC. But in retaliation the dear old Rhine Army have posted my batman to the other side of Germany.

PS Give my love to Molly when you see her – she's a very nice girl and I am sorry that she and James have broken up.
PPS Poor old Harry Brown has had a rather rotten home-coming after four years abroad. Sleet and snow in England and four cases of small-pox on his ship. He has been in quarantine for two weeks.

Stanley's use of the term, 'Stakhanovite', seemed more appropriate to our needs in this country. (Stakhanov was a Russian coal-miner who produced an incredible daily output by working two shifts out of three per day, instead of one.) It was a bitter February and coal was in short supply. The Government appealed to industry to save fuel as London only had a week's supply left. The Minister of Food told the House of Commons that the country would have to return to war-time rationing due to a world food shortage. Thousands in Germany were starving because their agricultural industry had been virtually destroyed by the fighting.

Bread would be darker and contain less wheat. The butter, margarine and fat ration would be cut from 8oz to 7oz per week. No rice was to be imported and the ration of meat, bacon, poultry and eggs would have to remain at the war-time level. A few weeks later the Ministry issued a recipe for squirrel pie.

GSI   *Thursday, February 14th, 1946*

Herewith photo taken at a recent Rendsburg dance. You'll be pleased to see I'm handling nothing more potent than a glass of gin. Don Campbell is on my left. I'm going with him and Bill Gill to Hamburg for the weekend.
Your legal query left me most embarrassed. Not only have I no recollection

of either of the cases you mention but I'm quite unable to answer your question. The point you made is rather a clever one but it is nothing unusual to have a set of facts which is irreconcilable with a supposedly fundamental theory of common law. In an uncodified system like the English it is often difficult to say what is the principle underlying the law. This is particularly true of the law of contract and the law regarding mistake and misrepresentation is notorious in this respect. Why don't you ask Glanville?

Applications have been invited from officers who want to bring their wives here. I think you'd quite like it in June, July and August but I have no intention of inflicting a German winter on you.

The comedy of my posting took a rather more serious turn yesterday when RA, Rhine Army, phoned up and said I was to report to them there forthwith. To which GSI said 'Do nothing'. It appears I am still in the Gunners and they can post me where they like! I'll soon be another headache for Monty or his successor. It's just fantastic for the Gunners to start demanding my body at this stage, after I've been in Intelligence for three months. The Colonel spoke gloomily yesterday of leaving military organisation in the hands of officers who are young and inexperienced.

On 14th March the International Olympic Committee announced that the games, suspended during the war, would be held in London in 1948. The same day an announcement of a new competitor in the field of speed was made. But this time it was a machine, which was capable of doing in seconds what a human mathematician took hours over. Called ENIAC and referred to as the Electronic Brain, it had eighteen thousand electronic valves but no moving parts. The announcement concluded by saying it might be possible to find some commercial applications for it.

GSI   **Friday, February 22nd, 1946**

The most interesting item of news in your letter was your talk with Glanville. I shall drop him another line today. Possibly he's more susceptible to a woman's influence than he thinks. I had some more good news today. I am going into Political Intelligence after all, probably at Lübeck. I shan't know for certain till Major Rolo, who runs that side of things, comes back from leave.

From the serious and occasionally dangerous work Stanley and his fellow Ib officers were engaged in, E mess provided relaxation if not always rest. Of discipline and sobriety, according to Hugh Carless, there was little but some tone was given to guest nights by the three General Staff Officers (G2s) – Majors Rolo, Randell and Russell Ross – who in turn assumed the office of Mess President and Entertainer in chief. On those evenings they were always acclaimed with the E mess song which lamented the slowness of promotion and had as its chorus line "I want to be a G2 too".

Of this remarkable trio Russell Ross, who later became a successful Suffolk farmer, presided over the poker table where the rules were designed to prevent anyone winning too much. Keith Randell, who stayed on in Intelligence, was a brilliant raconteur of barely credible stories. Hugh Carless quotes an example from the days when Major Randell was a security officer in North Norfolk. One winter evening, with snow on the ground, he apprehended a suspicious character loitering near Sandringham. "Your identity card" demanded Keith. As the only response was a stare, Keith continued, "Then I'll have to arrest you." "Bbut you ccan't dddddo th th that," was the stuttering reply, "Ii'm th th the Kking".

GSI   **February 26th, 1946**

Today was a really bumper day for me. I had five letters altogether: one from you, one from my mother and two from the Civil Service. But two and two only make four. Here's what the fifth one said:

"HM the King has approved the award to the above officers (Major Peter Lloyd and Lt S. A. de Smith) of the Chevalier of the Order of Leopold 11 with palm and of the Croix de Guerre 1940 with palm. The ribbon may now be worn pending presentation of the insignia at a later date."

I expect it is for some entirely imaginary exploits at the Escaut canal. The whole thing seems a little funny to me and if anyone asks you, you'd better say it was for something in Holland or somewhere. I phoned Peter Lloyd this afternoon and he too was tickled by the whole business but he didn't know any more than I did. I've no particular desire to see the citation because it would unquestionably be quite ridiculous.

Sergeant Norman Watt, who was in charge of one of 103 Battery's guns, received a similar award for action at Escaut. According to Sergeant-Major Jack Wilson, who was with Stanley almost continually throughout the campaign, none of the surviving members of 'A' troop to whom he has spoken recently can now recall anything untoward happening at the canal. However, Jack Wilson confirmed that there were many other occasions when Stanley exhibited extraordinary coolness and lack of fear in exceptionally dangerous circumstances. He also wrote, "Stanley was extremely well liked and one of my regrets is that our paths did not cross after the war." Jack Wilson later became Chief Superintendent of Police in Greater Manchester. Stanley ended his next letter with a few of Jack Wilson's words.

*I had a couple of letters from home today and my mother sent me an
address book knowing my propensity to forget addresses. She probably
doesn't realise that I shall lose it.*

*Talking of addresses, I'm very sorry about my mistake in sending you the
wrong letter. If my parents have got yours in its place don't worry – I don't
think there was anything revealing in it – or was there?*

*For now, as Sergeant-Major Wilson used to write to his missus, Yours till
hell freezes.*

The last of the trio of presiding majors, Paul Rolo, who was to become
Professor of History at Keele University, welcomed to E mess such notable
visitors as Major Hugh Trevor-Roper (later Lord Dacre), who was engaged
on the research which was later to provide the material for 'The Last Days
of Hitler', and Major Peter Ramsbottom, who was to join the Foreign Office
and, as Sir Peter, serve as British Ambassador to Iran and the United States.

Few evenings seemed to end without vaudeville and songs. Stanley writes
of one such evening when he wore his new Belgian medal ribbons.

*We had a big demob party here last night which was good fun. I managed
to get the two rather dazzling ribbons for my new 'gongs' and emerged in
full regalia. Keith Randell proposed the health of the member who has been
awarded 'The Order of Bourg Leopold'. (This was a notorious transit camp
in '44/'45.) They drank my health and sang the Belgian National Anthem
and 'For he's a jolly etc' and I replied in suitable manner – all a little
amusing, embarrassing and very unexpected.*

Some members of E mess would often retire to their rooms after dinner
to write or study and usually Stanley was among them. (Hugh Carless
comments that Stanley once impressed him by mentioning that before
sitting his exams at Cambridge he would make his way through the Concise
Oxford dictionary to put a sparkle on his wordpower.) But perhaps the most
brilliant member of that mess was Michael Ventris, then a Pilot Officer in
the RAF, who would work on his complex comparative language charts. A
few years later, before his early death, he was to achieve fame for
deciphering, together with John Chadwick, the Minoan linear B script, the
earliest form of written Greek.

                                                  Sunday, March 10th, 1946

Had some extremely good news from Glanville Williams. This is what he said;

'If you are interested in a lectureship at London would you call to see Professor Hughes Parry when next in Town? Give him as much notice of your coming as possible. I fear the salary would not be more than £500 to start, if that — I have no authority to mention any figure — but if you want an academic life I should be very pleased to have you as a colleague here'.

A week later a Select Committee of the House of Commons recommended that MPs salaries should be £1000 a year.

                                                  Tuesday, March 12th, 1946

I'm going to Denmark on Thursday with a Flight Lt and a Field Security Sergeant, both of whom are on the staff here. We're taking four political prisoners to hand over to the Danes. We will have to stay for three days.

Have you got my new address? It's c/o 270 Field Security Section, BAOR from Friday week. That'll be Pinneburg.

PS I've taken the first steps towards ensuring a leave date of 1st or 2nd of May. I approached a chap who is due for leave on April 30th and he's quite ready to swap with me if I can't get leave for our wedding.

In London the Government agreed that women would be admitted to the diplomatic service, but only if they did not marry. Another of my vague career ambitions went out of the window.

270 Field Security Section   Monday, March 25th, 1946

I'm not sure what work I'm supposed to do here; the job seems to be largely what I make of it. But I am doing a lot of reading. When I was in Copenhagen I bought a couple of books and have just finished Huxley's 'Brave New World', which I thought extraordinarily clever, and now I am beginning Joyce's 'Portrait of the Artist as a Young Man', his last fully comprehensible work.

Today I went to Itzehoe which I expect will be my home before many weeks have passed. We were trying to secure a decent Officers' Mess there but with a singular lack of success owing to the obstructionism of the Military Government. They really have the worst type of Military Government officer there: corrupt, inefficient and fit for nothing except fratting.

I hope to see Hughes Parry on May 10th. I'm sorry it will be during our

*honeymoon but I don't have much choice. Have you booked the hotel yet? I
think Crowborough sounds fine since we can't get away to the coast.*

270 Field Security Section   **March 27th 1946**

*Your delightful letter arrived today, together with your telegram and
birthday card. Really, you're spoiling me.*

270 Field Security Section   **March 29th, 1946**

*Last night we had a party for all the Intelligence officers in the Province —
about fifty people and one hundred bottles of champagne. Somebody in a
hilarious moment emptied a glass into my hat so when I feel thirsty I just
take a sniff. Paul Rolo, who runs Political Intelligence in 8 Corps, came here
yesterday but I didn't get much satisfaction from his visit — my position is
apparently even more anomalous than I thought. My chief interest at the
moment is in getting a third pip. If I'd got into Intelligence last May or June
I'd have one by now so you'd be marrying a Captain instead of a Lieutenant.
Do you mind?*

*Re: the wedding, we seem to be getting a lot of jolly useful presents but I
can't think what we are going to do with six electric clocks in a bed-sitter.
Did I tell you we are getting a coffee table from Aunt Annie? All we need
now is some coffee. Here's James' address. Do what you think best about
Molly but I think they would like to come to our wedding together.*

In the London Gazette, 4th April 1946, Stanley was 'Mentioned in
Despatches'. It was the so-called Cease-Fire List for North West Europe. In
Africa the Gold Coast became the first colony with a majority of Africans
in its Parliament. Other colonies were pressing for independence, too. In
India at the beginning of April, Sir Stafford Cripps met Mr Ghandi and other
national leaders, including the Moslem leader, Mr Jinnah, to discuss the
establishment of an interim government for India. But Stanley's thoughts
were not concerned either with the Mention in Depatches or with the
emergent colonies he would be dealing with in the years ahead.

270 Field Security Section   **April 5th, 1946**

*I think this is a very delightful time to get married. The weather is
marvellous and spring is just beginning to show on the trees. What a
contrast with last year. Heat, dust, ruins and death were all that one noticed
in Germany then. But when it's like this I feel strongly impelled to sign on
for seven years.*

*Do you remember I told you that Bill Gill was demobbed about four weeks
ago? Last week he was tinkering with some electric drill as he was so fond of*

doing when something went wrong and he was electrocuted instantaneously. The whole thing is very shocking and his wife wrote to Harry Duerr a rather pathetic letter. She'd got a little baby three months' old. At least if it had happened while he was in the Regiment she'd have got a pension. Now I don't know how she'll manage. I shall always remember him as a most remarkable character.

Three years previously I had met Bill Gill when I had visited Southwell. Of small stature physically, (he was known as 'Half-Pint') he was a character larger than life. His friendliness, combined with a wicked sense of humour, put me at my ease when I was overwhelmed with shyness in the presence of Stanley's fellow officers.

270 Field Security Section   *Thursday, April 18th, 1946*

I've just had a phone message from Kiel. It said I couldn't go on leave on April 30th and if I wanted to go before May 4th I'd have to present a compassionate case to the Brigadier. This is all very unsatisfactory but come what may I'm not putting off marrying you even for a day. Unless of course something unexpected happens like it nearly did last Friday. I slowed down to pick up a hitch-hiker and went into the most terrific skid. I finished up three inches from the edge of a ten foot drop and about five yards from a tree. I'm beginning to tick the days off.

You're quite wrong about officers' wives not receiving an allowance. They get four bob a day; which will be increased to half-a-guinea on July 1st. We shall be rich.

On April 21st John Maynard Keynes (Lord Keynes), the British economist who so profoundly influenced post-war monetary policies, died at the age of sixty-five. He had resigned from the Versailles Peace Conference after the First World War in protest against the plans for reparations. His major work, 'The General Theory of Employment, Interest and Money' formed a substanial part of my economics course. But, like Stanley's last letter below, my thoughts were far from work and economics.

270 Field Security Section   *Sunday, April 28th, 1946*

Unless something drastic happens this will be the last line I send you before I arrive back home. My leave date has been confirmed as May 2nd. My next letter to you, my darling, will after all these years represent the fulfilment of my dreams. It will be addressed to: Mrs Joan de Smith.

Epilogue

The wedding arrangements had gone very smoothly (though my father was slightly disconcerted when out of the four hundred and fifty guests who had been invited, four hundred and thirty two accepted). Our brief, but delightful, honeymoon was interrupted by Stanley's interview for a job at LSE where he was offered an Assistant Lectureship in Law at a starting salary of £400 a year. And a friend found us a one-bedroomed flat at £3 a week. Of his last few months in the Army Hugh Carless writes:

'On his return from compassionate leave as a happily married man Stanley de Smith became a member of Political Intelligence. His cup seemed full: and on July 4th, 1946, he enjoyed the bonus of being promoted to Captain.'

'Stanley and I inherited a spacious Ford V8 from Paul Rolo, when he left to go to Balliol as a young don. In this we travelled far and wide. In Aarhus we dined on whale steak. At Husum, the small grey town by the grey North Sea, we dined on scrambled (and rank-tasting) seagulls eggs which we had collected on the sandbanks. In Hamburg we saw a memorable show where a chorus of young women in black sang "Wir sind die Hinterbliebene, die hin und her Getriebene" (We're the ones who were left behind, who have been driven from pillar to post): an allusion to the war widows and refugees who still crowded into the British zone from the East.'

'In the Political Section there were many reports to prepare, the set piece being a monthly security and political analysis running to some twenty pages. Here Stanley's ability quickly to collate, analyse and draft came to the fore and he invariably wrote the major part. When he was demobilised in November 1946 I was left to edit the S-HIO monthly report. It took me more than twice as long.'

There were another fifty letters to me between June and November, 1946, and Stanley's remarkable written fluency and output continued unabated throughout his career. In 1946 he was promoted to Lecturer and six years later became Reader in Public Law at LSE. In 1954 he was given the Chair of Public Law, University of London, and finally became Downing Professor of the Laws of England at Cambridge, in 1970. He died of cancer at the early age of 51, in 1974.

He never lost his interest in constitutional and political matters, serving as Secretary to the Buganda Constitutional Committee in 1954 (at the time the Kabaka was deposed) and as Constitutional Commissioner for Mauritius from 1961-1968. At various times he acted as Adviser to the leaders of Malta, Western Nigeria and Kenya and in 1962 we spent a year in Australia where he was Visiting Professor at the Australian National University.

It is for his written scholarship that Stanley will chiefly be remembered. He was the joint editor of the Commonwealth and Dependencies volume (3rd ed.) and the Administrative Law volume (4th ed.) of Halsbury's Laws of England. He wrote frequently for the Modern Law Review and edited the Cambridge Law Journal from 1973-4. His publishers in the UK were Stevens and his major publications included:

The Vocabulary of Commonwealth Relations, 1954
The Lawyers and the Constitution, 1960
The New Commonwealth and its Constitutions, 1964
Microstates and Micronesia, 1970
Constitutional and Administrative Law, 1971

But I shall always remember most his magnum opus, which he finished in 1959, after eight years of evenings in his study, pouring over references and writing notes in his minute script, often on the backs of cigarette packets. The book, Judicial Review of Administrative Action, became a classic in its own time. In the preface to the first edition he wrote the words that, along with his letters, I shall always treasure:

'I am indebted most of all to my wife for asking pertinent questions on obscure passages, helping in the work of preparing tables and reading proofs, and bearing with me during the phases of almost obsessive preoccupation that accompanied the later stages of my writing.' S. A. de Smith, April 7th, 1959.

Bibliography

CAEN – The Brutal Battle and Breakout from Normandy
by Henry Maule, pub. 1976, David & Charles
CHRONICLE OF THE SECOND WORLD WAR
ed. Derrick Mercer, pub. 1990, Longman
CHRONICLE OF THE 20TH CENTURY
ed. Derrick Mercer, pub. 1988, Longman
DESPATCHES FROM THE HEART – An Anthology of Letters from the Front
ed. Annette Tapert, pub. 1984, Hamish Hamilton
DESPATCHES FROM THE HOME FRONT* – The War Diaries of Joan Strange
ed. Chris McCooey, pub. 1989, Monarch Publications
ENTERTAINING ERIC – Letters from the Home Front, '41-'44
by Maureen Wells, pub. 1988, Imperial War Museum
GREAT BATTLES OF WORLD WAR 1
by Anthony Livesey, pub. 1989, Michael Joseph
GREATER LOVE, LETTERS HOME 1914-18
ed. Michael Moynihan, pub. 1980, W.H.Allen
HALLIWELL'S FILM GUIDE (6th Edition)
by Leslie Halliwell, pub. 1987, Grafton
KEESINGS ARCHIVES 1943-46
pub. Keesings Publications Ltd.
ONE FAMILY'S WAR
ed. Patrick Mayhew, pub. 1985, paperback, Futura
A PLACE CALLED ARMAGEDDON – Letters from the Great War
Michael Moynihan, pub. 1975, David & Charles
SECOND WORLD WAR*
by Martin Gilbert, pub. 1989, Weidenfeld & Nicholson
THE SECOND WORLD WAR (6 Vols)
by Winston Churchill, pub. 1948-53, Educational Book Co.
THE SECOND WORLD WAR
by John Keegan, pub. 1989, Hutchinson
TRUMPET CALL – The Story of the DLOY
by Lt. Col. J. D. Bastick, pub. 1973, by DLOY
THE WORLD AT ARMS Readers Digest Illustrated History Of World War II
ed. Michael Wright, pub. 1989, Readers Digest Association

Unpublished documents:

NORTH WEST EUROPE CAMPAIGN – The 77th Medium Regiment RA
by Major L. Thomas, DLOY Regimental Museum, Preston
THE WAR DIARIES OF THE 77TH MEDIUM REGIMENT, RA
Public Records Office

Abbreviations

AA	Anti Aircraft
APO	Army Post Office
ATS	Auxiliary Territorial Service
BAOR	British Army of the Rhine
BC	Battery Commander
BLA	British Liberation Army
BWEF	British Western Expeditionary Force
C-IN-C	Commander in Chief
CAGRA	Commander Army Group, Royal Artillery
CATS	St Catharine's College, Cambridge
CLJ	Cambridge Law Journal
CO	Commanding Officer
DLOY	Duke of Lancaster's Own Yeomanry
DSO	Distinguished Service Order
ENSA	Entertainment National Service Association
FUSAG	First United States Army Group
GSI	General Service Intelligence
GTC	Girls' Training Corps
LSE	London School of Economics and Political Science
MT	Motor Transport
NAAFI	Navy, Army and Air Force Institutes
NCO	Non-Commissioned Officer
OCTU	Officer Cadet Training Unit
OP	Observation Post
OTC	Officers' Training Corps
POW	Prisoner of War
PT	Physical Training
RA	Royal Artillery
RAAF	Royal Australian Air Force
USAF	United States Air Force
VC	Victoria Cross